HUMAN MUSIC

For my Mother

CONTENTS

INTRODUCTION

It is the 1998-99 season of the San Francisco Symphony and I am on the stage of Davies Hall sitting behind my cello with the harpsichord on one side and the tenor soloist on the other. We are about to take part in a performance of the St. John Passion by J. S. Bach. The gentle smile of our conductor, Herbert Blomstedt, greets us as he raises the baton and I sense that I'll need the back of the chair to secure me for the wave of energy that I know is coming. The music begins with repeated, pulsing notes from the basses, cellos and violins. The basses play one booming note for every four notes that we play in the cellos as the violins spin out a line that revolves around ours. When I am sure that the tempo is synchronized I close my eyes and feel as if I am lifted from behind by a wave, like a surfer before standing. Soon there is a lump in my throat and as the choir sings "Herr" I experience a glorious rush.

(Later in the same season)
We are in a rehearsal in Berkley with Metallica. I am to play lead cello for the S&M concerts where the San Francisco Symphony merged with the iconic heavy metal band. The auditorium is surrounded by the band's sound and lighting support trucks. Lead singer James Hetfield rides in on a gleaming, gold 'n chrome custom Harley Davidson. Each of the guitar-playing members has a dozen instruments lined up offstage looked after by his own guitar squire. Lead guitar Kirk Hammett's lovely wife is standing among his collection holding their even lovelier baby. Meanwhile bass guitarist Jason Newsted's mom is backstage (she thinks

their music is too loud). Guys are roaming around with video cameras on their shoulders to take footage for a documentary.

There are a number of technical, musical, and psychological kinks in the bond between the heavy metal band and the orchestra that need to be worked out. While the band members display a strikingly serious commitment to the music and the rehearsal, many in the orchestra approach these concerts as mercenaries – paid participants in a completely unfamiliar genre. A few of us, such as Doug the harpist who sports tattoos on his arms and myself, are living out an adolescent dream. While I am having a conversation with drummer Lars Ulrich one of the cameramen approaches for a close-up and we turn away because the conversation concerns difficulties we are having connecting the sheet music-free band with the sheet music-dependent orchestra.

I am seated on the edge of the stage nearest the center. As we play "Devil's Dance" the deep repeated notes from Jason's bass guitar can be felt in the floor and in my chest. The dark power of the music evokes a thrill in me that is unlike anything that I have felt before. Like it or not it takes you by the shirt, pins you against the wall, and forces its way inside of you. I would later write to the guys in the band: if you take the fruit of rock music and cut away the sweet fleshy part, leaving only the hard, dark pit in the center, that is Metallica at its best.

It makes me wonder how this music is capable of evoking emotions that do not exist in nature. That is to say: if you had spent your life in any other time in history and had never heard music like this you could not have experienced this particular kind of emotion. It's not exactly anger or fear or thrill, but it seems to be a synthetic hybrid of all of these and more.

I close my eyes again to remove the distractions and to take a reading of my senses. The rumbling repetition of the beat seems to be the central power station for this brand of emotion. If the deep pulse were to be filtered out of the sound, if the lyrics and singing and guitar chords and cymbals would remain but the boom taken away, the impact would be much weaker. The pulse is the ride, and a deeply felt pulse is a ride on a Harley.

These concerts are a starting point for an investigation that will come to obsess me in the ensuing decade. Why do we respond to music in this way? How is it possible for music to trigger emotions, especially emotions that seem to be supernatural? There must be a place deep within us that we share that is reached and ignited by sound.

(A few years after that)
I am on stage in the Kennedy Center for the National Symphony Orchestra's performance of my own composition *Fuga Eroica*. I hear the repeated notes in the basses leading up to the climax and I breathe deeply as the music gradually gets louder and more complex over the insistent pulse. This passage begins with a quote from Beethoven's violin concerto where the hypnotic first notes are simply four regularly spaced heartbeat-like "booms" (D naturals) on a kettledrum. When I wrote these pulses and the music that surrounds them I felt as if I was following them. Like a novelist who invents characters, puts them in a situation, and then writes down what they do and say, I set the pulse, pointed it toward the a mountainous thematic return in the distance, and then wrote down the music that I heard building and swirling around it. By hearing the music first in the imagination, leaving the details of the design to be filled in later, the music seems to form itself. This growth has its roots in the same place that is lit up when we hear the music – the emotional center. It was in that half conscious, half sleep, emotionally directed state of mind that an insistent pulse made itself an inevitable part of the long, pre-climactic crescendo in my fugue.

After a few years of investigation and rumination, I was convinced that I had discovered why repeated pulses touch our emotions: because we listened to them in the womb for four months before we were born as our brains were being organized.

(In 2003)
As a test of this and other aspects of my theories, I wrote and recorded music for tamarin monkeys. In one of the tamarin songs I tapped my thumb on the body of the cello at a pace of about 200 thumps per minute, the pulse rate of an adult monkey. They were calmed and attentive to my little tamarin ballads; it was the first time any species other than our own demonstrated a response to music in a controlled study. Could it be that the little beasts were moved in a similar way to how I was moved by the pulses in Bach, Metallica, and the Beatles? Could these sensations have their origins in the wombs of each species?

Human Music

(Finally, in May of 2010)

I am speaking at the Washington Academy of Sciences' annual awards banquet, describing my theory: that the sounds heard by the fetus in the womb provide a basis for music. There is an approving rustle to my immediate right, which I later discover came from Karl Pribram, one of the most important and influential neuroscientists in the world today. I mention in the speech the prominent role in musical appreciation of the brain structure that I think of as the dealer in the game of emotions, the amygdala. Pribram later delights in telling me later that he was almost kicked out of Yale for proposing that the amygdala is central to our emotions.

My approach to the questions of the origins and affective processes of music was not unlike my approach to musical interpretation and composition, that is: more inside-out than outside-in. Theorize first, ask questions later. Make the logical connection, then look into the body of knowledge to see if it had already been discovered. Luckily I had not yet read that the connection between human pulse and pulse in music had been thoroughly discounted. I would later discover that the reason this connection had been set aside was simply because the possibility of it forming in the womb had not been adequately considered.

OVERVIEW

Until now, research into the inner workings of music in the brain and on our emotions has focused on examining music as a complete entity. The ideas presented in this book are the product of a different viewpoint: rather than examining the whole of music as we hear it, I asked the question of each ingredient in the recipe: "Why would this trigger an emotion in humans?" I began by identifying some twenty-six elements such as pulse, meter, pitch range of melodies, etc., that are each indivisible and contain definable features. After a few years of questioning, conjectures, probing and research, I felt that I had accumulated plausible answers as to why each would trigger an emotional response and had a workable theory that would explain the fundamental origins of music and why it affects our emotions. Since any good theory is testable, I set about confirming the ideas by writing species-specific music for other animals. If the ideas were sound, then this music should be able to affect their emotions and behaviors. The study that I conducted with Charles Snowdon at the University of Wisconsin demonstrated that species-specific music works and earned us a fair amount of press and the New York Times #1 idea of 2009. This book is about the ideas behind that study; it is about how music can only be understood when it is seen as an art form that is designed by humans to appeal to human perceptions.

Seeing a complete picture of the origins and functions of music requires connecting dots from a variety of disciplines. Composers see the pattern dots most clearly while scientists see the neurological dots. Singers, instrumentalists, and instrument makers each have a good view of the musical issues relevant for each. This theory connects vocal dots with cellist dots and composer's dots with neurological dots. Taken as a whole, this book comprises a picture of music that shows these interconnections. The ingredients of music can be categorized into four families of origin: our vocalizations, environmental cues, those borrowed from visual processing, and those based on the sounds of the womb.

Womb Music

The centerpiece of Human Music theory is an explanation for the fetal origin of the fundamental building blocks of music: pulse, meter, and melody. Making this discovery was like finding a translucent paper with drawn-to-scale sketch of a great painting. When I placed the sketch over the painting I could see that all of the features lined up proportionally. All of the sounds heard in the womb are represented in the music of all cultures.

The sounds heard by the fetus for four months before birth permanently etched the foundations of music into the subconscious brain. This midbrain is made up of the collection of structures known as the limbic system. These structures are primarily responsible for our emotions and are almost fully formed at birth. All of the features of fetal development that make it possible for the fetus to hear sounds, remember (subconsciously) those sounds in adulthood, and respond to them emotionally have been known for some time. I realized that when these features are added together and compared to the construct of music, it becomes apparent that the part of our brains that is responsible for emotions remembers the sounds of the womb.

There are a number of features of the human music theory that represent somewhat novel paradigms. When an idea is presented in this book that belongs to the theory but is not commonly recognized, it is printed in bold lettering.

MAP OF MUSIC'S PATH TO THE EMOTIONS:
(BEGIN AT BOTTOM LEFT)

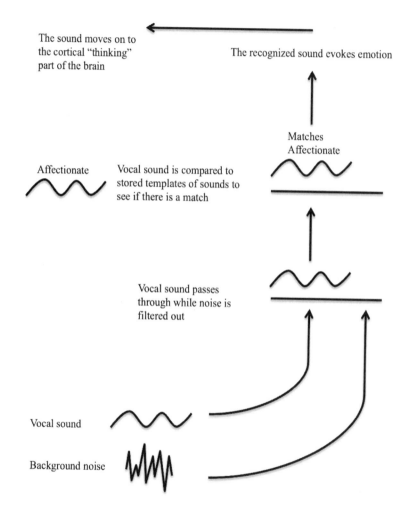

The sound moves on to the cortical "thinking" part of the brain

The recognized sound evokes emotion

Matches Affectionate

Affectionate

Vocal sound is compared to stored templates of sounds to see if there is a match

Vocal sound passes through while noise is filtered out

Vocal sound

Background noise

1

PULSE

Much like the Beethoven violin concerto and J. S. Bach's St. John Passion, the Brahms Requiem begins with evenly spaced pulses played in the deep, low register. Similarly, the first beats of the song *Can't Take My Eyes Off You* by Bob Crewe and Bob Gaudio are presented in a cushioned bass note (F) in precisely the *lub-dub* pace of a beating human heart. My friend and editor Jennifer Ryan remarked to me that the first beats of that song trip her into a glorious pleasure.

You were listening to pulses before you were born. If you were conceived in January and born in October then you heard your first sound in June of that same year. In-utero research and analysis has consistently shown that the fetus responds to the sound of the mother's heartbeat. Sound measurements taken in the womb by one of the leaders in the field, Denis Querleu along with a group of French researchers, have shown that the sound of the mother's heartbeat in the womb is 25db above the baseline noise, that's about the same as a TV set at normal volume three feet away from you in a quiet room. So three and a half months before you were born your hearing had improved enough to be able to pick up the sound of her heartbeat. At this point you weighed about a pound and a half and the limbic structures in your brain were about the size of the tip of your little finger. The fact that you were hearing the heartbeat for most of the growing time of these structures is an important point. Not only is the limbic system responsible for our emotions, but also it is able to retain information long before the parts of our brains that we use to remember things like shopping lists and phone numbers. This Grand Central Subconscious Station of your emotions was absorbing and retaining information about our emotions long before you were born.

The salient feature of brain development that makes all of this possible is this: information that enters a developing brain structure will tend to remain. Just as the sand mixed into the brick mortar will be there for as long as the building stands, information that is incoming as a brain structure is growing will become a part of that structure's organization. The sounds of the womb are indelibly dyed into the very fabric of the subconscious mind and have formed templates of subconscious recognition.

Your feet and hands and limbs and the upper part of your brain still had a lot of growing to do after you took your first breath. Don't we all feel a gentle thrill when we hold a baby's hand in our own and marvel at how tiny it is? You would feel a somewhat opposite thrill if you were able to hold the baby's midbrain and compare it to your own; they would be almost the same size. 3D brain imaging technology used by scientists in Baltimore in 2006 showed that the structures of the limbic system are almost completely formed at birth.

Every species has certain abilities that will be necessary for infant survival to be operable at the moment of birth. Large prey species such as antelope are on their hooves within minutes. Have you ever seen a transparent fish egg a week or so before hatching? The eyes of an embryonic clownfish, for example, are huge relative to the developing body and they are already twitching and looking around from inside the egg. The shell is transparent in order to allow the embryo to get a head start in developing sight before it breaks out. Fully functioning eyesight is necessary for most fish from the moment they hatch. The emotional centers of the human brain are something like the eyes of the fish; they are almost completely developed by the time the baby exits the womb. It will take years for the upper "thinking" part of the brain to catch up. This is one reason why early childhood is such an emotional roller coaster. Yesterday my three-year old son cried when he was told that he couldn't have a lollipop but within minutes was beaming with delight when I printed a dinosaur for him to color. He has adult-sized emotional structures but too little of the countervailing prefrontal cortex.

Human Music

It often helps us to get a perspective on ourselves when we compare *Homo sapiens* to other species as if we were aliens from another world comparing newly discovered life forms. The narrow spectrum of types of sounds that we humans respond to becomes apparent when we compare our time scale to other species. Think of how quickly and easily small, darting birds fly through tangles of branches. If we imagine ourselves in the bird's body it is only possible to follow such a path if we slow down the flight enough to see and react at our own pace. The ruby throated hummingbird has a resting heart rate of 250 beats per minute (bpm) and a feeding heart rate of up to 1200 bpm. Let's imagine that hummingbirds had their own music. It seems likely that it would be incomprehensively fast to our ears. The repetition rates of the pulses found in human music on the other hand (40 – 240 beats per minute) coincide with the slowest (respiration) and fastest (footfalls of running) pulses that can be heard in the womb. **Human music is built to the human scale.**

We do not have conscious access to our fetal memories, but if we did we would remember that there wasn't much to do in there. Most of the senses brought in little that was new or interesting; eyesight, smell, and taste were certainly limited and there were few touchable items. Tactile sense does play a role in some of today's music, and the fetus could certainly have felt as well as heard the mother's heartbeat. Hearing is the exception to this dearth of information. *Sounds* are always present; the patterns of speech heard in the womb are constantly changing and are learned by the fetus.

During the summer months before you, October-born reader, emerged to take your first breath, during the entire long, hot summer as friends smiled at your mother and as the more experienced mothers among them sympathized with her having to endure part of her third trimester in the August heat, as you grew from the size of a grapefruit to your eventual birth weight, you were hearing the uninterrupted cadence of your mother's heartbeat and breathing. You heard these sounds ceaselessly all summer long, as the brain structures responsible for your emotions grew from the size of an almond to approximately the size the size they are now. Occasionally you also heard your mother speaking. All of these sounds informed and attuned your brain as it developed.

Human Music

Keepers of the Pulse

The timpani (kettledrum) player in an orchestra is a percussion specialist, the Prince of Percussion. He or she will choose sticks that are harder or softer depending on the style of the composition. A military style calls for hard sticks, the sound produced by them is loud and clear in keeping with the needs of field drums that conveyed information to distant troops. Most music sounds best, however, when the timpani are struck with cushioned sticks that soften the blow. I have had the pleasure of working with some real artists behind these drums, including Jauvon Gilliam in the National Symphony. If the role of the timpanist is Prince of Percussion, he is the King and Field Marshal.

The first time we heard Jauvon was in his audition. The finals were held with the entire orchestra onstage. We played the opening of Brahms' Symphony #1. (If you are not a classical music lover and plan on skipping the classical samples available online you want to make an exception for this one. I must confess a stab of jealousy when I think of someone who will have the experience of hearing this overwhelmingly powerful music for the first time.) Our recently appointed music director, Christoph Eschenbach, instructed Jauvon: "In these opening moments, don't follow me. For a few seconds here, you lead the orchestra. You are the king." Jauvon took to this instruction like he was born to the throne. The notes he played became a sonic electromagnet for the rest of us to cling to. Part hammer blow, part heartbeat, he clearly established the target center, the fulcrum, the focus, the *meaning* within this music of Brahms.

That regular beat could be kept with the sound of a stick hitting a table, but it wouldn't sound "good" to us. Over the centuries of the development of instruments musicians found that stretching a skin over something round makes the sound die away more slowly (longer decay). It was also discovered that elongating the round skin holder into a cylinder made the sound more resonant and could give it a pitch (the tube resonates and lengthens the decay even more). And if it were struck with a cushioned beater the beginning of the sound would be less sudden (longer onset). Each of these modifications was made in order to create a pulse sound that we perceive as "good". Recognition is the key point here. Why does a drum sound "better" than a stick hitting a table? The answer is: because **we *recognize* the drum sound, each of us who can hear heard it constantly for four months before we were born.**

Perhaps you are wondering if the sound of a drum and the sound of the heartbeat from inside the womb are so similar by coincidence. Consider the history of the drum. It is highly doubtful that it was a singular invention that spread from a single point. For that to be true a drum would have to have been carried by each branch of the original migration of *Homo sapiens* out of Africa 60,000 years ago. (As improbable as this seems, I rather like the idea that a musical instrument was important enough to tote around on a migration.) It is far more likely that drums were invented concurrently in different cultures. Disconnected peoples came up with the same basic drum design. Three thousand years ago as the Greeks were drawing images on vessels of people playing the tympanon, the Chinese of the Shang Dynasty were making drums out of clay and stretched alligator skin. These parallel developments occurred well before the silk route had established a connection between the cultures of the East and West. Meanwhile the cross-rhythms of the Niger-Congo peoples were being played on djembe drums that would not be seen by Europeans until the 15th century. That was around the time Westerners began invading the Americas where they found that drums had been made by all of the aboriginal Americans: from the Inuit and Ojibwe in the North, to the Lakota in the plains, the Aztecs between the continents and the Incas in the South.

To explain such a parallel development of one musical instrument with a singular, basic design and meant to be struck in repeating patterns of pulse and meter requires a commonality among all people. This commonality must be fundamental enough to supersede all linguistic, racial, and cultural differences. Furthermore, since all emotional responses begin with recognition, and since the preference for the sound of the drum is universal, then it is most logical to conclude that the template of sound that is recognized was formed in an environment that we all share. Emotional responses follow salient recognition. Our task is to discover the reason our emotional centers recognize the sound of the drum.

We can often get a clearer picture of what is plausible by looking at what is implausible, like seeing through the eyes of alternative viewpoint guru Steven Wright. He says that he likes to skate on the other side of the ice because it's less crowded down there. Consider my new invention: the not-a-drum. It is a bunch of stones in a bowl played by jabbing a stick into it. It creates is a consistent and repeatable "chk" sound. It's very easy to build; anyone can get pebbles and a stick. Smaller round pebbles make a softer "shk" and bigger sharp-edged stones make a harder "KCH"... but would that sound good to others? Would we find versions of my easily made rhythm-producer in other cultures? No. I don't think there will be a line at the door for my not-a-drum concerts. My instrument creates a peculiar and repeatable sound, but the brain's emotional center remains uninvolved because it does not recognize the sound.

Perhaps the best example of the sound of the heartbeat in music is produced by the pedal drums in Western popular music. Don't let all the sweat and manic passion of the drummer lure you into thinking that they aren't very careful about getting their drums to sound exactly right. The time it takes for the sound of a strike to die away is important, usually a pillow is placed inside of the pedal drum to kill the sound a little faster than it would die away without it. This sense of "just right" comes from the maternal heartbeat. Below are a few figures and descriptions that outline the development of the drum:

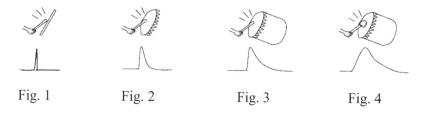

Fig. 1   Fig. 2   Fig. 3   Fig. 4

The graduated onset and elongated decay of a pedal drum strike (Fig. 4) make the amplitude contour resemble that of the heartbeat as heard in the womb (onset .02s, decay .06s). Fig. 1 above shows the spike of a transient sound made by one stick hitting another; this sounds "not so good" to us. In Fig. 2 a skin is stretched over a round collar and struck by the stick and the elongated decay created by the vibrating skin sounds "good". When the stretched skin is placed over a cylinder the decay is elongated further and sounds "better". Finally, when the drum is struck with a cushioned beater, the onset is graduated as well as the decay and this sounds "just right" to us. The feelings of "good", "better", and "just right", like all emotional responses, begin with recognition. In this case we recognize the sound that was imbued in our growing brains.

Feeling the swing

There are compelling pulses all around us as well as within us - in the waves approaching an ocean shoreline, in the passing of the days from light to darkness, in the change of seasons from the long-day warmth and color of summer to the cold dormancy and horizon-skimming sun of winter. The evenly spaced timing and implied movement of the pulse is connected to our perception of movement by the swinging pendulums that we see and feel in the world around us.

The movement of a pendulum is a musical concept that relates to the feeling on a swing. Imagine you are looking down from the rear high point on a swing, moving forward and gaining velocity as you descend, you feel the gravity sink you into your seat as you speed pass the ground. This movement and feeling can be translated into music. The Germans call it "schwung". The best example I can think of is in the Scherzo of Brahms' piano concerto #2. You can hear an example if you visit www.davidteie.com and click on the link: Brahms 2 or hear track 1 on the CD. Listen to the three-dimensionality of the rhythm, patterned after the rhythmic interpretation of Leon Fleisher. What I mean by three-dimensionality is: the swing doesn't just go back and forth, it sounds as if it goes up and down as well, the way a children's swing moves, slowing and weightless at the apex and speeding toward the nadir. It would seem reasonable to think that a perfectly regular pulse, like the ticking of a well-regulated clock, would sound the most inevitable. You may agree, however, that the slight ebb and flow of the Fleisher-style rhythm sounds even more inevitable than perfectly mechanical rhythm. When the tempo slightly speeds into the bottom strong beat and then slightly slows at the top weak beat, it gives the music a perceived velocity.

This variety also aligns with our fetal experience with pulse since the tempos of the heartbeat vary. We are well aware of our quickening pulse when we exercise, but we tend to be less aware that subtle variations in the speed of the heartbeat occur often. Even standing to go to another room will raise the heart rate a bit.

Mr. Fleisher is the musician who taught me how to compress rhythm (who learned it from Artur Schnabel, who learned it from Eusebius Mandyczewski, who was Brahms' assistant). Leon Fleisher is to the Peabody Conservatory what the wizard is to the Land of Oz. I also heard him compare the funereal pulse in the Chopin sonata to the swinging incense used in the priestly processions in a dark cathedral. These are times when, in the hands of a master, the pulse can evoke solemnity. If you want to get a taste of what it is like to be in the mind of such an artist as Leon Fleisher, take a moment to close your eyes and use your imagination to sketch, paint, and animate this image: In an evening service of a medieval cathedral, under the huge, arched canopy a priest paces in a floor-length white robe holding a silver handle connected to three long silver chains attached to an urn containing smoldering incense. The priest swings the smoke-trailing urn first toward and then away from the altar. Sometimes you can hear a "chink" when the chains catch the fall after loosening at the top. Pay attention to the graduated speeds of the urn: descending from the apex it gains velocity before speeding past the floor. The essence of hyper-inevitable rhythm is this accelerated movement toward the pulse. Now, while keeping your eyes closed and with the image still playing in your mind, imagine putting your hands on the keyboard and playing this slow, dark music of Chopin.

Pulse is hypnotic. Swinging pendulums or sudden loud, disorienting sounds are used by hypnotists to gain access to the subconscious. Music almost always begins its journey into our hearts by putting us in a trance-like state of mind. We have a variety of terms and descriptions for the many levels of these induced states of relaxation and altered consciousness ranging from temporary daydreams to deep meditation and hypnosis. Rocking, eye fixation, and progressive relaxation are commonly used to induce hypnosis. Music, the invisible hypnotist, swings his pocket watch before us. The concert halls are darkened (progressive relaxation) before the performer steps onstage, reducing distractions and concentrating the focus of the audience (eye fixation) while enhancing the sense that they are witnessing something from another, magical world. Whether it's the rhythmic, repetitive, instrumental figure that introduces the vocal line or the disorienting crash of an opening chord followed by run-pounding beats, rhythmic pulses can open the door to the soul. The pendulum pulse is the big skeleton key on the ring of keys that open the door to the subconscious, granting music access to the secret emotions hiding in the limbic system rooms. Once inside, passion, beauty, love, conflict, grief, resolution, and peace can all resonate within us.

Musicians who are good musical hypnotists know that the pulse has to be "in the slot". If the tempo is a little too fast or too slow the music will lack the feel of a natural ride that will buoy the melodies and harmonies and set up a physical synchronicity with the audience. Try this demonstration of tempo just rightness: take a teacup half filled with water and swish it back and forth in time with the movement of the water. In the average teacup you will be swishing about 320 times per minute. If you do the same thing with a half-filled 2 ½ quart pot the right tempo is about 180 swishes per minute. There is one perfect tempo for every vessel, too slow or too fast and the swishing waves interfere with each other and the water churns. If you move it at just the right tempo the side-to-side movement and the side-to-side flow link-up like clockwork. That is how it feels when you play music that is cruising in a groove.

The Beats of Running

There is a link between the musical beat and the emotional scene that the musician is trying to construct. The adrenaline that is the driving force behind our fight or flight response induces behaviors that are fast and furious. Slow music, on the other hand, often creates scenes that are conducive to dreamy relaxation. Clearing out the adrenaline and rocking us while cooing a lovely lullaby, the slow tempos allow us to feel comfortable enough to pass from the hyper-attentive state encouraged by fast music to a slightly meditative state. Musicians who are keenly aware of the significant role that tempo plays in evoking moods and images will judge the acoustics of the room, sense the attentiveness of the audience, and find the pace that best suits the environment.

Most amplified bands will use the same tempos in the live performances as they used in the recordings because most audience members expect to hear the music exactly the same way as they came to know it. It can be a very problematic catch 22 when highly creative musicians must perform cookie-cutter replicas of their music night after night, year after year. When Jason Newsted left Metallica to form

Echobrain the driving force behind his exit was the fountain of music in him that demanded other outlets. He thirsted for the spontaneously interactive music making of alternative genres.

I mentioned to Jason that orchestral playing provides limited opportunities for personal interpretation since the conductor directs the flow and balance while the musicians follow. Many of us find playing in small "chamber music" groups to be rewarding in a way that is more personal. Although there is a thrill to being a part of the inertia of the great ship of an orchestra, there is also a thrill to being at the rudder of a four-man sailboat. Jason responded: "This (Echobrain) is my chamber music." Metallica's founding band members James and Lars felt that Metallica should have been enough for Jason. Perhaps this helps us to understand the ubiquity of band break-ups. The rock star is king of the popular culture hill, yet these people are regularly opting-out after standing up there for a while.

Another San Francisco bay area rock icon is Dickie Peterson, one of the founding members of the band that originated power rock music, Blue Cheer. Their music spawned a new genre that eventually led to grunge, metal, and punk. Dickie told me that he believes the machine-like click track pulse in contemporary rock music robs it of living, breathing variation. He plays in a style that allows the tempo to ebb just a bit and then flow again and drive forward when it feels right. Perhaps these concert-to-concert variations helped to provide the musical freedom that allowed Dickie to enjoy a long career playing very loudly.

Setting the Pace

Many classical performers calibrate the tempos of the music to the resonance of the hall, like setting the swishing water tempo to the size of the vessel. Music in a cathedral sounds clearer with slower tempos because the sound echoes around for more than five seconds. If the music is too quick the sounds blur together. Music in a dry auditorium designed for speaking needs to be faster to make up for the missing resonance. Playing in a very dry hall can be very unsatisfying. It's like trying to find the right swishing pace of a dry vessel.

The finest performers can not only calibrate their playing to the reverberation of the hall, but are able to sense the attention of the audience and create moments when everyone in the space hangs on a note like a crowd expectantly watching a droplet on the tip of a finger slowly getting closer to a still water surface, and then feel a little gasp of release as the droplet disappears in the blink of contact. Backstage at the new hall built for the Philadelphia Orchestra one of our players was telling pianist Emanuel Ax that he thought the hall didn't have any magic in it. To this Ax responded: "Isn't it up to us to provide the magic?" Within an hour he had made good on his own pronouncement in a memorable performance of Beethoven's piano concerto #2. There are places in this music where the tempo slows slightly and the notes may be caressed before the tempo returns, like the swing that has passed the nadir – the moment when you look up into the green, sun-speckled tree and become weightless near the branches before falling back again. In rehearsal Ax took time in these places, but in the concert he stretched some of them to the point of creating miniature ecstasies. It wasn't the kind of exaggeration that demonstrates a Great Performer's Great Expressivity; rather it was something akin to humility. The audience was stone silent and his timing was linked to their heightened attention. It was as if he had relinquished some of the control to them, not a note was played too soon. He and the listeners were together on a walk at sunset, stopping at the same time to bathe in the light of the rose-lit sky.

Metallica relinquishes control to no one. In our concerts the band was completely in charge. The music is dictatorial. The size of the club, hall, or arena does not matter since the amplifiers and technicians take care of all that. The tempo is right because Lars & Co. make it right. The fans expect to hear the songs the way they came to know them. Metallica also plays with an awareness of the audience, but in a different sense. While the classical and jazz performers adjust their playing to the room and the crowd in a kind of streaming flight where they will trim this and power that to stay airborne, heavy metal musicians are responsive to the passions of the fans who sing along with songs they have listened to hundreds of times by using exactly the tempos that were used on the recordings.

High-voltage amplification has made it possible for low frequencies to move a lot of air and a lot of ribcages. In Berkley I could feel the beat in the floor. I once asked Dickie Peterson about the origins of high-powered amplification. He told me that the reason they played so loudly was because they wanted the music to be felt. "We wanted to feel the beat." A powerfully amplified band can create beats that penetrate the body. Therein lies a new element of music introduced by the rockers: tactile response. I remember being near the stage in a concert by Alice in Chains where the movement of the air created by the sound was so strong that I could feel and see the hairs on my arm move to the beat.

Why do we want to feel the beat? We don't want to *feel* the piccolo. (Fine piccolo playing can be delightful from the concert hall seats, but if you have to sit close-by it can *feel* like an ear drill.) We want to feel the beat because we *felt* the beat. The maternal heartbeat creates a pressure wave that not only can be clearly heard but can also be clearly felt by the fetus. While growing inside your mother the pump of her liquid-filled heart created a pressure wave that traveled through the liquid-filled tissue of her womb right into and through the liquid-filled you.

The Meter of Breathing

Back to the fetal experience of the October-born reader: By early July you could hear your mother's breathing. The midsummer before your birth brought an additional repetitive sound into your forming brain. The differently paced and constantly overlapping pulses of heartbeats, inhalation, and exhalation create patterns of strong and weak beats. In the womb the inhalation is louder than the exhalation. When the inhalation sounds simultaneously with the heartbeat it adds up to the strongest sound, exhalation with the heartbeat is somewhat strong, and the heartbeat alone is weakest. As a result music tends to feel right when it has a repeating pattern of strong and weak beats that resemble those that we heard in the womb. **The combination of heartbeats and breathing forms the basis for musical meters.**

Meter in music is a repeated pattern of strong and weak pulses. The most common meter in Western music is 4/4 time; it's even called common time. It contains one strong beat followed by a weak beat, then a slightly stronger third beat followed by a weak fourth, all regularly spaced: **ONE** two **THREE** four. Now try this: take your pulse while counting your breaths. Does it come out to be about one breathing cycle for every four heartbeats? If so, you're not alone.

When respiration and heartbeat are combined we have:

ONE	=	inhalation + heartbeat
Two	=	heartbeat alone
THREE	=	exhalation + heartbeat
Four	=	heartbeat alone

or another way to see it:

Breathing:	SWOOSH		swiiiish	
Heartbeat:	PUM	PUM	PUM	PUM
Combination:	1	2	3	4

Common time is common to us all. And it is very commonly found in music. A few years ago I attended an excellent Nine Inch Nails concert in Prague and there could not have been more than two minutes of music during the entire concert that wasn't in 4/4 time.

Think about it: theoretically, the possible combinations of tempos and stresses that are available are infinite, yet the spacing, stresses, and tempos of common time are the very same as the combined pulsations that are often heard in the womb. The other meters that are used in music can also be traced to other combinations of strong and weak beats. The ratio of 1)STRONG – 2)weak is 2/4 time, and 1)STRONG – 2)weak – 3)weak is 3/4 time.

Other pulses that can be clearly heard and felt by the fetus can also combine with the heartbeat to create overlaps that augment the strength of some beats. Naturally, not all mothers have the same heart/respiration ratios and the synchronicity of the beats is constantly changing. The heartbeat is faster when walking and the pressure waves created by the footsteps of a pregnant mother are certain to be audible to the fetus. The faster pace of the heartbeat combined with the even pulses of footfalls creates a relatively quick 2/4 meter. Even the rarely heard footfalls of running are sure to be found in the developing brain's list of recognized combined pulses.

A weak beat placed in the silence between the duple pulses of the heart creates a triple meter. Here is a visual approximation using "lubb, dub", the traditional vocal approximation of the sound of the heartbeats used by physicians:

Regular beats: | | | | | |

       LUBB   dub (silence) LUBB dub (silence)

       ONE   two   (three)   ONE   two   (three)

These three beats may be unevenly spaced; in the heartbeat (and in the Viennese waltz) the second beat comes earlier than it would if each of the three beats were equal. It is spaced something like this: ONE, two, (three) ONE, two, (three) STEP, join, (turn) STEP, join, (turn). The waltz step is three-dimensional. The one beat is down slightly with bended knees, then the second beat is up. This rise on the second beat causes it to hover slightly before gravity returns the dancers to the dipping first beat. The sense of motion is similar to the swing of the pendulum. As a result of the uplifted hover, the second beat is placed just a bit early. At least this is the way it is played in Vienna. On this side of the Atlantic it depends on the knowledge/ignorance ratio of the conductor. Unfortunately, there are those that will have us play Viennese waltzes the straight and easy way, unable to manage the subtle intricacies that make this dance float.

The mixed meters are also traceable to the fetal sonic environment. 6/8 is a combination of triple/duple (**1** 2 3 **4** 5 6) combining the LUBB, dub, silence of a quickened heartbeat with inhalation and exhalation. If you like this kind of thing you could gather up a few more musical meters and do your own in-mom comparisons. I don't think you will find anything outside the human scale between the fast footfalls of running and the slow swishes of relaxed breathing. In fact, you won't find anything about music that is not anthropocentric; there is no facet of music that does not broadcast its very humanity.

Cultural Commonalities

It should be possible to confirm the fetal origins of music by comparing the sounds of the womb to the commonalities of music. If we find a match, then the connection would be supported. This question pertains to the centerpiece of Human Music theory: if music is indeed based on the sounds of the fetal environment then the characteristics of music that resemble the womb should be found in the music of all cultures.

There are often many differences between the music of one culture and the music of another. The patterns of pitches (musical scales), instruments, and use of harmonies all vary widely. Later chapters of this book will be dedicated to the many features of music that are not based on recollections of the sounds of the womb, but since they are based upon the environment in which each of us lives rather than the environment in which all of us were conceived they can be very different from one another. The many connections between music and speech, for example, have been widely researched. There exists a fairly well understood body of knowledge about the many links between expression in speech and expression in music that will be examined in later chapters in this book. There are, however, universal traits found in music that have evaded explanation and are clearly unrelated to speech. It is primarily the *differences* between music and speech that have made the origins of music so mysterious. One such difference that is often noted is that music contains regular pulses and meters.

Continuity

Here lies the answer to the question of whether the sounds of the womb are found in the music of all cultures: yes, all music contains regular pulses and meters. These underlying beats also provide another hidden universal characteristic of music: continuity. While speech stops and starts, music rarely presents any other than an unbroken rope of sound. So now we have another piece of the answer to the commonality question: not only is a regular and repeated pulse one of the universal traits of music, even though it is not found in speech, but nearly all music contains pulses, meters, and is *continuous*. **Nearly all of the music heard in all cultures is continuous.**

Continuity is key to musical appreciation, attention, and subconscious recognition. The womb solves this mystery as well. Even as the melodies may be presented in phrases that are separated from one another, there is continuity in the underlying pulse and accompanimental patterns. Your mother's voice came and went but the pulse and meter always remained.

Take a moment to hum "White Christmas" but instead of humming continuously, pause for a second or two every few seconds: "I'm dreaming… (long pause) of a white Christmas just like… (pause) the ones I used to know… (pause)" This is how speech sounds (this depends, of course, on the situation and people engaged in the dialogue. (If you time the silences between utterances to those found in the conversations between Northern Minnesota Scandinavian fishermen in a boat, the pauses will need to last at least 30 minutes.) Melodies come and go in one-breath phrases but the accompaniment nearly always continues, in the music of all cultures, until the song is over. There are exceptions to this when all the music comes to a stop and then resumes, but the silence will be brief and the tempo of the pulse nearly always remains.

We have seen that the acoustic parameters of the sounds in the womb are the same as the parameters of universal characteristics of music. What are the chances that this is just a coincidence? Is it possible that we don't create music based on fetal memories but have made music out of similar sounds by chance? No. It is about as close to impossible as anything can be. Consider just a few of the variables:

- The pulse could be irregular with any number of different variations in the durations between them.
- The pulse could be from minutes to milliseconds apart.
- There could be no pulse/beat at all; music could have regular or irregular squeaks, or gurgles, or swishes, etc.

The combinations of the accented beats that create meters could create other, less regular patterns, the possible number of these patterns increases exponentially with each added accent.

Additionally, we need to factor in the probability that these elements are the same in not just one culture's music, but every culture's music. The enormous coincidence would also have to include the parallel development in disconnected cultures of the peculiar skin stretched-over-a-cylinder instrument that provides those similar-sounding underlying beats. Perhaps you will agree that it is astronomically unlikely that all of these pieces fell into place randomly, but just how astronomical?

My dad once came up with the following image that helps to picture an individual's chances of winning the lottery: Imagine a wall that is covered by 1-inch square stamps. The wall is 6 feet high and 7 miles long. If you drive a car beside the wall and throw a dart out of the window, the chances of hitting the one hidden lucky stamp is about the same as your chances of winning the lottery. So, considering all of the variables, what is the statistical probability that the womb and music share the same sonic elements coincidentally? I passed this question by an MIT grad nuclear physicist friend after pointing out the long list of variables. She probably dreams up a few equations like these every morning before breakfast. She thinks the following image is in the ballpark: imagine closing your eyes and throwing a dart at a cluster of galaxies. You have a much better chance of hitting the one lucky atom.

In these variables we haven't even considered the most complex of the universal elements of music that is based on the sounds of the womb: melody.

2

VOICE

(September 26, 2010) Last night Renée Fleming sang the Four Last Songs of Richard Strauss in our opening gala concert. Portions of the melodies from each song have been caressing my mind all through the morning; they blend into each other as if they had been cut from the same dream. Christoph Eschenbach, in this, his first concert as our music director, managed to convince us to play this music with the transparency that can be created with feather-light bowing over the strings. Strauss' rich harmonies can easily seduce us into playing the accompaniment in sonorous tones that would eventually billow into singer-obscuring clouds of sound, but this was a performance where we were kept to our rightful place as the clouds that buoyed the voice.

A year ago she sang *Morgen* with us, a song Strauss composed for his wife. It tells of a time when they will "again unite amidst this sun-breathing earth". In this song a pure, timeless violin melody is played twice, the first time alone and the second time the soprano sings a countermelody that accompanies the violin. Most divas sing the countermelody much louder than the violin melody, assuming that any line of music that is not The Soprano Line must be incidental. The music is most affecting, however, when the vocal line humbly and tenderly floats around the violin melody. I was seated in the chair directly next to Miss Fleming's in the rehearsal of this song. When the moment arrived for her entrance she remained seated and sang as if to a child in a quiet room. I was reminded of my mother, whose voice took on a deep purity when she sang softly. A welling of emotion rose in my chest and throat and eyes. I absorbed the warmth of the music as I would the sun or mother's affection.

It is very likely that the first sound you ever heard was your mother's voice. If you were conceived in January and born in October then you heard your first sound in June of that same year. The sound you heard was your mother's voice. Her voice sounded louder to you in the womb than it did to the people she was addressing. A team of researchers from the University of Florida headed by Douglas Richards managed to convince eight bedridden mothers-to-be to have microphones inserted into the uterus and placed near the head of the fetus. The mothers were asked to speak in a loud voice as the intrauterine sound level was recorded. They found that the average mother's voice in the womb is 77.2 dB. That's as loud as traffic on a busy street. The intensity of the sound of the maternal voice in the womb is nearly four times greater than the intensity measured in the air for someone standing right next to her. The maternal voice is louder in the womb because liquids and bodily tissues carry sounds much more efficiently than air. The pitches from her vocal chords quickly and easily travelled the short distance to your little, budding ears. You couldn't hear her consonants very well; they are produced at the mouth opening (say: "shh" – all the sound is out front) and are mostly made up of high frequencies. Most of the sounds of her consonants had to go through the air and through her slightly extended belly. Very little of the sounds from your mother's consonants will have made it in to you since these upper frequencies do not transfer well from air to tissue. As a consequence the first sounds you heard will have sounded very much like your mother humming.

Remember the elementary school science experiment where we scraped a magnet on a nail over and over to align the molecules and made a magnet out of the nail? This is analogous to your mother's heartbeat calibrating your sense of time. Her voice also gave you a predisposition to the linguistic patterns of your mother tongue. Psychologists Jacques Mehler and Peter Jusczyk have shown that 4 day-old French infants responded to the French language but not to other languages. They used an investigative technique that observes how the rate of the infant's sucking changes with the sounds they hear. The newborns still prefer the French language when the speech is filtered to remove the consonant and vowel sounds, retaining only the melody. They removed these sounds in order to present maternal speech as it is heard from inside the mother. Just as the fish's eyes learn and calibrate from within the egg, you learned and calibrated your senses from within the womb.

Maternal Melodies

The maternal voice heard by the fetus in the womb is the foundation of melody. When we compare the features of maternal speech as it is heard in the womb to the features of melodies that are found in the music of a wide variety of cultures we find compelling similarities. Indeed, it is a supportable assertion that the contours and prosody of specific languages *as heard by the fetus* are nearly identical to the melodic contours of the music associated with that language. For most of us it is warmly illuminating to realize that your own mother's voice enabled you to enjoy melodies.

To get an idea of how speech sounds when it is pared down to only the melody, try this. Say this aloud in a feminine, appealing-to-husband tone: "Honey... (he didn't respond) HONEY!" Notice how the second time you say "honey" the word creates the same melodic motive as the first "honey" but higher in pitch. Now do what the clever French psychologists did: use the same pitches that you used when saying "Honey", but this time just hum. There it is: melody. **All of the commonly found features of musical melodies are present in the mother's voice as it is heard in the womb.**

The newborn French infants do not show a preference for the melody of the French language when it is played backwards. This means that a near term fetus already recognizes the contours of melodies, and that the development of musical taste has begun. Newborns not only recognize melodic contours of language, they use them. Kathleen Wermke of the University of Würzburg in Germany studied five-day-old infants and discovered that they use the contours of their own mothers' language in their cries. We are learning the shapes of melodies in the womb and ready to use them from the moment we start breathing. No wonder music seems to be such a natural part of our world.

Each language has its own commonly used contours. Perhaps the clearest example of melodic contour in the English language is the upward-ending question:

<pre>
                    here?"
               me
     you   help
   "Are   going to
</pre>

If the speaker is irate and feeling overworked it may not go up at the end, the expressive contour of the last three words might sound like three low car horns:

<pre>
          you
   "Are   going
              to
          help me here?"
</pre>

To get an idea of just how unusual-sounding a backwards contour can be, let's reverse the notes of that sentence and listen for the unnatural contour:

<pre>
                 you
          going   are"
           to
   "here me help
</pre>

(Star Wars fans: Yodaspeak.) This creates an odd-sounding contour in the English language but it may be typical of another language.

Human Music

Cultures and Contours

The melodic contours of a culture's language also tend to be reflected in that culture's music. Researchers have recently discovered that the pitch changes between the syllables in spoken English are wider than in spoken French. When they examined the contours of French and English music they found that matching preferences are found in each culture's music as well.

Musical contours may be thought of like bias relief sculpture. That is to say, the important figures are brought to the fore and the less significant figures are carved into the background. Take, for example, a little melody made up of two short notes followed by one longer note. When a fine instrumental musician interprets three notes like this he or she will decide the intent – the spirit of the music – then imbue the playing with the appropriate tone colors and phrasing.

Instrumental musicians don't have the opportunity to read the lyrics to help us to interpret the music; we must listen for meaning in the score and project that meaning through sound. If the composer has indicated, for example, that the notes are to be played smoothly and the harmonies that accompany the melody are warmly consonant, the interpreter may imagine that the notes should be played as if the melody had been set to the words "I'm in love". In that phrase the first two words set up the central point. The player carves the first two notes into the background and the third note, the word that carries the deepest meaning, is emphasized. A less skilled and artistic musician will tend to leave out these nuances and the three-note phrase may sound like an instrumental version of "I'm in bed".

The composer who is widely considered to be the master of the interconnections between the notes, words and emotional intent was the songwriter's songwriter Franz Schubert. He wrote melodies that are so natural and affecting that composers and performers since his time (1797–1828) have regarded him with awe and envy as well as sadness that his life ended when he was only 31. One of the prominent features of his melodic style is that he gave each syllable in the lyrics only one note. Other composers will often put two or more notes to a syllable: for example in the hymn *Silent Night* there are two notes sung on the first syllable. Irving Berlin, who was described by George Gershwin as

"America's Schubert" used the same one-to-one note/melody standard as Austria's Schubert. Hear how the words match the notes in *White Christmas*: "I'm drea-ming of a white Christ-mas just like the ones I used to know..."

This intimate and absolute union of notes and syllables is natural to us. Those of us who use Indo-European languages (including Schubert's German and Berlin's English) nearly always place a single pitch with a single syllable in our speech. Other languages use some contoured syllables where the voice changes pitches on a single syllable, but all languages are made up of predominantly single-pitch segments separated by consonants. As a result, since the origin of melody is the mother's language, the music of all cultures uses predominantly single-pitch segments.

Discrete Musical Notes

You will not find music from any culture that consists primarily of sliding frequencies. American emergency vehicles' sirens use sliding frequencies; music uses notes. A wide variety of mammalian vocalizations do create of these kinds of slides, such as the cat's meeeooooowww. But music never sounds like a succession of ascending and descending slides. Why not? Because it doesn't sound "good" to us, we don't recognize it. We do, however, recognize the chained together single-frequency segments that we heard so clearly from our mother's speech as it was heard by us in the womb. Remember that the high-frequency consonants created at the mouth opening such as "ch", "t", "s", and "sh" did not get to your ears inside your mother's belly, so what you heard sounded something like humming. The subconscious part of our brains in charge of spotting good sounds remembers and recognizes *notes*.

Discrete, single-frequency segments (notes) are found in the music of all cultures. Syllables, and their musical offspring: notes, are so much a part of our world that we take them somewhat for granted, so much so that this commonality in music has eluded discovery until now. In order to fully appreciate how distinctive the note is it may be helpful to take it apart and compare it to other naturally occurring sounds. The principle characteristics of the note are:

- It is discrete, that is to say it is separate from what came before and what comes after it.
- It contains a single, fixed frequency as a fundamental pitch.
- That fundamental pitch is enhanced by a resonator.

We'll need to include a little acoustic primer here since a lot of the information to come is based on the overtone series. Without getting into distracting details, the basic outline is this: each of the tones created by a voice or an instrument produces a fundamental frequency (periodic sound) that we hear as its pitch. This pitch is bundled with a collection of overtones sounding at the same time that are directly proportional to the fundamental. Let's examine a tone in the lower range of a man's voice. If the fundamental pitch created by the folds of the larynx vibrates 100 times per second (100 Hz) then the overtone series above this fundamental pitch includes the frequencies that are multiples of that: the octave (200 Hz), a fifth above that (300 Hz), two octaves above the fundamental (400Hz), a third above that (500 Hz), a fifth above that (800 Hz), a minor third above that (900 Hz), etc. Generally, lower overtones are stronger than the higher overtones. As the number and strength of the overtones increases the timbre becomes more complex. In other words, the reason you can tell that one tone is harsh (an electric guitar with a fuzz box) and another is pure (a flute) is because your auditory processors distinguish between the complex overtones of the guitar and the simple overtones of the flute. A tone without any overtones at all, such as the one that used to accompany the test pattern on the televised "This is a test of the emergency broadcast system" is called a sinusoidal wave (not often found in nature).

The relative strength of the various overtones gives an instrument its recognizable timbre or tone quality. The open "aaay" as in "say" vowel lets out a lot of overtones. The stronger presence of many overtones in this vowel gives the pitch a complex quality such as the timbre of an oboe. A nearly closed, circular mouth opening reduces the strength of the overtones that escape and we hear a relatively pure "oo" vowel. The relative lack of overtones in this vowel produces a purer quality such as the timbre of a flute. Every voice and instrument has a different timbre resulting from the "voiceprint" of the relative strengths and weaknesses of the overtones. I'll plant the seed here of a concept that will come up often in this book: threats are made of complex timbres, while affectionate and submissive utterances are purer.

Open mouth + loud + bared teeth = most complex timbre
Nearly closed lips + quiet = purest timbre

These fundamental tones and overtones are not perceived independently unless you have been trained to hear them. They are taken in as a single entity and perceived as a tone color. Tone color is roughly analogous to visual colors. In much the same way that the wavelengths of three colors may be combined to create the perception of a single color, there are a number of different wavelengths of sounds that are "translated" by our auditory processing into a single tone color. In each case a variety of wavelengths are taken in, but a single color is perceived.

In most animals, including our species, the vibrations of the vocal folds create the fundamental pitch and a resonator that is unique to each species "colors" the sound, making it recognizable. We can tell the difference between a cow's "moo" and a guy saying "heey" even if the pitches are exactly the same because the shape, length and size of the resonating cavities of the throats and mouths recognizably modify the waveform of the pitch. The difference we hear between the cow and the guy are primarily due to these modifications. The guy also has a variety of mouth shapes that are unavailable to the cow allowing him to produce vowels. If he sings the vowel "oo" on a single pitch, then sings the vowel "ee" on the same pitch, the periodic sounds created by the vibrating folds in his larynx would be the same, the change would be in the overtones created by the resonance of the upper vocal tract. He created a resonance-enhanced periodic sound.

Resonance-enhanced Periodic Sound

If I were to set this prose to music I would highlight the end of that last paragraph with a startling chord change and a booming, shimmering percussion that gradually gets softer until only a single note remains. The resonance-enhanced periodic sound is perhaps the largest and oldest key on the ring of keys to the locks that allow music access to the heart. Its origins date back to the time when mammals were a rarity and birds were evolving from dinosaurs.

Our auditory system classifies most sounds in the natural world as ignorable noise: the clicks and pops of one object striking another (transient sounds) or the white noise of the sound of rainfall (non-periodic sounds). These sounds produce random waveforms that are filtered out of our attention in much the same way as our visual processing filters out the random movement of tall grass waving in the wind. Each of these auditory and visual perceptive filters serves the same purpose, to allow heightened attention to sounds and movements that might be important to us. There is one particular type of sound that is given top-priority status in the human auditory system: the periodic sound, otherwise known as pitch. In the natural world periodic sounds are almost always produced by vocalizing animals. Since we are a natural predator as well as potential prey, Mother Nature has made sure that our ears perk up when they are visited by periodic sounds.

On the map at the beginning of the book you can see that the first territory that music follows on its journey to the heart of emotional response is through the primary auditory processing. Pitches that are modified and enhanced by some kind of resonating chamber are treated as the sounds that are given the highest priority; we are designed to take notice of resonant pitches. The attention that our brains pay to vocal sounds is noticeable in our daily lives. If you are trying to read this on a bus, even if you are seated near the noisy engine and hear loud traffic outside, it is the person on the cell phone that diverts your attention. If you are folding clothes in a laundry room with both machines going and the meow of a cat can be heard through the din, it will probably register in your mind. Psychologists categorize these as attentive emotional responses. Vocal sounds are chauffeured in a fast limousine though a traffic-cleared course straight to the emotional center of the brain. This limo also carries music because **nearly all musical instruments create resonance-enhanced periodic (vocal) sounds.**

Music benefits from the priority treatment given to vocal sounds because musical instruments produce sounds that resemble voices. Even the orchestral kettledrum, normally not thought of as a particularly vocal instrument, produces a resonance-enhanced periodic sound. If we compare the parallel development of musical instruments in a wide variety of cultures, the similarities are just as striking as they are for the drum. The following instruments have strings tuned to pitches in the range of the human voice attached to resonating boxes: the West African kora, the Chinese guqin, the Indian sitar, the North American Apaches' tsii'edo'a'tl, and the European violin. The flute may be even more ubiquitous. Fossilized bone flutes have been found that date back more than 30,000 years. Many musical instruments have been invented and modified over the years to create the kinds of resonance-enhanced richness that remind us of the human voice.

Perhaps the most vocal of all instruments is my chosen instrument, the cello. Thanks to the inherently human qualities of the instrument, but also thanks to the superlative playing of many notable cellists over the years, each of whom advanced its status and recognition, the cello is an audience favorite. We live in a golden age of the cello. Yo Yo Ma is the most famous classical instrumentalist of all time, and the four-cello heavy metal band Apocalyptica had a number one song on American rock radio in 2009.

Surely one of the reasons that I was drawn to the cello is that we were all singers in my family. My dad was a singer, voice teacher, and choir director, my brother followed in his footsteps, and my mom was the best singer of all of us. She had a voice like purple velvet. She provided the blend and color to the sound of any alto section that was lucky enough to include her. To envision the effect her voice had in a choir's alto section, imagine a canvas that was painted with a brush that was a little too dry – you can see the white canvas beneath. Mom's voice filled in these spaces with warm, blending color. It was impossible to identify her voice in the section, but it was also impossible to miss the rich blend that her presence brought to the section's sound. I have given you a chance to imprint your own lasting memory of her remarkable voice by putting a Norwegian folk song duet that she sang with my father: "Ola, ola" on the website at: www.davidteie.com and click on Olaola or listen to track 2 on the CD. If you hear it you will understand why my brother and I are musicians. With this kind of music making in the home, any other road just looks like any other road.

I am convinced that the successful unraveling of the fabric of music that underlies the ideas in this book was made possible by an intimate knowledge of vocal nuances that is uniquely available to one who has studied singing and has also implemented vocal nuances in string playing. Separating the ingredients in the recipe was the first step taken when formulating the theory of human music; this process is easier for those of us who have been examining and refining these boundaries for many years. An instrumentalist who is intimately acquainted with vocal technique is keenly aware of subtleties that define the boundaries between the vocal techniques of singing and the voice-like techniques of playing. Recognizing the importance of tone colors, for example is easier for one who plays an instrument capable of a wide range of tone colors and has devoted long hours to creating a wide-ranging tonal palette.

We Teies were the singers. If someone had a wedding or funeral in town it was our phone that would ring. I even dated singers. My dad came home one Saturday after judging high school soloists all day in Minnesota and announced that he only heard one good singer all day, but that one was a wonderful soprano from South St. Paul. A few weeks later in a combined choir concert I sang a solo with my Fridley High School choir and a girl from South St. Paul sang a solo with her choir. She had a shockingly beautiful voice and I realized that she was the singer that my dad had spoken of. Armed with an opening line "My dad judged you and came home saying that you were..." I asked her if I could call her. We went out a few times and I took her to our senior prom (shuttling her off to a concert that she had to sing between the dinner and the dance). A few years later my brother called me and asked the name of the girl from South St. Paul that I used to go out with. "Dorothy Benham", I said. "That's what I thought, she's Miss Minnesota!" So in September I watched on my little b/w television as she was crowned Miss America. I had not seen her as a beauty queen, what had attracted me most was her voice.

Cellists are able to play up in the range of the highest coloratura soprano (Dorothy is a coloratura) as well as the deepest bass. On our instrument we can play the music of any aria in any opera. In the hands of a master, the cello *becomes* the operatic character. The cello shares with the voice a highly variable timbre. If you float the bow on the string like a feather the cello produces a pure, breathy tone. If the weight of the bow-arm is relaxed into the string and drawn slowly it makes a gripping, snarling tone. The cello can weave satin as well as burlap, can paint pastel watercolors as well as vivid oils, and can sing Mozart's "Queen of the Night" aria as well as "In-A-Gaddda-Da-Vida."

Opera buffs, have you ever wondered why it is so difficult to understand the words when a coloratura soprano is singing in the extreme high register? One reason is because the audible complexity of vocal timbre diminishes in the extreme high register since most of the overtones that would identify the different vowels are too high for most of us to hear very well. It also happens to be very difficult to control the voice in that register; the constantly changing vowels and consonants tend to throw off the balance in the vocal apparatus. It is easier to sing if you keep a consistent air stream flowing and in order to achieve that the apparatus-modifying vowels and air stream-stopping consonants often get set aside.

Tones of Voice

Timbre can be changed within a single note. "You have to be able to make a career on one note!" the legendary cellist Piatigorsky once said to Stephen Kates who was my cello teacher at Peabody. When executed properly, changing the tone quality on a note is like looking into a face of one whose mood is changing: picture the change in the face of a boy waiting for his father. He looks expectantly at an opening door only to see a stranger walk in instead. Cellists want to be able to infuse a single note with so much meaning that it leaves an indelible mark in the listener's memory. These nuances are best produced while thinking about the character, the spirit behind the music.

Imagine the sound of the note created by the word "now" when the context is a frustrated father ordering a reluctant teenager to get dressed in this scene in a suburb of Detroit in 1965:

> Elmer, his wife Dottie, and their daughter Debbie were running late for the company barbeque. Dottie had called up to Deb's room repeatedly but had not yet heard an answer. When Elmer opened the door to her room he saw Debbie lying on her bed with her legs crossed talking on her princess phone saying:

"Oh, I know, he's just dreeeamy!"

Elmer could not contain his frustration:
"Deborah Pattison put down the phone and get dressed
(here is where you want to listen to the "musical" sound
of this note) NOW!"

Loud and in the upper register of his voice, this note sounds like a blast from a brass instrument.

One more scene: This time imagine the sound of the note created when this same word floats from the upward-turned face of a tenderly smiling high school girl in the arms of a boy... it's one month later and Debbie is dating Bobby, the boy she was cooing about on the phone:

Debbie and Bobby are sitting together on the grass in a secluded corner of a park. Bobby has been trying to have a respectable demeanor throughout the late afternoon, but when his face is close to hers he feels her body soften and forgets to keep up his mature façade:

"You know... I... I was wondering if... when I could kiss you?"

She tilts her head slightly looking at his lips through half-closed eyes and says:

(listen for it) "Now."

Intoned in a tender, hushed treble voice reminiscent of a breathy clarinet in a jazz ballad. More to the point – the breathy clarinet is reminiscent of the treble voice.

The qualitative difference between the sounds of these two versions of the word "now" is an example of the realm of human vocal expression and of the interpretive artist. Inflections in music approximate the sounds that we use in expressive speech. Music and speech draw from the very same well. As demonstrated in these contrasting examples, much of the expressive communication in speech is broadcast via tone quality.

Why is timbre so important in musical expression? The foundation of the answer is found in a pattern of communication shared by almost all vocalizing animals. Eugene S. Morton discovered that a wide variety of birds and mammals use the same types of timbres for certain expressions. Low-pitched, harsh vocalizations are threatening while high-pitched, pure vocalizations are affectionate. Naturally, the high and low are relative. A high pitch for a human is a low pitch to a squirrel, and a high pitch for a squirrel is a low pitch to a bat.

One of the keys to my ability to write effective music for cotton-top tamarin monkeys was the realization that what is high to us is low to them. Consequently, calls that sound low and harsh to them sound rather chirpy to us. At the other end of the spectrum, their high, pure, cooing-to-baby calls merely sound like whistles to us. One reason that we don't respond emotionally to their calls is because they are in a different perceptual range. When I slowed down the tamarin calls they told a different story. A tamarin threat slowed down eight times could easily be used in a horror show while the slowed-down tamarin mother-to-infant call sounds sweet and tuneful. It made sense to me that if I created melodies based on the melodic outlines of tamarin calls (much like the French composers create melodies based on the melodic outlines of the French language) then sped the music up eight times it would be more likely to be appreciated by them.

Timbres Trigger Emotions

Morton's discovery demonstrates that our emotional responses to different qualities of sound are even deeper than primal. We tend to describe our most basic human characteristics as "primal" or "primitive" or "primary" referring to qualities that were present "in the earliest age". In the context of our understanding of evolution these are characteristics that we share with other primates. But the common source of expressive communication through timbre can be traced to common ancestors that are much more ancient, going back hundreds of millions of years. If you approach a vocal animal with a loud, harsh voice using a pitch that is low for that species, that animal will understand your threat.

Guttural threats as well as affectionate coos originate in and are interpreted by the same area of the brain: the deep, midbrain, mammalian structures of the limbic system. The vocalizations of screaming, sobbing, crying, moaning, and laughing originate in one of the limbic structures, the amygdala. The most deeply affected person will not use speech at all, but will make sounds that have emanated from this emotional well. These primitive, mammalian vocalizations communicate directly from emotional center to emotional center, bypassing the language centers of logical and interpretive cognition; they are generated in a different part of the brain than language.

If I scream when I see a threat and you startle at the sound of my scream, the entire interplay between us progresses without any conscious thought whatsoever. Natural selection placed the production and reception of these emotional signals near the motor-function-governing brain stem for a good reason. Reaction time is critically important, there is no time for the conscious/thinking cortical structures to follow the complex reasoning process that would involve evaluating the sound, computing the need for action based on the possible threats present in the environment, and finally sending to the motor cortex instructions to respond. The adrenaline produced when we hear a scream is triggered directly from the nearby deep brain structures without waiting for the approval of reason.

Here is a simplified trail of the sound of a scream through the brain:

- The sound enters the ear
- It is recognized as a vocal sound and, as such, is given priority treatment in primary auditory processing
- The amygdala recognizes the voiceprint/timbre and initiates an emotional response by triggering the release of adrenaline.

Loud, harsh, periodic sounds (pitches) are short circuit emotional trigger sounds. The reaction to such a sound must be immediate; there is no time for conscious evaluation of threat potential.

Loud
+ Harsh
+ Fast
+ Vocal
= heart rate increase, eye dilation, and increased blood flow to the vital organs.

The brain will figure out where the threat-like sounds came from later, for now immediate response is the top priority.

Patients whose amygdalas have been destroyed often lose the ability to sing and properly enunciate vocal inflections. This loss of function can also cause great changes in the pitches and timbres of speech. Clearly this Grand Central Station of our emotions plays an important role in music. Considering the immediacy of sound-to-response, music not only affects us subconsciously, it affects us *pre*consciously.

Many animals are born with "hard-wired" emotional responses to certain calls. There are a number of species that have different warning calls for different threats because the defense must be appropriate for the attacker. Burrowing animals must keep a wary eye on both the skies and the grass. If the threat is a hawk, for example, the right defensive maneuver is to retreat into the ground. If the threat is a snake, however, retreating into the ground would be suicidal; dispersal or mobbing will more effectively foil the attacker. Accordingly, the warning call given when a hawk is spotted is different than the warning call for a snake. Now here's where this gets interesting and musically relevant: research has shown that although some of these calls are learned, others are inborn. In other words, a juvenile that has never seen a hawk and has never heard an alarm call scampers into the ground when it hears its first hawk alarm call. That is a preconscious emotional response. A young chimpanzee will appropriately react to a particular warning cry from its mother without having heard the sound before. Apes and monkeys with surgically muted mothers or reared in isolation produce appropriate complex emotional calls to convey information, including the presence of danger, and they will respond to these same calls with appropriate reactions *the first time they hear them*. Many of the fears triggered by warning calls are not learned by the chimpanzee, they are not learned by the prairie dog, and they are not learned by us; we are born with them already in place. Of course, these emotional sounds are species-specific. The warning cry of the prairie dog won't have any effect on a nearby cow.

Now imagine writing a film score for a prairie dog horror movie. The prairie dogs are sitting in their little seats in a darkened theater munching on bags of wheatgrass. The violins play a repeated motive that subtly imitates a snake warning call in the scene where a mad prairie dog with a bloody knife sneaks around a burrow corner. The eyes of the riveted audience dilate, their heart-rates go up, they are on edge and uneasy as they feel for the intended victim in the movie: "You gotta get OUTTA THERE!!" If you would compose the underscore using the snake motive in that scene you would be the Bernard Hermann of prairie dog horror films.

As Morton discovered, one of the primary differences between the various emotionally generated sounds is timbre. The qualities of sound that are activated by the emotional structures of the producer will activate an appropriate emotional response immediately and instinctively in the receiver. Harsh/fear is at one pole and pure/affection at the other.

Emotions Direct Us

In order to trace the pathways that music takes into our innermost selves, most readers will need to broaden their definitions of emotions. The division between thoughts and feelings is artificial. As a brief example of the complex relationship between them and of the processes and motives of the mammalian midbrain that controls our emotions we could examine the subject of so many songs: love. Few human activities fire up the midbrain to initiate such powerful behavior-directing mechanisms as mating.

Debbie has fallen in love with Bobby. She is euphoric when they are together as they were for the entire weekend.

(I won't bother to list the mood-enhancing chemicals released when an attraction turns to a crush, but they form a potent drug cocktail.)

It's now Tuesday afternoon and Bobby has not called since a short check-in Monday. Debby is feeling short of breath and distressed.

(She is going through withdrawal. The midbrain has identified a mate and will not allow her to lose him without a penalty.)

At this point Debby thinks about Bobby often. After she has been distracted by something that occupies her attention her thoughts return to him because her hormones are hard wired to continually nudge her about his absence. We will turn up more evidence of emotions directing our thinking as we forge our way into the mysteries of music.

The emotional centers of our brains have simple and effective ways to control our behaviors and communication. The primary tools are also polar: reward and punishment. If we behave in ways that provide for the success and propagation of the species we are rewarded by the dopamine class of euphoria rewards: eat ripe fruit, drink cool water, have sex, cuddle a baby and so on. The more important the behavior to the species, the stronger the reward: fat-filled comfort food brings out the "mmm, nice" while orgasm supports the only truly necessary act for propagation with an inner party complete with fireworks, an open bar, beautifying goggles, and bouncers posted outside the locked gate keeping out distractions.

The regulators of emotions deliver punishment by inflicting pain. It has been shown that physical and emotional pains both activate the same areas of the brain. The pain that you feel when you set your hand on a hot stove is a mechanism that helps to prevent you from damaging your body, and the emotions directing your behavior instill a fear of the hot stove that prevents you from touching it again. In the same way, and from the same behavior-directing parts of the brain, the grief that you feel with the loss of a loved one is a kind of punishment that is intended to direct you to protect your loved ones. In both cases, physical and social, the pain introduced by the emotional directors within us will tend to prevent the repetition of the action that brought on the pain.

The emotional centers are also capable of exerting direct control over our bodies. As a speaker becomes emotionally charged the conscious brain may still control the words, but the midbrain takes over control of the voice. The more highly charged the emotional state, the more control the emotional centers exert over the sound of the voice. In normal conversation the midbrain lays low and the contours and vocal qualities of speech adhere to the designs of linguistics. But when emotions swell they modulate the throat and vocal apparatus.

Moans have neither the loud sonic complexity of screams nor the soft purity of whimpers; they are centered between the two extremes and vocalized in the middle range. The best music of love is rich with feelings that moans inspire. The slowly moving contours of mid-range musical melisma will touch our inborn sensitivity to moaning and entice the same instinctive reaction that we would have to hearing a moan. The similarity between the sounds of moans caused by pleasure and those caused by pain may appear to be incongruous from the point of view of a person experiencing those diametrically opposed sensations, but the reason for the similarity is more obvious when we consider that both types of moans are intended to induce similar reactions from the listener: the moan of pleasure inducing feelings of love and the moan of pain inducing her sister feeling, sympathy. One of human's favorite pets, the cat, has a vocal communication that serves the same purpose as our moan. The purr is a sound that conveys contentment to the hearer, but cats also purr when they are in pain. It would seem that cat's purrs are roughly equivalent to our moans.

Screams are the human fear mongers. A loud scream is the warning cry that will induce hair-raising alertness in every human within hearing distance of the screamer in the blink of an eye. There's no reason to use much print here reminding us of the obvious evolutionary necessity for screams. The first time I ever heard a truly blood-curdling scream (made by my son) my body froze, my eyes widened, my heart pounded, and then I ran toward the sound. A fairly large group of children had been playing in the back yard and fun-related squeals and screams had been commonly heard that afternoon. This scream was different. I couldn't have said what the difference was at the time, but it was a sound that was impossible to ignore. He had caught his finger in a folding chair and we were soon to be on our way to the emergency room to stitch him up. Our highly developed and subtle sound processing capabilities allow us to detect minute differences in the tone colors of human vocalizations and the subtle difference between the sound of his scream and the sound of a happily screaming child in the yard was instantly recognized by my limbic system's "ears."

Think of the difference between the tones of voice of a professional wrestler over a PA system and a mother over her baby. Maternal cooing conveys peaceful affection and sounds like pure soft flutes, while the aggression that precedes battle is roared like the sound of a Stratocaster with a fuzz box - wild with overtones. It may help you to appreciate how naturally the sound fits the circumstance to mix the two images. Take the microphone out of the wrestler's hand and replace it with a baby and imagine the wrestler keeping the same tone he was using when he said: "I'm comin' to get you!" as he growls at the cherubic face: "I'm comin' to feed you!"

Music Plays Human Perceptions

Are there other musical elements that play this perceptive polarity? We know that the emotional vocalizations of love and submission are quiet and consist of purer waveforms while the emotional vocalizations that express the threats and screams that incite fear are loud and have complex overtones. Research has shown that the dissonant, atonal music of Arnold Schoenberg also induces a fear response. Do the timbres of threats have anything to do with atonal music?

Since atonal music is not widely disseminated or appreciated, perhaps a brief primer would be appropriate. In the early 20th Century Schoenberg invented a style of composition that produced music that is almost entirely dissonant and has no traditional key center. It is worth noting that he and his followers did not intend to be writing music that was consistently disturbing to listeners. It is also worth noting that this kind of music did not evolve slowly through the gradual adoption of appealing traits that were shared and passed on by many, but was an intellectually devised system that was the brainchild of one man.

If a contemporary composer of atonal music in 1960 were to have read in the science section of his morning paper that cognitive researchers discovered that the music of Arnold Schoenberg activated a fear response in their test subjects, the news might have made him feel a bit uncomfortable. But he could have picked up the phone and called Alfred Hitchcock's favorite composer Bernard Hermann and would have been told the same thing. Atonal music found a niche in horror movies long before the fear-confirming cognitive tests were even possible.

Since our emotions exist to direct our behavior it follows that music capable of eliciting emotions can direct our reactions to scenes on film. Try this if you doubt the power of music to instill a scene with emotion: rent *Psycho*, mute your television, and watch the scene early in the film where Marion is driving in the rain at night. Not much there, so, we've all driven in the rain. Now turn up the volume and watch it with Hermann's soundtrack. The panic of an escaping thief is represented *entirely* in the music. I hope you paid attention to all of the music; the white-knuckle emotions revved-up by this landmark score deserve notice. How was it done? With suddenly loud, heart-pounding runnin rhythms, and judicious use of that ancient purveyor of fear: dissonance.

Consonance and Dissonance

Conveying concepts of consonance and dissonance in prose is perhaps the highest of the many hurdles that must be cleared when writing about music. Defining the sound of dissonance in words is something like describing a color; it is difficult to do without a reference. For those readers who haven't spent much time in music theory classes, the best way to call your attention to consonance and dissonance in music is to hear examples (go to www.davidteie.com and click on Dissonance or listen to track 3 on the CD). You will discover that you already know the difference between them even though you may not have been familiar with the terms.

Consonant intervals are created by the simplest ratios the most consonant interval is the octave, a ratio of 1:2. If a guitarist plucks an open string (vibrating 200 times per second), then places a finger on the string dividing it exactly in half it will sound an octave higher (vibrating 400 times per second). If the finger is placed so that the string is divided in three parts it sounds a fifth higher, the 1:3 ratio of the fifth creates the second-most consonant interval. As the ratios become more complex the intervals created become less consonant.

Why does dissonance make us frightened? When I followed the clues that led to a plausible answer to this question I discovered that the dissonant-fear connection has ancient evolutionary roots. Simply put:

ordered communication conveys: "everything is ok", chaotic communication conveys: "everything is not ok".

The axis polarity of consonance and dissonance is the fulcrum of the art of harmony. It is one of the many elements of music that are universally understood and not subject to the tastes of individuals. The force that results from the polarity of consonance and dissonance is the force that drives music. It is to music what positive/negative is to electromagnetism. This polarity is enabled by the birthplace of the sonic differentiation between good and bad: the emotional centers of the mammalian brain. Dissonance activates the limbic structures responsible for fear while consonance activates the structures responsible for pleasure.

Why should the emotional centers, care about dissonance? It is not possible that the responses were placed there by natural selection for no purpose. It is also highly unlikely that it is some kind of sonic coincidence that includes not one but two different and opposing reactions, one to dislike the dissonance and another to like the consonance. Since the only pertinent use of intervals in our natural world is produced by human vocalizations the answer must lie there. **A dissonant chord is interpreted as the harsh vocal tone of a threat, a consonant chord is interpreted as the pure vocal tone of affection.**

Indeed, the foundation of this polarity is found in our emotionally generated vocalizations. The human vocal sounds that communicate threats and warnings that induce fear contain the harsh-sounding complex overtones found in open-vowel screams. At the other end of the spectrum, the vocalizations that express pleasure or induce pity are the pure waveform sounds of cooing and whimpering. The quality of sound of the treble melodies of mother's speech heard in the womb has a particularly pure sound. The sound-insulating belly of the mother attenuates the high overtones more than the fundamental pitch, leaving relatively pure waveforms for the fetus to hear. The screams of warning are loud for obvious reasons while the emotional vocalizations of love and sympathy are soft for equally apparent reasons. The complex overtones of the open vowels, the "a" family, are easily produced loudly while the purer waveforms created by the covered vowels of "oh" and "oo" are difficult to project over long distances.

The pure vocal tone is like the smooth flow of water from a faucet. If you put your finger in the stream the flow is disrupted. The closer your finger is to the faucet the more the stream is disturbed. A similar effect is produced in the voice. In a calm state the voice produces a clear, even sound. When we feel angry, however, muscles in the throat distort the vocal folds and disrupt the flow of the periodic sound, producing a harsh timbre.

Although a mutant gene that reverses these reflexes may exist somewhere, effectively, this response is never built backwards. No one enters a bathroom, turns on the light, sees a huge spider lurking on the corner of the mirror, feels startled and frightened, and then steps back and emits a soft "oooo". Accordingly, our natural responses to consonance and dissonance are also never built backwards. Composers may habituate themselves somewhat by constant exposure and rationalize the use of relentlessly dissonant music in the belief that they are producing something new and, therefore, valuable, but the templates of our understanding are inborn and not learned. The sound of fingernails scraping a blackboard sounds like the distilled essence of the harshness of a baby's cry, which is designed to be irritating. The complex overtones that it exemplifies will always sound disturbingly harsh to human ears.

Recognizing Voices

Voice recognition is one of the most important and well-developed human abilities. We are able to recognize individual voices with remarkable precision. One of the vocal characteristics that is key to recognition is the relative strength of the overtones that are present in the sound. Every voice has a unique mix of strengths and weaknesses in the overtones, called formants. Each of us has accumulated a mental library of voice templates that are used to compare and recognize. The process is very much like the barcode on packaging used at the checkout register. The variations in thin and wide lines on the barcode are read, compared to a stored template, and rung up when a match is identified: "BEEP It's my sister Alice in trouble again." When you hear a friend's voice, the relative intensities of the overtones are compared with the collection of stored templates in your mind and recognition occurs when a match is identified: "That is Alice speaking." This recognition is likely to be accompanied by a subtle emotional trigger. If you didn't expect Alice to be in town you may feel attentive. If Alice sounds like she's worried you may feel sympathetic. It's important to remember that the recognition and emotions often occur before your conscious evaluation. You may *feel* attentive before you *think*: "What is she doing here?"

While individual voice recognition is highly developed and precise, the tone-of-voice recognition of a stranger is necessarily much broader. Individual voices have identifiable overtone-series barcodes, but voices have qualities related to the emotional state of the communicator that need to be generally recognizable. If a stranger speaks in a threatening tone we need to be able to recognize that threat without comparing the sound to the normal tone-of-voice for that individual. For this general recognition we possess a set of templates that are hard-wired into our system at birth. If highly specific individual recognition is comparable to a barcode, general tone-of-voice recognition is more like fingerprint matching. A fingerprint contains identifiable turning points and curves called minutiae. When a latent fingerprint, such as that found in a crime scene, is compared to templates of complete fingerprints the investigators are looking for matching minutiae. A 10-point match is perfect. When a latent fingerprint is incomplete and imperfect it might be a 4-point match. In this analogy, you would feel an emotional response to a sound that only gets a 4-point match to a template of sounds stored in your auditory system.

Mother Nature has set these emotional responses on a hair trigger. No harm is done if adrenaline is introduced even if it turned out to be unnecessary. ("That startled me but it was just a bag of groceries falling off of the table.") But a species would bear a significant evolutionary cost if adrenaline were not introduced when it is needed. ("Hmmm, a crash at my door, I'll just finish this sentence before I look to see what it is. Oh, there's a rival tribesman in my tent holding a club.") Our emotional responses to vocal sounds are set to deliver when an incoming sound merely resembles a recognized type of vocalization. For example, the scream is a loud, high-pitched, shriek with an open vowel. If an incoming sound is loud, high-pitched, and has complex overtones, even if it is not clearly identifiable as a person screaming, the midbrain will tend to initiate the response that is appropriate for a scream (fear/attention) and then send the sound up to the areas responsible for conscious thought for further evaluation.

The previously outlined ideas bear reviewing here because the function of dissonance is so important to the production of music. **When two or more pitches combine to create the aligned overtones of consonance the sound resembles the relatively pure tone of voice of affection. When two or more pitches combine to create overtones that are out of alignment, the interference and disruption of the waveform caused by the clashing notes of dissonance resembles a harsh, threatening tone of voice.**

The relationship between tones-of-voice and harmony is fairly simple even though harmony itself is wonderfully complex. The aspect of harmony that is relevant here is the single moment-in-time quality of any given chord; it is the kind of CT scan of harmony that you would get if you could freeze an orchestra instantly and all the players would hold the notes they were playing at a given moment. The quality of sound contained in such a chord gets its emotional punch from the voice interpretation part of our auditory processing. Chords that contain more dissonances are perceived on the threat end of the spectrum while chords that contain only consonances are perceived on the affection end.

If our auditory processing picks up an ordered waveform of a resonator-enhanced periodic sound in the frequency range of the human voice it will send the message to the emotional centers of the brain that an affectionate voice has been recognized. Our emotional centers are closely linked to our auditory processing and respond with pleasure to the sounds of consonance and with fear to the sound of dissonance because Mother Nature has wired us up that way to interpret vocalizations.

This pure/harsh polarity is also found in the linear intervals of melodies. As I discovered when researching the vocal communication of the cotton-top tamarin monkeys, this is true of other primate communication as well. There is a clear relationship between the motivation behind the call and the consonant or dissonant intervals used in the call. Affective expressions such as mother-to-infant calls are consonant and harmonious while threats use random intervals that created many dissonant intervals. Music has taken the consonant intervals of loving, flirtatious speech and used them as the foundation of harmonious melodies and taken the dissonance of linguistic warning cries and threats and used them as the foundation of dissonance in melodies.

The consonant/dissonant polarity enables a broad range of expression in speech and in music. The following is an outline of its evolution:

1. Emotional vocalizations use simple/consonance to express submission and affection and complex/dissonance to express danger and threats.
2. The corollary qualities of these emotional vocalizations were adopted into spoken non-tonal language to communicate emotion.
3. Music has further adapted the qualities of simple/consonance and complex/dissonance to the expressive interplay of timbres and intervals.

Our intuitive recognition of the expressive difference between consonance and dissonance led creators of music to organize a system of tones that derives its internal conflicts-resolutions from combining and alternating intervals that communicate anxiety with intervals that communicate attraction.

Species-specific Music

The automatic recognition of the difference between the tones of voice used for threats and for affection are not reserved only for humans. It is a characteristic of animal communication that has been handed down to us through countless generations of countless species for hundreds of millions of years. Even lizards produce a complex, broadband "hiss" to communicate a threat. I found when researching the vocal communications of the cotton-top tamarin monkey that the pure order heard in the undisturbed sound of cooing and the disorder found in the complex sounds of shrieks is represented in the rhythms and tonalities of their calls as well. The smooth-sounding mother-to-infant calls use regularly spaced syllables and consonant, even Mozartean melodic intervals. In contrast, the rough-sounding threat calls use irregularly spaced syllables and random, dissonant intervals. This led me to propose that: **an order/disorder polarity governs animal communication.**

When I first approached the eminent primatologist Charles Snowdon with the idea of testing the validity of "human music" theory by composing species-specific music for his colony of cotton-top tamarin monkeys he was intrigued and interested but not inclined to spend much time or funding for a study. He agreed to it only after he read my response to a message that he had sent to me that included two newly discovered tamarin calls.

I had been studying and analyzing tamarin calls working with a collection that were contained in a large, online library of known calls and their contexts. Each call had a specific, often charming name such as the "chevron chatter" or the "ascending multi-whistle" - a lovely and quiet mother-to-infant call that sounds like birdsong. Dr. Snowdon sent to me two new calls, labeled "SLtrill" and "SLmulti". I assumed that the similar names meant that they were similar calls with similar contexts. When heard at normal speed each of the two calls sounds like a chirp. The procedure that I had been using to analyze the tamarin vocalizations was: 1) slow down the recordings 8X in order to bring the frequencies of the calls into the human vocal range, making them easier for us to "understand" (it's a bit like looking at something through a magnifying glass) and then, 2) create a written version of the calls, representing the pitches and rhythms in musical notation. I found that these two new calls were very dissimilar. The SLmulti uses a harsh tone-of-voice in irregular rhythms, randomly spaced intervals, and randomly interspersed directions between the syllables creating a jagged melodic line. The SLtrill, on the other hand, uses a normal tone-of-voice in very regularly spaced intervals in one direction creating a smooth, straight melodic line.

Hearing the slowed-down SLtrill was something of a revelation, representing a turning point in my understanding of the intimate relationship between natural animal vocalizations and music. The SLtrill is a descending E flat major scale beginning on G. The first time I heard it I was so stunned by its obvious musicality that I had to sit down. I played it over and over, laughing in dismay. (Perhaps my own laughter created a regularly spaced descending scale - it is quite common, after all.) Isn't it typically anthropocentric of us to assume that we humans invented the E flat major scale? You can hear the SLtrill and SLmulti calls in real time and slowed down at www.davidteie.com and click on Tamarin calls or listen to track 4 on the CD.

I wrote to Dr. Snowdon somewhat hesitantly, since he had not yet agreed to conduct a test of my species-specific music, stating that I didn't believe that the SLtrill and the SLmulti belonged in the same category and outlined my observations. As it happens, SL are simply the initials of the person who recorded the calls; they were not intended to be placed in the same category. The SLmulti is, indeed, a threat call that had been directed toward an intruder. The SLtrill is an "all clear" communication that was heard after the intruder had left the room. Chuck was pleased to find that I had been able to correctly interpret the general meanings of the calls through musical analysis alone without prior knowledge of the contexts. He agreed to test the effectiveness of my species-specific music for tamarins and it led to the first controlled study that showed any species other than human reacting to music.

We used two widely contrasting types of music in the study, hoping that that would give us a better chance of inducing observable responses from these active and vocal squirrel-sized monkeys. One type of music is based on aggression and is intended to excite them. Can you name the corollary style of human music that is based on aggression? (The answer will be found in a few paragraphs.) The other type of music is intended to calm them down – these are the tamarin lullabies and ballads. Specialists in new-world primate behaviors carried out the observations using a software program that collects and sorts the data. Anxious behaviors such as scent marking and increased movement were recorded as responses to the tamarin aggressive-based music, as were contented behaviors such as foraging and decreased movement to the tamarin affilliative-based music.

In May of 2007 I visited the University of Wisconsin-Madison to record tamarin calls and discuss the protocol of the study. As I was nearing the end of my recording on the second day I sang a little song to them as a human music control. As expected, they weren't at all interested. Then I whistled an improvised tune based on the frequency range and contours of their mother-to-infant calls. Every member of the family stopped where they were and looked at me. They were as still as statues even after I had finished. These are normally jumpy little critters. They hop around and chirp to each other regularly as a defensive strategy; it is beneficial for them in the wild to be moving targets in constant communication with one another. When I whistled to them in their own musical "language" they were hearing the first musical communication designed for their species. We were, all of us in the room, monkey and human primates alike, stunned by the effect. I have posted the actual recording of this session at www.davidteie.com and click on Stunned silence and on track 5 of the CD. Listen for the movements of the tamarins bouncing around in the cage before I whistled, then during the whistled tamarin ballad you will hear a couple of little leaps before everything stopped (then that's me saying "wow" under my breath). The memory of this frozen moment - I was staring at them staring at me - will stay with me until my ability to remember is gone.

Following that I tried a version of the tamarin agitating music. I produced random "ch" rhythms and broadband "chh" (as pronounced in "chutzpa or Bach). I didn't move at all as I was doing this, I remained a still as ever, but the tamarins began moving all over the caged place. They were literally bouncing off the walls and yelling wildly. So the first tamarin heavy metal music concert was also a complete success. Yes, that's the answer to the question I posed earlier: heavy metal music is the human music of aggression. You can hear this improvised tamarin concert at www.davidteie.com and click on Improvised tamarin metal or listen to track 6 on the CD. The family became so vocal and agitated that I stopped doing it, fearing that the entire wing full of tamarin families would start to freak out. After my successful personal concert for the tamarins I bounded into the lab office and did a song and dance for the bemused lab techs: "I may be just a schmo to you, but to these tamarin monkeys I am Elvis!"

I will not be writing agitating music like this for other species. We only used music based on aggressive vocalizations briefly in the test; in the formal study each group only heard the 30-second tamarin "heavy metal" song once. When writing and recording music for other captive species (including the captive feline you may have in your apartment) I will only present calming or enlivening music.

A week or so after the testing had begun I was eager to know how things were going so I wrote to Chuck and waited for a reply. He responded that he did not know and would not ask because the tests were being conducted by someone who was naïve to the results we expected to find. Chuck would not taint the impartiality of the researcher by asking questions. I admit that I was disappointed in the lack of information, but at the same time I felt the cleanliness of true, double blind testing. (Double because not only did the primate behavior specialist not know what we expected to find but, strictly speaking, the tamarin monkeys didn't know either, did they?) In the summer of 2010 news of scientific impropriety in the hallowed Ivy League halls would shake the primatology world. In the wake of the news of data-altered cotton-top tamarin studies coming out of New England, the value of Chuck's insistence on strict methodology that he insisted upon in Wisconsin would serve us well when the time came for the impressed but incredulous music cognition scientists to pore over our data looking for leaks and smudges.

The study demonstrated that the tamarin monkeys were agitated by the tamarin heavy metal music and were calmed by the tamarin ballads. They were, as usual, indifferent to the human music that was presented to them as controls. This was the first demonstration in a controlled study that any species other than human could show an appreciation for music. You can hear the tamarin music by visiting www.davidteie.com and click on Tamarin music or listen to track 7 on the CD.

The one apparent anomaly was that they were calmed by the human speed metal that we used as examples of human agitating music: *Of Wolf and Man* by Metallica and *The Grudge* by Tool. That result is consistent with the theory even though it was surprising to us at first. The harsh tones are probably only dimly received by the monkeys since the low tones of this music are well out of their own vocal range. The pulses, however, would have been clearly heard. As it happens, the tempo of human speed metal pulses are about the same as the resting pulse of an adult cotton-top tamarin monkey. This finding tends to support the idea that womb music is effective for monkeys as well as humans, that is – as long as the musician matches the right womb with the right animal.

The musical analysis of tamarin communication revealed much about the common sonic ground that we share with these little beasts and other animals. The consonant sounds and ordered rhythms of the SLtrill communicate the return to order of an "all clear" call. The dissonant intervals and irregular rhythms heard in the threat/alarm SLmulti call represent chaos. The tamarins use random intervals between the pitches of the syllables when communicating threats; this randomness produces noticeably dissonant intervals. The rhythmic spacing of the syllables is irregular, as is the contour of the melody. In contrast to the straight-line order of the SLtrill, the SLmulti creates a zigzag melodic line that goes up and down randomly. It is the chaotic nature of the SLmulti call that led me to conjecture that it is a threat.

The order found in communication that sends the message that everything is okay extends beyond vocalizations. We also use regularly spaced, smooth-onset gestures when we stroke animals to comfort them and show our affection. Gentle rocking is another example of ordered, repetitious movement that conveys and promotes a sense of wellbeing. The pure vocal tones that a mother uses to soothe her baby are a sonic version of the smooth repetitions of stroking and rocking.

Order/Disorder

Light – dark, hot – cold, consonance – dissonance, these are all apparent polarities that actually involve only the relative presence of a single entity. Absolute darkness emits and reflects no photons and every increment of increasing brightness indicates an increase of the amount of light. Similarly, absolute zero is a state where the molecules are stationary and the increments of movement above that represent increasing degrees of heat. Vocal communication and music are based on a similar apparent polarity that represents varying degrees of a single quality: order.

If you were to whistle a constant pitch you would have something approaching the zenith of ordered sound, the pure waveform. It consists of a single, undisturbed oscillation. A two-dimensional representation looks like this:

If you were to simulate the raspy hiss of a threatening reptile the waveform would look more like this:

Cats threaten with a hiss produced with a wide-open mouth and bared teeth. It produces a very disordered "white noise" sound. Dogs threaten and warn with barks and snarls. The barks are harsh, loud, and so disordered that the pitch of the vocal tone is often not discernable. Their snarls are made with bared teeth and use a harsh tone in the lowest vocal register. At the other end of the spectrum cats express contentment or need for sympathy with the nearly perfect order of a purr. The cat's purr is an extremely regular pulse of about 28 cycles per inhalation or exhalation. Dogs express submission and need for sympathy with the highly ordered pure tones of whimpering. Cotton top tamarins have an extensive vocal range and dozens of calls that are used in a variety of contexts. The broad expressive vocabulary of these primates allows us to see how the order/disorder expressive polarity extends to rhythms and pitches as well as tone quality.

Inclusive Expressivity of Ordered Sound

Ordered communication is associated with inclusion; increasingly ordered communication represents increased social inclusion. The random, chaotic sounds of threats are meant to exclude. Normal in-group communication is more ordered and insinuates a general acceptance. The most highly ordered communication is reserved for the most intimate in-group members. This principle governs vocal communication in birds and even reptiles and reaches a level of highly evolved and subtle communication in the animals with the most sensitive hearing: mammals.

When we lay out all the elements of vocal expression and music a pattern emerges that is consistent across a broad range of categories of sounds including rhythms, melodies, and harmonies. The pattern seems to be inviolate. Just as no one would coo softly when seeing a snake in the bed, no animals express threats in soft, pure tones. Nor are there examples of maternal invitations to suckling that are expressed in loud, harsh barks.

The apparent polarity of Order/Disorder can be understood as the primary governing rule of expressive communication.

ORDER	DISORDER
Inclusion	Exclusion
Affection	Threat
Simple waveforms (in vocal timbres of affection)	Complex waveforms (in vocal timbres of aggression)
Consonant intervals (of affection)	Dissonant intervals (of aggression or distress)
Consonant harmonies	Dissonant harmonies
Regular rhythms	Irregular rhythms

This universally understood distinction represents an important expressive foundation of music that is profoundly linked to the communication of distant evolutionary ancestors that formed many millions of years ago. The expressions of the contented cat, the submissive dog, and the highly ordered music of Mozart are all derived from the universally understood communication of intimate acceptance. This recognition is as much a part of your nature as are the vertebrae in your spine.

Human Music

Dissonance as Spice

It is important to note that nearly all music that we hear contains some dissonance. It is a popular notion among armchair musicologists that the "progress" of Western music involved the gradual inclusion of ever more dissonances into musical textures. It is true that 17th and 18th century music contained fewer dissonances than 19th century music, and that most 20th century concert hall music is rife with it. On closer examination we see that Johann Sebastian Bach (1685-1750) used more dissonances than Mozart (1756-1791). This move toward tamer harmonies was led by none other than old Johann Sebastian's sons Carl Philipp Emanuel and Johann Christian. Some students of Johann Sebastian who were devotees of the earlier Baroque style thought that the ensuing Classical music of his sons was rather sissy.

The primary difference between the dissonance in early music and the dissonance in 20th century music is in its function. Dissonances in the music of the early masters nearly always resolve, meaning: the dissonant note that doesn't fit into the chord moves to a nearby consonant note that does fit into the chord. These movements provide tension and release and give the listener the sense that there is direction in the musical line. For instance, the note in the melody in *Happy Birthday* that falls on the first syllable of the name of the birthday celebrant ("Florence") is a dissonant note that does not fit into the chord but is immediately resolved to a consonance on the second syllable: "Happy birthday to you, happy birthday to you, happy birthday, dear "Flor-" (dissonant) "ence" (consonant), happy birthday to you." The dissonances associated with 20th century composers are unresolved and are often presented in unbroken succession so that nearly every moment contains a dissonant sound. The perception of direction that results from the movement from dissonance to consonance is erased when the listener is faced with static dissonance.

Just as the classical composers created music that was primarily intended to be beautiful and uplifting, many 20th century composers (perhaps we could refer to them as the "disillusionists") were intent on reminding us of the Grim Realities. They were successful. Unfortunately, the subliminal price we in the concert hall have paid for this revulsion is a general reluctance to return to the place of discomfiture. Since human nature abhors chaos perhaps it is fitting that so many of us abhor relentlessly harsh music.

Composers who adhere to a style of consistent dissonance have well-practiced rationalizations for writing music the way they do. I don't mind letting a secret out here about composition: the close relationship between randomness and dissonance means that it is much easier to compose dissonant music than consonant music. Of the twelve possible combinations of two notes in Western music, five of them are consonant, three of them are dissonant, and four of them are somewhere in-between. Two random notes have a 41.7% chance of creating a consonant interval. The chance that a third random note will be consonant relative to the first two is reduced exponentially. The chance that a fourth random note will be consonant relative to the first three is further reduced. **Randomness creates dissonance.** This ease of style has let some composers into the "often-heard club" who have more talent for creating scores that look beautiful on the page than music that sounds beautiful to the ear. The audience assumes that the composers know what they are doing since many of them discuss music in lofty terms, fostering the notion that they hear on a superior level. It is well known among musicians that many contemporary composers cannot tell when a player plays a wrong note in one of the composer's own compositions. One hilarious instance in our orchestra involved a clarinetist who played all of the rehearsals and the first concert on a clarinet in B flat before discovering that the score called for clarinet in A. That means that every single note that he played throughout the week, with the composer conducting, was wrong.

Musical Roller Coasters

Most musicians make music that moves them and hope that it will appeal to others in the same way. When we get "goose bumps" from music, the reward structures in the brain are stimulated. These are the same areas that activate when a hungry person eats or an aroused person has sex. While dissonance triggers a fear response from the amygdala, the brain's fear center, pleasant music tends to inhibit its activity. There are some musicians, however, who have managed to tap into this fear in a way that produces a thrill. They have discovered fear-inducing elements of music that make people want to come back for more rather than stay away.

Human Music

In the right frame of mind, for the right group of rebellious people, with the right drive in the pulse, fear can thrill in music the way fear of falling can thrill on a roller coaster. Music encompasses more than beauty; there are occasions for it to express anger, desperation, and even violence. Hormone-driven teens that seem to be genetically required to be rebellious prefer music that compliments their feelings. Power/hard rock is music of rage and rebellion. Not many rainbows there. Everyone in the room of a heavy metal concert will feel the raw energy of the driving rhythms, the screaming vocals, and the extraordinary volume of sound. This music is synchronic with the break out psychological forces at work in adolescence and powerfully draws on our hard-wired reactions to sound. Hard rock music contains emotional triggers that were made possible by amplification. They differ from the kinds of emotional responses that had previously been elicited by music.

In the 1930s and 40s Leo Fender and Les Paul created an electric guitar that allowed music to be played very loudly without feedback and in 1947 the transistor was invented. These coincident technologies have allowed for the development of a style of music that affects the listener differently than any other music. In the past, throughout the centuries-long flowering of folk songs and religious music, an entire family would hear and listen to the same music. There was, to be sure, different music for different groups and occasions: wooing troubadours, drinking sailors, hymns in churches, dances in barns, dances in ballrooms, ancient chants in synagogues. Then, as now, the characteristics of each kind of music reflected the different environments and purposes, but one generation listened to the same music as the next in the same places. This was still true in the early 20th century when everyone could gather 'round the vacuum tube radio and listen to Big Bands and Rachmaninov in the same evening.

The transistor made music portable and this portability allowed adolescents to carry the music that suited their desires. One of those desires, it seems to me, is separation from the nest. Robins kick their juveniles out of the nest when the time comes for them to learn how to forage and fly. Human parents usually don't kick the kids out of the home, but we do seem to have a genetically implanted time bomb that explodes in late adolescence causing them to doubt the authority of their parents and yearn for a release from house rules. I have had children in the house of this age and I also remember the sense of restless idealism that propelled me from my own parent's home. The transistor radio allowed adolescents to have their own music: music of rebellion. The emotional responses triggered by rock music are attuned to adolescent desires. The transistor era brought the dawn of a new family of music, whose branches include metal, punk, grunge and garage, that excites a different emotional response and for different reasons than other kinds of music.

Power rock music had its beginnings in the late 1960s. Among the most well-known and influential bands in its advent were Black Sabbath, Led Zeppelin, Iron Butterfly and Deep Purple. The melodies and harmonies are almost exclusively minor/modal. Metallica is one of the stylistic progeny of the early power rock bands. In the concerts that the San Francisco Symphony performed with Metallica, I remember hearing only a couple of major chords in two hours of music. The sound of this music is very dark. The darkness that we perceive augments the ominous assignation that our inner auditory interpreters give to low sounds and minor modalities - all of these combine to contribute to an atmosphere of attentive fear that makes a fitting transport for the lyrics of rage that are often found in this music.

The excitement is produced by three elements of this music that were new and unavailable before the advent of amplification. The first element is the volume. Very loud sounds trigger a genetically embedded fear response; an infant will cry after hearing a very loud noise even if it has never heard one before. Ask any aficionado of heavy metal and he will attest that this music must be *loud* - the kick you can get out of it disappears if it is heard softly. Once, when my son Andrew was only two years old, he told me to turn up the volume after the music in the car switched from the soft rock of James Taylor to the hard rock of REM. Not only does increasing volume increase our alertness, it also serves to increase clarity; the easiest way to make the music coming out of your loudspeakers more distinct is to turn up the volume. The louder the music is, the more attentive it will make the listener - up to a limit. That limit is crossed by power rock music. Once the music becomes loud enough to trigger a fear response, the attention dial is turned up to startle.

There is an additional attentive response that is associated with very loud music: it obliterates other sounds. This sonic masking makes people uneasy. The sense of hearing is, first and foremost, an early warning system that is always alert, even during sleep. When our primary early warning station gets so much interference that it can't tell what is out there our attention is heightened, like a warning system that has shifted from code green to code yellow.

The second element is the powerful bass sound that dominates power rock music. Sopranos and tenors, the high voices, are the lovers in operas, the villain is a bass. If we were able to break into the rooms with the files of sonic templates of our primary auditory processors like cat burglars sifting through the drawers with flashlights, we would find the that the file containing the combination of 1) vocal sound, 2) low register (signifying a mature male), 3) loud, and 4) harsh tone is stamped in red across the front "BEWARE." These are the sonic components of a male threat for our species.

The amplification of these low frequencies requires a lot of energy. The days of Rudy Vallee amplifying his voice with a cone had been left far behind by the late 60s when it became possible, for the first time, to fill a large hall with bass-register sounds that were loud enough to exceed the threshold necessary to induce a fear response.

The third element that accesses fear is the growling, screaming, and yelling in power rock music. The vocals in the grunge band Atreiu growl, Ian Gillan of Deep Purple screams (check out *Child in Time*), and System of a Down vocalists yell with only (intentionally) approximate pitches. These are all threat and fear inducing primal vocalizations controlled by structures in the brain stem and limbic system. These screams and yells trigger the fight or flight reaction in us; they are instantly understood at the emotional level as warnings from those in danger, rivals who would threaten us, or from enemies in battle.

The Electric Guitar

In order to enhance the impact and weave a consistent fabric of sound, musicians who expanded the sonic range of instruments created devices that paralleled the quality of the scream by increasing the complexity of the instrument's overtones. The fuzz box is the most obvious example. The sound of an acoustic guitar, such as the introduction and accompaniment of JT's *Fire and Rain*, is relatively pure. The fuzz box adds threat to that sound by adding distortion, the very same kind of distortion that your vocal chords produce when you speak in a harsh growl. Today the computer-enhancements available to recorded and amplified sound allow music producers to electronically increase the overtones of the vocal lines as well. The raspy vocal quality that is fits so well with power rock music is now available to every naturally crooning singer in every band at the push of a button.

This is another instance where we can see the issue more clearly if we look at it from the opposite side, like looking at a film negative. In your imagination, extract the pure tones of Julie Andrews (singing from an Alpen mountain in *The Sound of Music* "The hills are aliiiiive with the soooound of muuuusiiiiic...") and paste that quality of sound and her singing "Inna-godda-da-vida." into the center microphone of a dark stage with Iron Butterfly behind her.

The cello is well-suited to producing the low, grinding vocal sounds that are woven into hard rock music. I used a complex mix of overlapping low cello lines in one of the songs on the debut album of Echobrain, the band formed by Jason Newsted with Dylan Donklin and Brian Sagrafino while Jason was still the bass player in Metallica. Jason asked me to write and play the string arrangements for their first CD. Most of the music that we worked on was very different from the music of Metallica; it was that very difference that Jason craved.

A musician like Jason needs variety in his musical world. When he taps into the dark corners of his psyche while playing *Devil's Dance* the rage he feels is genuine, but he also feels the warmth of the summer sun on his face and needs to be able to express that kind of experience in his language, which is music. For Metallica to be his only and exclusive musical outlet would be the same as living with a voice that usually sounds low, loud, and harsh.

One of my favorite Echobrain songs did not make it onto the album. It was the heaviest chart on the list; perhaps that explains why it was cut, it may have been too close to the heavy metal music from which Jason was branching out. I composed the introduction with sinews of deep cello lines in the frequency range of a serious speaking voice of a mature man. The low range and slightly snarling tone quality of the cello turns on the beware sign in the listener's midbrain, setting the mood for the dark expression of the song. You can hear some of our music at www.davidteie.com and click on Echobrain or on track 8 of the CD.

Rock 'n Growl

Just as the violence in films plays on our hard-wired fears to give us an adrenaline rush, the mixture of growling bass, screaming vocals, and extreme volume in hard rock music excite genetically implanted reactions, causing adrenal fluids to flow and provide the kick that is felt from the music. This adrenal response may be interpreted differently by those who aren't predisposed to want to hear music of rebellion. They will feel the heightened state of response to the music but it will cause them to think: "I want to get out of here." For them the fear response is not a thrill, it is a source of discomfort; in the fight or flight simplification, they would rather take flight. This may help to explain why hard rock music has enemies as well as fans. There are people who don't enjoy jazz but it would be hard to find someone who hates it. The same cannot be said for hard rock music. Those who find the evoked sensation unwelcome tend to react to it with intense dislike.

The fear-response-based stimulation of hard rock music also may explain why so many of its fans turn to other forms of music as they grow older. Part of the migration is surely due to the dissipation of youthful rebelliousness, but there is another culprit: the reticular activating system (RAS). As mentioned earlier, sound passes through the emotional center of the brain first and triggers an emotional response without consulting our rational mind. The RAS, however, sends signals from the thinking brain back down to the emotional center to let it know that "It's only a bass player, nothing to be scared of." It is the same principle at work when we get used to a sound that is noticeable at first hearing. When the new automatic icemaker turns over a tray it triggers an (emotionally generated) attentive response. As time passes you hear the sound often and it is consistently identified as "not a threat" and eventually you habituate to the sound. The RAS has turned off the emotion that once made you perk up your ears. Eventually habituation desensitizes the listener to certain sounds. Many of those who have listened to a lot of hard rock music will find that they no longer get the same kick out of it that they once did. Habituation may explain why the audiences for this music tend to remain young even as the bands age.

By the way, the rockers also have a head start on eliciting the emotional responses that drive people to camp out in the ticket lines. Researchers have discovered that monkeys will "pay" rewards to see images of high-ranking monkeys. It would seem that the success of glam-gossip magazines is based on our primal instincts to keep tabs on those higher up than ourselves. The monkeys can teach us something about the broad appeal of some of the higher-ranking humans. Taking his place at the highest echelon of Western civilization, the rock star has elicited an attentive response before he has sung a note.

3

SPEECH AND MELODY

The Rhythms in Melodies

Perhaps you have heard a poem or a prosaic style described as "musical." Although the complimented authors may be flattered to have their prose compared to music, it's the musicians who did the stealing, not the poets. Poetry isn't musical, music is poetical. Music is the daughter of speech. All of the components of melody are based on human speech. Of all the elements of speech stolen by musicians, perhaps the most obvious theft is the one where we are caught red-handed with the loot in our instrument cases: the rhythms of speech.

To help us see the perfectly human-scale of music it helps to look at the range of other species' vocalization rhythms. As I noted previously, the rhythms of some tamarin calls are too fast to be perceived by us. The rhythms of some bat calls are not only too fast to comprehend, they are too high for us to hear. As it is with all other elements of music, common melodic rhythms are understandable to us because they are scaled to our voices and perception. Melodic rhythms are based on the rhythms of speech and complete musical phrases often last about as long as a spoken statement lasts between breaths. We heard these rhythms and melodies in the womb and now that we are out and we know the language, we can start writing some ourselves.

The two dimensions of musical rhythms are time and intensity. Melodic rhythms are made up of simple combinations of notes with varied durations and accents. Most music presents these rhythms in strings of segments formed from recognizable patterns. Here's an example: say out loud the word "because." Now repeat it a few times in close succession: "because, because, because…" The first note formed by the syllable "be" is short and unaccented; the second formed by "cause" is longer and accented. That is a rhythmic motive. Composers have been stringing rhythmic motives together for as long as there have been composers. Now you can dance into the next paragraph to the music of Harold Arlen "because, because, because, because, becaaaause, because of the wonderful things he does. (dittle-it-da-da-da-da-da-dum dee-dum) We're off to see the wizard, the wonderful wizard of Oz."

The rhythmic commonalities of speech and melody are most apparent to songwriters. The stresses of pitch and pulse sound the most natural when they align with the natural stresses in the syllables of the lyrics, otherwise the ac-CENT will be ON the wrong syl-LA-ble. Some sophisticated and urbane songwriters have purposely turned natural stresses upside-down with charming effect as Jerome Kern and Oscar Hammerstein II did in "Bill":

…so comfy and <u>roo</u>my,
seems natural <u>to</u> me.

It is hard to imagine that anyone had more intimate knowledge of the common territories of speech and music than Richard Rodgers. In the first of his famous collaborations, Rodgers would send the music to Lorenz Hart, who would then add the lyrics. In his second, even better known collaboration, Oscar Hammerstein would write the lyrics first and send them to Rodgers who would then set them to music. Rodgers had an uncanny ability to hear melodies in lyrics *and* write melodies that were so poetically rhythmic that they could be seamlessly paired with lyrics.

The natural rhythms of speech and the repetition of patterns in lyrics are often adopted wholesale by composers. The iambic meter of the line: "The rain in Spain falls mainly in the plain." written by Alan Jay

Lerner (no it wasn't G.B. Shaw) has a natural rhythm that Frederick Loewe left unchanged in his musical setting.

Can you name this tune if you say with exuberance: "mit heilige, lustige…"?

Answer: Theme from the first movement Allegro of Beethoven's seventh symphony.

The music of each culture contains rhythmic characteristics of its language. The strength and placements of accented syllables varies widely. Words of the Germanic and Romance languages have fixed accents. One of the common features of these languages that is often heard in the music of their cultures is the unaccented article preceding a noun: "*die* MAIN-acht, *the* GAR-den, *la* MER, *los* LO-bos". The grammatical placement of the article before the noun created an accentual pattern that found its way through folk songs and into the music of these cultures in the anacrusis or upbeat. These lesser notes that lead into the beat give shape and movement to the musical line. Paul McCartney, for example, establishes the pace of his song with the first word: "*The* long and winding road…"

Two-note versions of the upbeat can be formed from prepositional phrases:

O-oh say can you see
by the dawn's early light
what so proudly we hailed
at the twilight's last gleaming

And in Marian the librarian's lovely love song by Meredith Wilson: *There were* birds *in the* sky.

The Russian language is accent-free, the stress can be placed on any syllable. This is something that is often difficult for those of us who speak a fixed-accented language to grasp when trying to speak their language. I have often been asked where the accent should be placed in the names Shostakovich and Rostropovich. "Is it ShostaKOvich or

ShosTAkovich?" The answer doesn't fit into the schema of the English language: "It's Shostakovich."

In the Czech language the first vowel of every word is always accented. If language is the mother of music, then we should find that Czech melodies begin on the beat. If you get out your collection of recordings of the great Czech composer Dvorak (if you are lucky enough to have one) and try to find melodies that begin with upbeats you are in for a long night.

Italian is still used as the language of performance indications in printed music owing to the historical significance of Italian music. The entire category of Western music can be traced to origins in Italy; the Italians were the premier musicians of Europe throughout the first half of the second millennium. The Italians invented the piano and contemporary musical notation and we still use Italian as the internationally understood language of musical performance indications such as Allegro, piano, forte, etc. in printed music. The "musicality" of the vowels and consonants in the Italian language certainly played a role in putting "musicality" in music. It is difficult or impossible to produce a vocal inflection on a consonant, whether the consonant is vocalized, as in "z" or aspirated as in "s". Inflection and intonation color the vowels - and all Italian words end with vowels. Italian speech uses predominantly open vowels, quickly sounding simple consonants like "b, t, and l", and lilting accented phrases - all of these are perfectly suited to singing.

Emotionally inflected speech is more rhythmic and contains more extreme melodic/dynamic contours than normal speech. If the line "Your hair is so beautiful." is delivered in an expressionless monotone by, for example, a stage director instructing an actor to follow a cue in rehearsal the pitches and syllables will simply repeat: dit-dit-dit-dit-dit-dit. But in the voice of a lover in a rowboat the rhythm will sound more like: "Your hair is sooo beauuutiful." And the melody of that little love speech will sound a bit like Mozart.

Our perception of pitch itself is strongly tied to the pitches that the human voice is capable of producing. We are able to hear sounds that are higher and lower than our voices are able to sing, but we are unable to tell what the pitches are. Very high notes sound like squeaks and very low notes sound like rumbles. A few months ago I indulged my curiosity about this and created a recording of pairs of computer-generated tones that are lower than any human can sing. One pair formed the consonant interval of a major third; the other formed the dissonant interval of the minor second. I was interested to find that our perception of these intervals is indiscriminate and can even be turned on its head when the frequencies are outside of our vocal range. Amazingly, every musician I asked said that the major third sounded more "dissonant" than the minor second. Since these frequencies are not perceived as pitches, the minor second sounds relatively smooth compared to the distinct rumble created by the major third.

Human Art

I'm pulling off the road of music here for a quick spin into the land of philosophy. When I first began delving into the questions of human emotional response to music the first books I opened were written by philosophers. Music philosophy is a bit of a hot topic in the early 21st century. It is clear to me that an assessment of our emotional involvement in music must reflect an understanding of the impressive body of recent research into the cognitive processes involved in music, but this research seems to be invisible to most musical philosophers. It is understandable that most scientists are not trained in music, and that most musicians do not have a PhD in science, but a balanced understanding of how music affects us can only be reached if someone who is well-versed in one discipline is willing to spend a few years learning about the other. Musical philosophers need to stitch all three disciplines together; they need to know as much about Beethoven and about the brain structures of the limbic system as they already know about Wittgenstein. Unfortunately, such philosophers are very rare.

Does art transcend? If so, how far beyond our mere selves does it reach? I would simply argue that all art is human art, created by us for ourselves and for our perceptions. The awe, beauty and truth that can be felt when we listen to music, read poetry, see dancing, paintings, sculptures, architecture and photographs, and taste cuisine, often seem to be beyond the territory of human knowledge. Since we have no conscious access the inner workings of the emotional centers that respond to art, we conclude that the art has transcended our understanding.

Every art form appeals to a fairly narrow bandwidth of human perception. Visible light is an example. Most of the wavelengths of electromagnetic radiation are either absorbed by or reflected by earth's atmosphere. A narrow band of radiation that we call visible light penetrates deeply enough to reach the surface. We who inhabit this planet have evolved the ability to absorb this energy and use the reflected radiation to perceive details in our environment. We cannot see gamma or radio radiation, we only see in the wavelengths that are bouncing around on our earth's surface. Accordingly, Vincent Van Gogh painted with colors that reflect radiation in this visible range just as musicians play music in the frequency range that is audible to us. I'm the only fellow that I know of who has written music in ultrasonic frequencies. We can't even hear it, but cats might get a kick out of it.

The bandwidth of music that appeals to us is actually much narrower than our hearing range. Human hearing is most sensitive in the frequency range that is used to produce consonants. It is important for us to be able to tell the difference between an "ss" and a "sh." These sounds occupy the range from 2-4 kHz, or 2,000 to 4,000 vibrations per second. Despite this sensitivity, our melodies are usually in the fairly narrow range of 200 to 800 Hz. Below is a graph of the approximately 10-octave spectrum of human hearing. The ranges of the human voice, the adult female voice, and our highest sensitivity are highlighted.

20 kHz – highest percieved sound
10 kHz
5 kHz
2.5 kHz – most sensitive hearing
1.25 kHz
675 Hz – human upper vocal range (women)
366 Hz
183 Hz – human lower vocal range (men)
90 Hz
45 Hz
23 Hz – lowest percieved sound

Human Music

Mother of Melodies

Most instruments that carry the melody play in the range of the treble clef, the musical symbol for the range of notes between the frequencies of 262 to 880 Hz. Among the hundreds of instruments in this range are: the Western Violin, Flute, Oboe, Clarinet, traditional Chinese Arhu and Dizi, Sitar and Bulbul tarang from India, and the Japanese Koto. Instruments have evolved to play melodies in this range because this is the range of the melodies that we heard from our mother's speaking as our brains were developing in the womb. Simply stated: **the maternal voice established the frequency range of melodies.**

The following is a list of the most common features of melodies:

- they are made from resonance-enhanced periodic sounds (vocal sounds)
- they are presented in discrete, single-frequency segments (notes)
- they are in the frequency range between 200 – 800 Hz
- they form contoured phrases.

All of these features are identical to those of the maternal voice as heard in the womb. The concept of melody itself was created in the developing brains of each of us as we were floating in amniotic fluid.

We like to hear the occasional, midrange baritone but we seldom go out of our way to order the CDs put out by very low bass singers. Have you ever wondered why we tend to like the singing of men with high voices? The Three Tenors attracted millions of fans. The Three Basses would have trouble selling out the local pub. Male singers with voices that are high enough to be in the maternal vocal range are the ones we apparently most enjoy. There is ample crossover territory between the high male and the low female voice. My mom could sing almost all of the Beatles songs in the original octave and key. Her natural range was low for a woman - about the same as Paul McCartney's.

Melodies normally consist of sequences of consonant intervals relative to a tonal center, or key note, which is often the last note. "Love me tender, Love me sweet, Never let me go. You have made my life complete, And I love you so." The note sung on the word "so" is the key note; if that note is an F the song is in F.

A spoken sentence is a musical phrase and the pitches of speech tend to center on keys just as melodies do. If you say: "Love me tender" you are creating your own melody. The more emotionally charged you feel, the more affectingly melodious your speech will be. We tend to use ordered, harmonious, consecutive consonant intervals in our speech. Dale Purves at Duke University studied the intervals between the pitches that we use in our conversations and discovered that human vocal communication is primarily consonant.

The discovery of exactly which intervals convey particular expressions in each language is the subject of ongoing research. It may be some time before we have a complete picture of the relationships between emotions and the intervals used to express them. Researchers at Tufts University found that the descending intervals of the minor third and minor second are used in spoken English to communicate sadness.

You can hear this vocal music by setting up a little theater in the mind: Imagine a sweet-tempered girl of fourteen standing nearby and looking down toward the ground in front of you. She is looking at a puppy that is hobbling on a paw that has a thorn in it. She says: "Awww."

You probably heard a descending interval from the girl; perhaps it was a minor second or minor third. Her sympathy was expressed through a relatively quiet, pure tone in a melodic fragment that descended. Every aspect of this kind of emotionally generated vocal expression can be described musically because every aspect of it has been incorporated into music.

We are not alone in the animal kingdom when we communicate expression through pitch intervals. Many birdsongs are consonant and key-centered. I discovered that the cotton-top tamarin monkeys also use consonant intervals when communicating affection. I suspect that in years to come as we have a better understanding of whales and dolphins we will discover manifestations of the order/chaos polarity as well as consonance and dissonance in their complex communication.

Inflection

Inflection could be described as the combination of the three vocal variables of tone color, pitch, and volume. Although the individual characteristics of the European languages vary a great deal, they all share these musical components.

Human Music

Expressive inflections provide the natural seeds for the tended garden of Western music. The tonal languages of the Far East, on the other hand, use intonation as an indicator of word definition. In Mandarin, for example, a given sequence of vowels and consonants can have any one of the following three intonations:

Beginning high and descending	Beginning low and ascending	A single, fairly low pitch

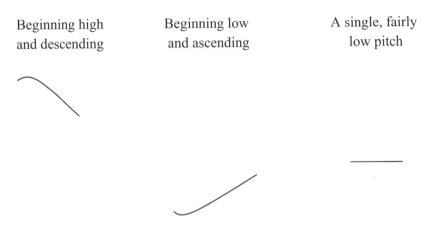

A single word such as "ma" intoned with each of the above inflections has three completely different meanings. Expressive shadings in spoken tonal languages are communicated primarily through the volume and timbre. The wide variety of linguistic contours in different languages accounts for many characteristics of music that are specific to each culture.

In the Indo-European languages pitch intervals between the syllables and the resulting melodic contours are used to convey personal expression. Since the intervals used are primarily consonant, and since an interval is relative, they must be consonant relative to a tonal center. The non-tonal nature of European languages provided the framework that allowed for the development of key relationships: the changing of tonal centers. The ability to move from one tonal center to others made large-scale musical structures possible. When a single musical work could contain diverse keys and move to other tonalities it could take the listener on a journey. This made possible the fulcrum of musical (and dramatic) structure: the return home.

There is compelling evidence that key center changes are found in highly emotional speech. When a tonal center shifts to another key musicians refer to it as a modulation. **We modulate tonal centers in our speech as we shift into more highly emotional states.** This shift is communicated by raising the pitch center. Actors may do this consciously, but the highly charged speaker thinks nothing of the shift; the midbrain regulates the pitches surreptitiously.

> Debbie has dressed in clothing that is a bit too exposed for comfort considering the cool weather, and heads for the door saying:
>
> "Daddy, I'm going to meet Bobby at the drive-in."
>
> Her father stops her at the door with the words:
> "Not tonight you're not. Aunt Flo is coming over for dinner and she is looking forward to seeing you."
>
> (higher in pitch) "But I told Bobby that I would be there at 6:30!"
>
> "Well, not tonight you're not."
>
> (higher still) "Daddyyyy!"
>
> "Go to your room!"
>
> (highest and using widely spaced dissonant pitch intervals) "This is so unfair! You are ruining my life!"

The way you feel charges your voice, broadcasting the sounds of your emotions.

All of the aspects of speech that can be varied to express emotion are included in music. In the broad outline: excited speech is higher pitched, faster, and uses shorter, more explosive syllables, while subdued, sad speech is slow, lower pitched, and uses longer, contoured syllables. Alarm speech is loud and dissonant, angry speech is low and harsh, affectionate speech is high, quiet, consonant and pure. In keeping with these innate alignments, loud, dissonant music and low, harsh music makes us attentively fearful while high, quiet, consonant, pure music soothes us. The expressive tonalities of the spoken Indo-European languages were forged by musicians into the tonalities of Western music.

Expressive Function of the Elastic Larynx

One of the most important variables in emotionally charged speech is the tone quality change that occurs when the voice box (larynx) is stretched to be higher or lower in the throat. It's interesting that it was the actors, not the scientists, who discovered the expressive importance of this change and harnessed it to convey feelings on the stage.

When we experience emotions, our subconscious brain modifies the sounds of the voice by manipulating muscles in the section of the vocal tract where sound originates. The vocal folds of the larynx (contained in the Adam's apple in men and in a similar place, though less prominent, in women and children) tighten and loosen to raise and lower the pitch, and the higher or lower placement of the larynx in the throat diminishes or enhances the resonance of the sound. A lowered larynx extends the resonating cavity of the throat, deepening the quality. A raised larynx reduces the length of the resonating cavity giving the voice a brighter, sharper quality.

When a person feels uplifted, his or her larynx rises. Bright sounds convey lively feelings. Laughter is an example of bright, quick communication that is normally accomplished with a raised larynx. One of the ways we can identify a fake laugh is when the laugher does not have a raised larynx and the vocal quality is normal. Most people can't raise or lower it voluntarily and are unable to consciously identify the tone qualities of raised-larynx and normal sounds, but all of us instinctively hear and recognize the differences.

Loud, high, open vowel calls with a raised larynx are cheers. When a moment of victory is achieved in sport, for example, the body produces instinctive responses. One of them is to raise the arms into the air. It has been noted that congenitally blind participants in sports also use raised arms when celebrating a victory. Since they had never seen the gesture, they could not be mimicking a celebration that they had witnessed. Body language communication such as this is innate and shared by all of the great apes. The vocal equivalent to the raised arms is the cheer. Just as we intuitively understand the meaning of the gesture, our auditory processors and our emotional centers understand what is conveyed by a loud, high, open vowel, raised larynx "AAAAYY!"

Brass instruments in the upper register create waveforms that are similar to the raised-larynx cheer. When a brass section plays a high, bright, loud, sustained major chord it creates a waveform that is close enough to that of a cheer to be understood as such by our ever-vigilant vocal sound interpreting brain. The emotional lift that we feel when we hear the triumphant brass chords at the conclusion of symphonic works is partially due to the uplifting "AAAAYY!" that brass instruments can produce. A musical victory played only by woodwinds and strings might only conjure up images of the cheering associated with, say, the groundbreaking ceremony for a new library.

When we examine the tone quality of a lively speaker and compare it to the tone qualities in lively music we find many similarities. And when we examine the tone quality of a grieving speaker and compare it to the tone qualities in somber music we also find many similarities. The tones-of-voice used of these modes of speech match the corollary modes of music.

The experience of sadness or grief causes the larynx to lower. The lower larynx allows more of the throat to act as a resonator, giving the tone a darker, slightly covered, hollow quality.

When I listen to the opening melody of the slow movement of the "New World" symphony by Dvořák I often feel a lump in my throat. Part of that feeling is due to the dark resonance of the English horn that naturally and instinctively engenders sympathy within me. The difference between the sound of a note sung with a normally placed larynx and a lowered larynx is similar to the difference between the sound of the oboe and the English horn. Both instruments use vibrating double reeds to produce the sound. The English horn has a longer resonating body with a bulbous end. If you were to hear each instrument play the same pitch, you would notice that the English horn sounds darker, more covered and hollow than the oboe. Listen to a demonstration of the sounds of the oboe and English horn compared with the sound of normal and lowered-larynx singing at: www.davidteie.com and click on Oboe comparisons or listen to track 9 on the CD. Composers use the variety of orchestral colors such as these to enhance expression. Dvořák gave the first melody in the slow movement of his

"New World" symphony to the English horn, this orchestration of the melody can make some of us feel an enigmatic sense of sympathetic longing for Dvořák's home.

The English horn is notably "darker" than the oboe and is often described as a more somber instrument. The sound qualities of the oboe and the normal-larynx voice are similar, while the English horn more clearly resembles the lowered-larynx voice. The sound interpreters in our brains make comparisons very much like this when incoming vocal sounds are evaluated. The voiceprint is compared to a template and, when a match is found, appropriate emotional responses are triggered. It hears the English horn, the sound is a match to the sound of a lowered-larynx voice, and our emotional centers initiate a saddened emotional state.

The lump that you sometimes feel in your throat results from emotions that have lowered your larynx to a place that feels tight and, well, lump-like. When you witness or hear about something that moves you to feel pity, grief or sympathy, your emotions are communicated by the tears in your eyes and the lump in your throat. The tears make the sympathy visible, and the lowered larynx makes it audible by modifying the resonance of speech in a way that is instinctively recognizable to listeners. A person who is in a state of pain speaks with just such a tone quality. When a sister hears that speech she feels sympathy; she feels a lump in her throat. When that sister speaks herself, her voice will have taken on the same deepened quality.

This sympathy can be strikingly contagious, as I witnessed while on tour in Fargo, North Dakota. Kristin Rudrüd, who played the role of the murdered wife of the car salesman in the Coen brothers' film "Fargo", attended a screening of the film with us and agreed to tell us about the making of the film. She told us how she added elements of tension to the scene where she was to be kneading dough in the kitchen while talking to her husband (who had already arranged to have her killed). She asked the directors if she could be cutting up vegetables with a large knife instead of kneading dough, which they agreed to, and she decided to load her speech with stress. She demonstrated one of the techniques that she used to accomplish this by lowering her larynx while talking to us. Even though the words she used while doing it were merely explanatory, I was shocked to find that I was moved by her speaking voice. I felt a lump in my throat, gasped slightly, and even felt the beginning of welling in my eyes.

She exhibited no other signs of emotion, it was the tone quality alone of her voice that triggered a sympathetic emotional response in me. The quality of her voice sparked my automatic stress recognition and nudged my tear ducts to reciprocate before my language-interpreting brain had any idea what she was saying. My reaction to the sound of her voice was instinctively sympathetic. I wondered: Could this be one of the emotionally activating processes of music?

Emotions connect us through sound. To demonstrate the immediacy of the connection, come with me into a dark forest for a moment. At times such as these, emotion spreads from one to others allowing a group to be instantaneously alert when one on the periphery of the group is alarmed. You are sitting near a campfire warming your hands. I am a few paces away from you looking out into the tangle of branches. I see a dark mass move that outlines the silhouette of a bear. I scream. Your heart rate goes up immediately, your eyes widen and dilate, and you jump to your feet while turning toward me. My scream enabled you to feel fear without seeing anything frightful. Adrenaline that is flowing in my system allowing me to fight better or run faster is flowing in your veins as well. You feel my emotion.

We would not have to be in a potentially dangerous place for this transfer of emotion to take place. In another scenario: I am in a room with a pillage-veteran Viking accustomed to drinking the blood of the vanquished from his skull. I have been introduced to him as a sensitive musician. He is standing holding a sword and shield while I am seated with my legs crossed and my hands folded on my lap with a nervous smile on my face. I scream – his heart rate goes up. Even though he has nothing to fear from me, the sound enters his auditory processing, is identified as an alarm call, the amygdala responds by stimulating his adrenaline. Once the sound has been sent up to his conscious brain for evaluation and given the "nothing to worry about" assignation, he may laugh (I hope) at his own reaction. He could not have prevented it, however. We are connected to each other's emotions, and one of the connecting cables is sound.

Human Music

Sympathetic Sound

This sympathetic response is analogous to the acoustical phenomenon of sympathetic vibration: if two strings are near to each other and tuned to the same pitch, plucking one of them will cause the other to vibrate as well. Similarly, if someone in your family speaks to you with the tone of voice created by the lump in her throat, you will tend to get a lump in your throat sympathetically. When we are moved by music, it is not that the music transmits emotion the way language transmits ideas, rather it causes a resonance within the listener. Music does not have the power to express feelings, the way language can express "I love you", but it does have the power to evoke those feelings, to excite emotions within us.

The connection that allows the rising emotion in one person to be communicated through sound, causing the rising of emotion in another is the magical conduit of music. Composers write music that is filled with emotionally charged sounds. The process is not unlike speaking. You would say the words "I'll be there" one way if you are speaking 1) in a flat, informational tone to an irritating colleague at work, but you will imbue them with a very different music if you use the same words when speaking 2) to your lover asking for a tryst or 3) to a child. The emotional component of your communication is provided by tone-of-voice: 1) stop bothering me, 2) I love you passionately and desire you, 3) it makes me happy to spend time with you. You feel the feeling, the words are formed in your mind, and your emotions color the words as you speak them.

Composers do the same. We feel the feeling, the notes are formed in the mind, and our emotions guide the choices of instrumental timbres to color the sounds. Just as you hope that the listener understands the emotional undercurrent of your speech, composers hope that the listeners feel when hearing the music as we do when writing it. In music and speech, the sound quality itself is expressive.

Emotionally affected vocal quality is important to music because it is capable of inducing a sympathetic response in the listener. The heartfelt sympathy that is triggered automatically when we hear a voice with a deeply lowered larynx forms one of the finest emotional kicks that music can produce. Trained singers work rigorously on using this technique to touch their audiences. One of the most commonly heard instructions for voice students is to open the throat and lower the larynx, increasing vocal resonance by using the very technique demonstrated by Kristin Rudrüd.

The Timbres of Voices and Instruments

A study conducted by my father, Ernest Teie, (one of a rare breed of PhD singers) at the University of Minnesota compared the overtone series of the voices of trained and untrained singers to determine what effect training has on vocal resonance. He discovered that the region around the fourth overtone, known as the singer's formant region, was significantly more prominent in trained voices than in untrained voices. Training affects the tone quality, and tone quality affects our emotions.

Instrument makers create instruments that have sonorities that sound human. I propose that they have modified them to resemble the timbres that sound expressive to our ears. I tested this idea on my instrument, the cello. I compared the tone prints of factory made cellos with those made by such great old Italian masters as Stradivarius, Testore and Joseph Guarneri. Although the resonance of the instruments of the masters is generally superior across the entire frequency range, the region that is most enhanced is the fourth formant region, that very region that singers strive so hard to develop. I also found that the resonant formants are lower on the great instruments than on the cheap instruments indicating a deeper resonance similar to the sound of the larger resonating cavity of a lowered larynx singer. Voices and instruments that resonate in these formant regions sound expressive to us because they simulate the tone quality of an emotionally affected speaker.

There are many differences between normal speech and sorrowful speech: the pitch center goes up, the resonance of the voice increases, the tone quality becomes purer, and the intervals used are much more consonant. When we are grievously pained the voice shifts into the highest gear and the most musical of all modes of speech.

There is an overdrive shift for deeply pained speech: **at the extreme end of grieved speech is the lowered larynx combined with a pure, high, falsetto voice.** This is the kind of whimpering speech that Stan Laurel used when he was being chastised by Oliver Hardy. This type of speech is rarely heard in everyday life. Many people will go for years without saying anything in this vocal mode, and many who find that they have begun speaking this way will stop themselves out of embarrassment. I have posted examples of this mode of speaking so that the reader might have a clearer idea of how it sounds (out of respect for the aggrieved speakers I did not post the genuine examples that we are using for our studies).

The most remarkable and musically relevant feature of this grieving overdrive speech mode is that the intervals used are highly consonant. The melodies of this type of vocalization are the most consistently consonant and key-centered of all human vocalizations. The clarity of the tonal center and ubiquity of consonant intervals in this type of speech present vocal melodies that could have been written by Mozart. If we were to extract some of Laurel's self-pitying comments and set them to an accompaniment we would hear that Stan's whimpering has all the classic traits of a completely tonal melody.

When I was first discovering the musicality of these vocal modes I was listening to the speech of a man who was deeply saddened and profoundly remorseful. The sentence that I was listening to didn't have anything in the words themselves that would indicate that he was sad. He was saying: "I went to visit them because…" When my five-year-old daughter heard the speech she asked me when the man's wife had died. She didn't know anything about the context or what he was talking about. At the age of 5, *before she had personally experienced genuinely grieving speech*, she knew the meaning in the man's voice.

We are imbued at birth with the ability to recognize the sound of pained speech and that we respond sympathetically to it. I found that I was strongly affected and troubled by these types of speech when evaluating them. In order to create a detailed notation of the contours, pitches, timbres and formant analysis of the speakers, I had to listen to them many times over. After an hour or so of working I felt that I needed to take a break. Even though I don't know personally any of the people involved and was concentrating on creating a musical representation of the speech, I was so affected by sympathetic feelings that it interfered with my concentration.

Human Music

Pitch-Center Shift in Emotional Speech

Whether the emotion is gleeful, saddened, excited, or grievous, the vocal pitch is raised. When the larynx is stretched out of its normal placement the added tension raises the pitch. The raised larynx of a lively mood causes the pitch center of our speech to go up:

(higher)
"Wonderful!"

"yes"

(lower)
"Can you come with us?"

The larynx is also stretched out of its normal placement when it is lowered. This lowering creates an enhanced resonance and shifts the pitch center 2–5 semitones higher. To get an idea of how far that is, it is about the distance between the first pitches in "Happy birthday":

(5 semitones higher)   to

(2 semitones higher)   birth
            Hap-py   day

The grievously pained speech that combines a lowered larynx with a falsetto vocal production further raises the pitch center an additional 5–17 semitones.

(much higher)
"Oh no!"

"Little Bobby"
    (higher)
    "Was anyone hurt?"
(lower)
 "There was an accident."

Human Music

Music in Grief

As speech becomes emotionally charged it is imbued with characteristics that make the emotions identifiable. The extreme emotion of grief induces speech that is highly organized and musical. We perceive it as "musical" because music itself has extracted these emotional characteristics of speech.

I have created some samples of these strata taken from witness testimony, a press conference, and a memorial service in the public domain. These samples are available at www.davidteie.com and click on Lowered-larynx speech or on track 10 of the CD. You will hear only the pitches of the speech of three individuals. I have filtered out the upper frequencies to hide consonants and the identities of the speakers. In each case the vocal changes resulting from increased emotions were clearly identifiable and consistent. The normal speech was relatively monotone while the grieving speech was clearly organized in discrete tonalities and consonant intervals. I have presented here one man and one woman. First you will hear a brief example of the person's normal speech as a baseline for comparison. You will hear that neither of these speakers have animated, sing-song voices. Then you will hear three versions of each individual making highly charged statements: 1) the speech alone, 2) with the cello shadowing the voice to point out the pitches, 3) a musical setting of the speech that highlights the highly organized tonality of the grieving speech.

The higher pitch areas are terraced. In other words, the shift from one mode to another is not gradual, but immediate, like a gearshift. If musical structure is borrowed from speech, then we should expect to find a tendency for musical phrases to follow the same pattern of terracing. **Terraced pitch centers are hallmarks of emotional variance in speech and corollaries of these terraces are found in music.**

Pitch Center Shift in Song Structures

Songs usually have two sections: the verse and the chorus. Many songs have yet a third section called the bridge. I wondered how often the second section has a higher pitch center than the first. If song structure mimics the strata of the shifted gears of an emotionally charged voice, then we should find that the second section of songs are higher than the first.

Before tallying up the number of times a shift in pitch center transitions from lower to higher in song structures, let's consider the number of possible song contours. The statistical probability that no discernable contours could be discovered at all is overwhelmingly great. If music only follows the typical contours of normal speech, then one would not be higher or lower than another except by random coincidence.

When we examine song structure, however, we find a remarkably strong correlation between the pitch center transitions of emotionally affected speech and the pitch center transitions in song structures.

I examined the top 10 songs of all time from three sources: 1) the top 10 selling songs of all time, 2) Rolling Stone magazine top 10 songs, and 3) the top 10 songs of the 20th Century compiled by the Recording Association of America and the National Endowment for the Arts. Added together these total 24 songs since some songs appeared on more than one list.

I found that 18 of the 24 songs clearly contain a second pitch area that is higher than the first and the transitions between the first and the second are terraced. That means that 76% of the most popular songs reflect the tiers of emotionally charged speech. 9 of these 18 songs have a higher-still third section and all 9 of these follow the ascendant pattern of increasingly emotional speech: low, higher, *highest*. Of the 24, 4 songs stayed at the same pitch level, and only two had descending melodies. 3 of the 4 songs that maintained a consistent pitch center are fast Rhythm & Blues dance songs, which partially explains this lack of terracing since consistency is an important feature of dance music, providing a rhythmic ride.

Below is a list of the songs and the pitch-related structure of each. The songs are listed alphabetically and only the composers are credited:

- "American Pie" by Don McLean – the second section is higher: "man, I dig those rhythm 'n blues ooh, I was a lonely teenage broncin' buck…"
- "Candle in the Wind" by Elton John – the middle of the second section is highest: "and I would like to have known you…"

- "Coração de Luto" by Teixeirinha – this song repeats one continuously descending melody
- "Good Vibrations" by Brian Wilson of The Beach Boys – second section is higher: "good, good, good, good vibrations…" the song also modulates a whole step up toward the end of the song
- "Hey Jude" by Paul McCartney of the Beatles – second section is higher: "anytime you feel the pain…" third section is highest: "na, na, na, na, na, na, na…"
- "If I Didn't Care" by Jack Lawrence sung by The Ink Spots – the second section of the melody is higher: "If this isn't love…" and the third section is higher still: "And what makes my head go 'round…"
- "Imagine" by John Lennon – second section in the latter part of the melody is higher including head voice: "living for today ooh, you may say I'm a dreamer…"
- "In the Year 2525" by Rick Evans – there is no chorus, but each repetition of the verse is a semitone higher
- "It's Now or Never" ("O sole mio") by Eduardo di Capua – begins with high chorus: "It's now or   never…"then the verses are lower: "When I first met you…" the later choruses are higher than the first
- "Johnny B. Goode" by Chuck Berry – the second section is the same pitch level as the first
- "Like a Rolling Stone" by Bob Dylan – second section is higher: "how does it feel?"
- "My Generation" by Pete Townshend of The Who – each repetition of the verse is repeated in a higher key
- "Over the Rainbow" by Harold Arlen – the second section (bridge) is higher: "Someday I'll wish upon a star…" (In the little known original version the song opens with a verse: "When all the world…" that is followed by the higher chorus: "Somewhere over the rainbow…" and the bridge is higher still.)
- "Respect" by Otis Redding as sung by Aretha Franklin – end of the song is higher with improvised vocals

- "Rock Around the Clock" by Max Freedman and James Myers recorded by Bill Haley and His Comets – there is no second section
- "Satisfaction" by Mick Jagger and Keith Richards of The Rolling Stones – second section is higher: "I can't get no…"
- "Silent Night" by Franz Gruber – second section is higher: "Christ our Savior is born…"
- "Smells Like Team Spirit" by Kurt Cobain, Krist Novoselic, and Dave Grohl of Nirvana: end of first section is lower: "Hello, hello, hello, how low…" the second section is higher: "With the lights out, it's less dangerous…"
- "This Land is Your Land" by Woodie Guthrie – this song has no second section
- "We Are the World" by Michael Jackson and Lionel Richie – the second section is higher and the later chorus is a semitone higher
- "What'd I Say" by Ray Charles – constant pitch center. It does contain some higher notes in the last verse but is not counted as one of the terraced structure songs.
- "What's Going On" by Marvin Gaye – second section is higher: "What's goin' on?"
- "White Christmas" by Irving Berlin – there is no second section
- "Yes Sir, I Can Boogie" by Ralf Soja sung by Baccara – the second section (chorus) is higher

Dance music is much less likely to reflect the terraced pitch centers of emotionally charged speech. Music that is intended to get you hopping to the dance floor tends to follow a steady course. Dance music has a different agenda than the sing-to-the-heart structure of love songs and emotional appeals. There are some hybrid forms – my favorite dance-floor moment of all is the raised pitch shift that occurs in "Play That Funky Music". I've found myself airborne before landing on the downbeat of the chorus in that song. It is, in fact, a good example of a pitch center shifting into high gear: "Yeah, they was dancin' - and singin' - and movin' to the groovin' - and just when - it hit me - somebody turned around (listen for the shift into high here) and shouted 'play that funky music white boy!'"

It is worth noting that the second section in songs is often paired with lyrics that represent the emotional heart of the song. The opening section, the verse, establishes the characters and situation ("Once upon a time you dressed so fine...") then the second section, the chorus, expresses the core meaning ("How does it feel?") As you will read in the following chapter, the structure of our stories follows the same logical progress of introducing the characters and situation before the telling of the event. The chorus usually comes after the verse and could be thought of as the reason the songwriter wrote the song.

Verse: There comes a time
        When we heed a certain call...
Chorus: We are the world
        We are the children...

There are times when our speech flits into and then out of one of the higher strata. In the middle of a phrase the voice can shift into a high falsetto for a syllable or two and then the speaker brings the sound under control again, returning to a normal pitch center. When the voice cracks like this it makes a sudden leap upward into the falsetto, or head voice. The interval covered by a cracking voice is at least a perfect fourth. These notes that leap upward are often found in the haunting music of the Celts.

They are also found in many of the melodies of Elton John:

```
                         aa-

            maaa-
                    aaa-
        et                  a-
    Rock-                   a-
                        an
```

and Dave Matthews:

     space

             ween
The   bet-

Colors and Textures of Speech

Spoken communication can be written down in letters like the ones you are looking at now, but we all use modifications and enhancements added by pitch, inflection and timbre to imbue our language with personality and feeling. These elements provide the colors and textures that make the paintings of speech personal and emotionally charged. Written language is like a pen and ink drawing of speech. What was lost in the transcription from sound to ink was found by creative souls who forged the sonic elements of speech into the pure expression of music.

The languages of Europe contain a host of expressive variations that cannot be transcribed and have received relatively little attention by linguists, they are the nuances of inflection. While grammar, syntax, context, vocabulary, and etymology each has its own large shelf in a library, a pamphlet on how inflection can radically alter, or even reverse the meaning of a phrase in speech is difficult to locate. Written language, when viewed on the evolutionary time-line of *Homo sapiens*, is a recent addition to human society. Despite its newness, it is often confused with language itself. The elements that are missing from the written versions of these languages are often the most expressive facets of the original spoken languages. As the reader already knows (perhaps he or she doesn't *know* that she knows, but will soon be reminded) inflection is often more fundamental to expressive communication than vocabulary. The words we use often matter less than the tone we use. Is she truly sad that her friend left town, or secretly happy to be rid of him? Is she trying to cover up her feelings? Has she learned to modulate her pitch like a radio personality? Does she use the high-flighty sing-song that she hopes will attract athletic men? Is he uncomfortable expressing his emotions? Is he a tough guy? Does he want to sound like a tough guy? (not very musical) Is he demonstratively gay? (extremely musical) Is he a demonstratively gay tough guy? The point is: the nuances of pitch and inflection are the very elements of speech that identify our personalities, and are, therefore, individual by definition, obscuring the commonalities.

But without commonalities none of us would be able to "read" a stranger, and we know that, to an extent, we can. The ability to perceive character, truthfulness, intention, social station, attraction, threat or danger in speech was vital enough for natural selection to have consistently weeded out those who couldn't do it. Survival will have depended on a fellow's ability to tell that this man is a disguised enemy or that woman wants to have him. Improved perception fostered improved deception: "If I can better mask my hatred of him, he will let me remain in the group. Then I will undermine and supplant him." Deception, in turn, allowed the more perceptive to prosper. The rising parallel towers of competing perception and expression created a species capable of extremely varied and precise vocal nuances.

The process of learning these nuances is one of gradual refinement that begins before we are born. (Remember that you were learning before you were breathing.) Just as children begin building with blocks, then Legos, and eventually computer chips, so do they learn the broad outlines of the pitches and tones of voice before graduating to more subtle expressions. The inflections of small children tend to be exaggerated; the rising pitch at the end of a small child's question will often soar into a charming little squeak. The expressive uses of pitch and inflection are learned along with vocabulary and the specific organization of grammar. Fully mastered inflection is often very subtle; small nuances allow dense collections of vocal contours to be capable of communicating complex meanings. Music borrows from the inflections of speech, and borrows most from speech that is charged with emotion.

The expressive linguistic elements of intonation, inflection, volume and timbre have received a great deal of independent attention from non-linguists, however, unaware that they were examining the distilled extraction of inflected vocal expression when they were studying music.

Human Music

Singing: The Distilled Expressions of Speech

Singing itself can be thought of as stylized speech. The sounding note of a vowel is the pitch; in music the pitch is determined by the composer. The subtle and varied nuances that are used to approach, color, and ornament a pitch will be referred to here as inflection. Musical inflections are in the purview of the performer.

An emotionally affected speaker who has lost control of fine motor function is the root of another melodic turn: the quivering melisma or ornament. In this kind of speech the lower lip quivers and the voice flutters over an uncontrolled pitch range and volume and often leaps into the high, falsetto head voice. This kind of vocal flutter is referred to in music as an ornament. I think the "ornament" is egregiously misnamed: the name evokes images of tinsel and curlicues and fails to represent the gravity of this deeply evocative type of melodic contour. It is often heard in the most emotionally charged part of a tune. The melisma has long been a hallmark of virtuoso technique. It is prominent in the music of Moorish and Arabic influence and that found in countries closest to the Near East the melodies are highly affected by these musical eddies. It is also used heavily in contemporary popular female vocals such as that found in the stylings of Christina Aguilera, but the genesis of the melisma is found in the birthplace of many musical elements, emotionally inflected speech.

Inflecting Thespians

It is time to raise the curtain on your imaginary stage again and call your actors back from their coffee break – we need them to demonstrate expressive intonation in a few more skits.

Version 1: The scene takes place in the front hallway of a nice, middle-class home. Elmer, wearing a suit and carrying a briefcase is headed for the door. He is content and self-confident and calls out to Dottie, whom he made love with the night before:

```
---                    L E A-
---                          viiiing!"
---
---
---          "I'm
```

The pitches are high in his vocal range and the sound quality is pure and loud enough to be heard by her in the bedroom. The octave between "I'm" and "lea-" and the minor third between "lea-" and "ving" are nicely tuned. This kind of speech sounds something like Alpine yodeling.

Version 2: Elmer heads for the door after having an argument with Dottie:

```
---
---
---
---          "I'm lea-
---                    ving."
```

The pitches are low and descending, the quality is complex with a bit of a snarl in the sound. In this version he is still angry and wants to get away. He has not said it loudly enough to be heard clearly, but he doesn't care.

Version 3: Elmer heads for the door after having an argument with Dottie but is willing to talk later.

```
---
---
---                    lea- viiing."
---          "I'm
---
```

The pitches are not quite so low, the quality is less snarly and he holds the last vowel long enough for her to understand him.

Version 4: Elmer heads for the door, but has been delayed by his wife and will now be late for a tryst with his lover.

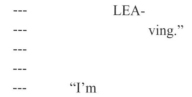

It sounds something like his first incantation, but the stress-induced tension in his vocal folds causes the intervals to be a bit out of tune and the last vowel is cut short by his need to swallow. She wonders why her husband hasn't been himself lately.

Let's compare the quantity of information contained in the language itself with the quantity of information contained in the tones-of-voice in these four versions. The language conveyed: 1) he (subject), 2) is (in the process of), 3) leaving (action). Now consider the enormous quantity of information contained in his various inflections. Transcribed language is often only a sterile shadow of speech. In an emotionally charged moment, it is the inflections, not the words, that convey the true expression. When we extract inflections from language we have music.

Now that you have the hang of it, supply the inflections in the following snippets of human interaction yourself. We will do away with words altogether now – listen to how these imaginary characters respond to the following situations by saying an open "ōōō" (rhymes with "shoe"):

-----A young woman sees an adorable baby in a carriage….

-----A catty, gossip-loving man sees two people he knows that had recently broken up entering a restaurant holding hands …

-----A 21 year-old man drinking beer and watching football with his buddies sees a receiver who had leapt for the ball over the middle get nailed by a flying, horizontal linebacker…

-----A man is told that his friend had a concrete block fall on his toe…

-----Same story – the toe had to be amputated...

You're good at this! Actually we all are - which is one reason why music is so widely appreciated.

The pure vocalization that you imagined in those situations is somewhere between language and emotionally generated vocal expressions. These exclamations have little to do with language but have a lot to do with music.

Now for our dramatic finale: imagine a scene where a woman is pleading for her husband not to leave her. The opening argument is moderate as they exchange low, short utterances. The moment she realizes that his intention to leave is serious her voice takes on a higher pitch and more dramatic quality, then cracks a bit. The pitch varies widely as her pleading gets ever louder. After the door slams behind the departing husband, she emits a high, piercing wail. Any resemblance between the "music" of that scene and an Italian opera is absolutely not coincidental.

4

THE STORYLINE

Verse and Song

My dad remembers where he was when he heard the news that his hero, Yankee's first baseman Lou Gehrig, had died. Any of us who were alive and sentient remember where we were when we heard that President Kennedy had been assassinated. The strong emotions that accompany news of important events burn the entire experience of hearing the news into our memories. I guess that this is an indication of how important music is to me: I remember where I was the first time I heard the clarinet concerto by Aaron Copland.

It was an overcast afternoon. I would have been about 12 years old, in the back seat of our blue Belvedere driving through the tall pine forests of Southern Manitoba. We must have been tuned into Canadian Broadcasting Corporation Radio out of Winnipeg. When the first few plucked bass notes in the harp awoke me from my empty staring at the sky it was like seeing a glimmer of gold in a dim cave: "What's this?" The clarinet floated like a grey bird over the ride of the bass, drifting effortlessly up and over and down again. All the while it was somehow heartbreaking, this music.

I also remember that I was staring into the fireplace in our cabin in Springsteel, Minnesota when I first heard Issac Hayes' rendition of *By the Time I get to Phoenix*, I was skating on an outdoor rink at night the first time I heard *Crimson and Clover*. And I was being driven home one night in Randy Terry's dad's car the first time I heard *Hey Jude*. We had pulled up in front of my house somewhere in the middle of the song and I asked Mr. Terry if I could stay in the car until the song was over. My best friend, Randy, already knew of the song and said that it lasted 9 minutes. Mr. Terry let me stay anyway. I could hear that the song was something about not being afraid and making things better, but the real message for me was in the music. The cheer, the hope was in the mantra of the refrain: naaaaaaaa naaaa naaaa naa na naa naaaa... I wouldn't learn until decades had passed that Paul McCartney penned this song in his car as he drove to visit Julian Lennon after John had moved out. It is a rare occasion when a songwriter feels that the expression in the music is so complete that words are unnecessary.

In *Hey Jude*, the verses top out on the same pitch as the refrain, but the refrain stays up there, long and loud, at the height of the phrase. In the terminology of voice teachers this difference is called the tessitura. In this song the highest note of the verse and the highest note of the refrain are the same pitch, but the tessitura, the mean pitch, of the refrain is much higher. It is possible to hear this refrain as a stylized cheer: an open vowel centered on one or two long, loud, high notes.

We have seen that the higher pitch centers of emotionally charged speech compared to normal speech appear to be the bases for tiered pitch centers in song structure. There is also another facet of the structure of speech and that is found in the structure of songs, and it is related to how we organize our stories. Just as a person telling a story introduces the characters and situation, then follows with the events and ends with the emotionally relevant point, so do song structures often contain the character/situation in the opening and the emotionally charged heart of the story later in another section. The songwriter tells us:

Here is the story: ----(lower pitch center)-----   verse, verse...

and <u>here</u> is how
I *feel* about it: ----(higher pitch center)----   chorus/b section.

This pattern is often repeated, giving us more of the story and giving us the chance to feel/sing along with the chorus the next time it comes around. Our sympathetic emotional doors have been unlocked by the introduction of characters and situations and are opened in anticipation of the emotional expression that we sense will ensue. Most contemporary songs follow some variation of this ABA form. You could turn on a radio now, tune in to a popular music station, and have a good chance of hearing an example.

Here are a few notables:

VERSE   B SECTION

Can't Take My Eyes Off You
(by Bob Crewe and Bob Gaudio)
"You're just too good to be true..."   "I love you, baby..."

Bridge Over Troubled Water
(by Paul Simon)
"When you're weary..."   "Like a bridge over
                                                troubled water..."

Independence Day
(by Gretchen Peters)
"Well she seemed alright..."   "Let freedom ring..."

Si, mi chiamano Mimi
(from Puccini's opera *La Boheme*)
"Mi chiamano Mimi"   "quando vien lo sgelo
("Call me Mimi")   sole e mio il primo
                                               bacio..." ("when the thaw
                                               comes the morning sun and
                                               my first kiss...")

The Renata Tebaldi performance of this famous *la Boheme* aria is a guaranteed magic carpet ride for me. Around the 3:00 minute mark when the harmony shifts my skin flushes and it feels as if the breath that has been taken from me; it lightens my body and shifts my equilibrium as I close my eyes and submerge.

Words and Lyrics

My brother and I grew up as goose bump addicts. It wasn't just music that we listened to; a recording of excerpts from the speeches of Winston Churchill were a regular fix for me. After his death, a commemorative issue of Life magazine contained a small, plastic record that could be removed and played on a phonograph (with a coin on top to hold it in down). I listened to it like music. It never failed to thrill.

In these passages, as in musical passages, a setup is necessary for the success of "the chills". If we were to hear Churchill speaking only the words "their finest hour" we might feel little more than a little twinge of excitement, but when these words are heard in context, the preparation makes the words "their finest hour" an arrival of monumental meaning, a moment in history. These quotes are presented below in blank verse to highlight the use of poetry and rhythm that Churchill learned from his literary ancestors Milton and Shakespeare. In order to enhance the musicality and rhythm and to better appreciate the cadence that he used in the original version of this speech, pause momentarily between the lines as you read:

"Let us therefore brace ourselves to our duties
And so bear ourselves
That if the British Empire and its Commonwealth
Last for a thousand years
Men will still say
This
Was their finest hour."

The rhythmic cadence is even clearer in his tribute to the pilots of the Royal Air Force:

"Never in the field of human conflict
Was so much owed
By so many
To so few."

In the Parliamentary speech that became a call to courage that braced his nation: "We shall fight on the beaches" he uses as many musical elements as can be found in a well-designed melody. His tone-of-voice is deep and determined, the dogged stubbornness that Churchill personified is expressed in the rhythm and repetition, and, perhaps most remarkably, the pitches that he uses are squarely in E flat major. To demonstrate how absolutely tonal this speech is, I wrote and recorded a musical setting of this speech that may be heard at: www.davidteie.com and click on Churchill or on track 11 of the CD. The sentence "We shall fight in France" begins on an A, rises in discrete scale steps to peak on F on the word "air", and cadences at the end of the sentence. The second sentence begins on a G on the phrase "We shall fight on the beaches", follows a chromatic ascension to "we shall fight in the fields", prepares the final cadence with an F on the words "streets" and "hills", then ends with the emphatic highest pitch of the entire passage as he cadences in E flat major with the words "we shall never surrender".

"We shall fight in France,
We shall fight on the seas and oceans,
We shall fight with growing confidence and growing strength in the air,
We shall defend our island,
Whatever the cost may be.
We shall fight on the beaches,
We shall fight on the landing grounds,
We shall fight in the fields and in the streets,
We shall fight in the hills,
We shall never surrender;"

Of course, ideas themselves have the power to stir our emotions. Let's look at this power in the context of the following premise: emotions have been placed by natural selection to induce behaviors that provide for the survival of our species. When we are rallied behind a cause, when we sense that we are aligned with one another, when we strengthen the cohesion that improves our society's chances for survival our emotional centers reward us with chills of euphoria and tears of empathy. Every societal species has mechanisms that ensure the alignment of the group. Human emotions make us attentive when we look up to our leaders, punish us with guilt and stress when we betray our group, and reward us with euphoria when we align behind a common cause. In 1940 in Britain the cause was defense; in 1968 in the United States the causes were peace and unification. In all cases the singularity of purpose that strengthens a society is supported and promoted by the emotional directors deep in our subconscious minds. Our mid-brain limbic behavior guidance system provides us with the euphoria of unity. These emotions are felt even more strongly by listeners who are already in an emotionally heightened state from the fear that often accompanies the grave circumstances of unifying speeches.

Needless to say, the unity of common-cause euphoria that strengthens the will and fabric of a given society is not always beneficial to humanity. There was plenty of unity-fueled euphoria felt in rallies on the other side of the Channel in 1940. I can't bring myself to put in the listening hours necessary for a musical analysis of Hitler's speeches, but it is well known that he was adept at building effective climaxes. One striking quality is the absolute brutality in the tone of his voice. Viewed in the context of Morton's rules of mammalian vocalizations, his loud, harsh tone clearly expressed threat and aggression. In the Nazi rallies the underlying common cause expressed partly through tones of voice was aggression.

The salient point concerning the parallels between oratory and music is that the impact of Churchill's ideas are greatly enhanced when they are housed in cadences such as his. He could have said: "We shall fight in France, on the seas and oceans, with growing confidence and growing strength in the air, in the fields, streets, and hills, on the beaches and landing grounds..." but such a laundry list would have little chance of making it into the books of great quotations.

When his linguistic rhythms and structures are stripped of their meaning and purpose the effect is somewhat different:

He shall put on his boxers,
He shall put on his trousers,
He shall put on his shirt and his jacket,
He shall be fully dressed,
He shall never go naked.

I include that travesty to illustrate the point that music only serves poetry and prose that is imbued with emotion. Have you heard of anyone setting the Pythagorean theorem to music?

Great oration and music often contain symmetry, repetition, and climactic melodies. These two forms of expression are so intimately connected that it is occasionally impossible to tell where one leaves off and the other begins. Someone listening to Martin Luther King's "I have a dream" speech who does not understand English will hear a melodic design, will hear him singing.

The pairing of words and music can be like tying shoelaces, connecting two ends of one string. It is an intertwined dance between the partners poetry and melody. As speech becomes more emotional it becomes more musical and the emphatic point of a story is highlighted melodically. When these two focus points converge in a song they may create a memorable whirlwind pairing: producers call it the "hook". Often used as the title of the song, it is the sing-able, memorable union of a melodic high point with a key turn of the phrase. If you have heard any of the following songs more than once you will probably have the hook spinning in your head as you read the titles: "Take the last train to Clarksville", "(good, good, good) Good Vibrations", or "YMCA".

Inside the music business there is a mercantile association between the hook and record sales; the catchy hook sells. This shouldn't blind us to the artistically pure territory in the heart of the songwriter that often welds words to melodies. Although it may be true that the music business can be like Hunter S. Thompson's view of TV: "... a long plastic hallway where thieves and pimps run free and good men die like dogs, for no good reason." it is also true that creative musicians and lyricists tie together poetry and melodies that genuinely affect them. Songwriters often pair words and music in a moment of inspiration, as if they were hearing rather than inventing it.

John Lennon told of his experience writing "Nowhere Man": "I'd spent five hours that morning trying to write a song that was meaningful and good, and I finally gave up and lay down. Then Nowhere Man came, words and music, the whole damn thing as I lay down."

The expressive power of the pairing of a strong idea with a moving melody was eloquently described by the wonderful lyricist and songwriter E. Y. Harburg who said: "Words make you think a thought.

Music makes you feel a feeling. A song makes you feel a thought." The pairing of the essence of the music in a motive and the essence of the meaning of the song in a word is capable of inducing flurries of concurrent stimulations in the hearts and minds of listeners. When we hear the synthesis of music and story neurons are working overtime back in the information-sorting room of our brains. There, beyond the reach of consciousness, emotional speech is registered, sympathy and empathy begin to glow, and anticipation and attention are cranked up as the story unfolds. As the singer delivers the point of the song we feel the connection and understanding tug at something within. The tip of the point is sharp and barbed, the hook is set, and our hearts are reeled in.

Story Structures

The emotional connection that is provided by the story is personal, instinctive, and profoundly sympathetic. Story structure can be a powerful foundation of expressive communication. Just as the motives, intonation, and inflections of music are drawn from speech, many musical structures are replicas of the structure of our stories. From the shapes of musical phrases to the designs of large-scale works, composers tell stories in the way we are all designed to hear stories. People are always telling them and are almost always telling them the same way, and that is: introduce the characters and the situation and then describe the event with emotional inflection.

Of the many events that each of us witness in a day, it is the emotionally charged events that we will most often relate to someone. In the story-structure, the event comes near the end of the story and is given appropriately emphatic intonation. This progress is the introduction–expectation-fulfillment design used in much of the music written after 1800. We are moved by music that follows the natural progress of our stories.

The structural recipe for most dramatists, novelists, and composers is: setup and deliver.

Set up: characters + situation
- then -
Deliver: the emotionally charged event

In speech and literature, the phrase, sentence, paragraph, chapter, and book are often best communicated with the emotionally resounding point near the end. The musical extractions of these spoken elements are: the motive, phrase, thematic area, movement, and multi-movement work. Music that sounds expressive often shapes each of these elements so that the emotional emphasis is prepared.

A template for listening seems to exist in our minds: it predicts that the central, emotional point will be near the end of the story. In actual storytelling the focus of the story could be a piece of news, a feeling, a conclusion, an action, a place, a quality – whatever it may be, the point of the story is delivered with emotionally charged inflection.

The progression of character/situation to event is a pattern of speech that is possibly related to an inborn grammatical template that we all possess. Recent research has given us a fuller understanding of the true nature of language structures. Predispositions for nouns and verbs and modifying adjectives and adverbs seem to be inherent in humans. You might say that when a baby is born the grammatical dinner has yet to be served, but the table has already been set. There has been relatively little study of the large-scale tendencies related to inherent grammatical designs, but there is reason to believe that we are predisposed to hear and tell stories in a certain way.

Our mother's speech that we heard in the womb contained story structures. Remember that the study of infants born to French mothers demonstrated that they preferred the French language, but not if it was played backwards. The difference between backwards and forwards is the shape of the phrase, the musical structure of the story.

The following story follows the expected progress:

Dottie tells Elmer about her experience with their 5 year-old son Harry at the store:

"Harry went with me to the store today. He GRA-bbed a GLASS VASE and would NOT LET GO!"

Harry – in the store – grabbed a glass vase, these are the set-up and the action, but the emphatic climax of the story is the emotional response. When we listen to a story we naturally listen with this story-structure in mind. Similarly structured music conforms to our natural ability to follow the flow to the emotional crux.

The naturalness of the progress of our stories can be made more apparent when we take notice of how unnatural it sounds when we change the order:

> "Harry grabbed a glass vase and would NOT LET GO
> when he went with me to the store today."

That version ends with a bit of a thud.

One often-heard variation of this story structure puts the emotionally emphatic point at the beginning and then tells the story with the second fully explained emphasis at the end:

> "HAR-ry was AW-FUL TO-DAY!
> We went to the store and he GRA-bbed a GLASS VASE
> and would NOT LET GO!"

The structure of "O Sole Mio" (the melody of "It's Now or Never") is patterned with this variation. Elvis sings: "It's now or never" in the pleading opening and then begins the story that makes sense of the plea "When I first saw you with your smile so tender…"

Sometimes we introduce the point…

> "You will NOT be-LIEVE who I saw in the Dairy
> Queen today!"

> "Who?"

> "FRANKIE VALLI!!! (SQUEEEEEAL!)"

> "(SQUEEEEEAL!) OH my GOD! (SQUEEEEEAL!)"

…before getting to the story:

> "I KNOW! I was going up to see Timmy… People
> seemed all WEIRD and stuff, and when I went up to the

counter Sherri looked at me 'OH MY GOD' and she whispered: 'Look behind you, look be-HIND you!' And I TUR-ned a-ROUND and THERE in the COR-NER WAS "FRANKIE VALLI!!! (SQUEEEEEAL!)"

"(SQUEEEEEAL!) OH my GOD! (SQUEEEEEAL!)"

The introduction to a song often plays as if the performer is saying: "Come over here and hear my story". The establishment of the key, pulse, characters and situation in the verse allows the listener to attune his or her attention and sympathies to the singer. You look into his face, set aside distractions, and slip into a kind of matching wavelength of communication. The in-group connection between the teller and the hearer is essential to the sympathetic reception of the communication. We tend to pay less attention to the story of someone from the "other" group, an enemy or anyone who is distrusted. The elevated social status of the singer is also conducive to heightened attention and sympathy from the listener. Social hierarchal mammals pay attention to the alpha male, people pay attention to the rock star.

The transfer of emotion from one person to another is a topic that will come up often in this book. It is an underlying premise that allows music to be infectious. We tend to smile at people who smile at us, and a person who is smiling tends to feel uplifted. When we listen to the opening of Beethoven's fifth symphony it is likely that it makes us feel much the same way that he felt when he wrote it. We are designed to empathize with the emotions of members of our group. If a member of a tribe returns from the forest and tells of the saber-toothed tiger he has just seen, the other tribe members will sense the fear in the speaker and feel fear rising in themselves; every member who hears the story will be in an attentive state. We also may be inclined to sympathetically respond to the emotional expression that lies in the emphatic climax of a storyline.

The emphasis may also be expressed through delicacy. When you play the following in the theater of your mind, hear it in a feminine voice intoning the last word more softly than the rest of the sentence and with a quality that is melodiously drawn out and breathy:

"I had this home-made vanilla ice cream, and they served the warm chocolate sauce on the side and it melted the ice cream a little when you poured it on... it was de-li-cious!"

Music has carved out a significant part of human culture by harnessing the power in that kind of communication. Musicians have borrowed the emotional expressions from our speech and combined them with story-structures that are natural to us, delivering emphasis where the emotional high point of a story would be communicated. Music resembles an emphatic story; it draws our attention and awakens our empathy. To put it simply: music is an art form that contains the extracted essence of emotionally generated communication.

Musical Partners

The pairing of music with other disciplines deserves its own place in an examination of music and illuminates some of the powers that music possesses. When music becomes a bride to an existing form, the structure of the groom will dictate the structure of the music. The only exceptions to this are when music plays a primary or significant role in the art form as it does in opera and musical theater. Operatic music places necessary elements of character and situation in the recitatives, where the dialogue and information are presented quickly. Musicals use speech in place of recitatives, but both operas and musicals use the story structure to present the emotional point in the most memorable music of each genre: in the operatic aria and the musical's song.

Mythic Journeys in Music

The arching, rainbow path of the myth: from home to the adventure-journey to victorious return may be the most famous, elemental, and resonant of all storylines. It is found in the animated feature film that shows the hero nearly defeated by the villain before miraculously winning the day. It is in the chick flick that follows the playfully-caught-in-the-rain-and-falling-in-love montage with a near break-up before the couple gets back together and meets at the altar in true, tested love. And it is the backbone of nearly all of the dramatic adventures. These stories are built upon the same ancient foundation: home – conflict – return.

Music was empowered to create this structure when musical key relationships were introduced about two centuries ago. Before the middle of the eighteenth century a single piece, movement, or song usually contained a single set of motives in a single key patterned into a movement or song that was intended to express one basic expression. The songs of drinking, sailors, troubadours, and children, as well as the arias of Handel, Pergolesi and other Baroque and pre-Baroque composers were primarily of a single-character in a single key. Sophisticated composers would imbue these single movement-single character works with wonderfully varied facets and dimensions, but contrasting sections in distant keys were unavailable. Each movement or song had to revolve around one key area because the instruments were tuned to sound good in one key, but would have sounded out of tune in distant, unrelated keys.

The invention of equal tempered tuning in the mid-eighteenth century enabled musicians to play in modes based on any one of the twelve keys without having to stop to retune the instruments to other keys. The composers of that era were able, for the first time, to change key centers as the music unfolded. Introducing new tonal centers and new melodic material in the same movement allowed for the telling of musical stories that had different characters in storylines that journeyed to distant areas. When the sons of J.S. Bach and other early classical composers created a second melody in a second key that was a contrast to the first within a single movement, it was like putting another character on the stage.

This variety of tonal centers could evoke the natural shifts in tonal centers that we hear every day in conversations. As noted earlier, we speak in primarily consonant intervals. It follows, then, that the relative consonant intervals of each speaker tends to imply a tonal center. Each of us who speaks in one of the non-tonal languages possesses something akin to a key center to our speech. When we are excited or moved that tonal center is raised – it is this rising that is evident in the verse/chorus song structure outlined previously. When two people converse they are likely to be using two different tonal centers. The varied tonal centers found in speech were ultimately adopted and stylized by those giants of organized sound, Haydn, Mozart, Schubert, and Beethoven.

Mind you, not one of them did this consciously. There is nothing that I know of in the record that indicates that any of these composers analyzed the pitch centers of speech and then used the principles to guide their own designs. But they did communicate verbally, they told and heard stories, and they had no less intuition than Lennon or McCartney. What these classical geniuses did do was to set about composing music that was primarily natural, vocal, and dramatic.

The ability to move between different keys also enabled the perception of progress and development in musical storylines. The most commonly-used musical structure in Western music from the middle of the 18th until the end of the 19th century is the sonata-allegro form. The primary elements of this structure are:

1) A – Exposition, the first theme is introduced in the main key and a second theme is introduced in the secondary key (for example, in "Oh, Canada" the third note sounding on "da" is the main key note and the secondary keynote corresponds to the note sounding on "Cana").

2) B – Development – this is usually a turbulent section where the themes are expanded and presented in distant keys.

3) A – Recapitulation – a restatement of the Exposition, but this time both the first and the second themes are presented in the main key.

The sonata-allegro form is the myth storyline represented in musical structure. To listen to the first movements of most of the works of Haydn, Mozart, Schubert, Beethoven, and Brahms is to listen to music with a mythic storyline. The A section introduces the themes, the B section provides the conflict and develops the motivic material in other keys, and the moment of return to the A section is the moment of arrival, the point of emphasis in the story, the return home. Songs and symphonies, midsize structures and large structures use this kind of ABA form. Since music happens over time and is not appreciated as a single shape, perhaps it is better to describe it less as a form than as a cyclic journey.

In the song that has been called the greatest song of the 20th Century "Over the Rainbow" from *The Wizard of Oz*, the journey of the song predicts the journey of the story itself. The song encapsulates the story: it begins with a statement of hope – dare to dream – then move to another place – away up where the bluebirds (of happiness) fly – then we return home. In the coda, as the scale ascends: "why, oh why, can't I?" Dorothy, in her daydream, becomes the bird. The rainbow song expresses the same journey as the lyrics and the story itself. In the film, the Kansas home "A" sections are black and white and the "B" section, the dream, is in vivid color. We can't help but notice that the color and drama and beauty and fantasy are in the dream, in the adventure, in the journey to the other place - where the girl next door (mythic hero) finds and slays the wicked witch (dragon).

The dream/journey-B section in music is a favorite colored brick road for musicians where everything is possible: witches terrify, Munchkins giggle, and heroes conquer. This structural fulcrum is a fantastic place where we can slay our own personal dragons and become the people we wish we were. It is in the bridge, on the rainbow, where musicians open our hearts.

Puccini's opera *Tosca* gives us another example where the form of a melodic line predicts the character and storyline of the entire work. The expression contained in one brief melody in *Tosca* is a breathtaking example of the loving genius of Puccini. This is one place where hearing eight seconds of music will provide more understanding than reading another few books on the subject. If you go to www.davidteie.com and click on Tosca or listen to track 12 on the CD you will be able to hear this melody. In eleven notes of a solitary clarinet accompanied by only a single note in the bass Puccini prepares the flow of the drama and presents a portrayal of the title character that offers a glimpse of her tragic fate.

Timing

Some stories take moments to tell, some take hours. The length of a story is usually discernable by its introduction: if, two minutes into the telling of a buccaneer's excursion, Blackbeard hasn't left the saloon yet to board his ship you might want to get comfortable. The scope of the set-up and delivery in music must be presented similarly. The length of the motives and phrases and the speed of the harmonic movement often indicate the proportion of the design. The magnificent size of the structures of the St. John Passion, B minor Mass, by J.S. Bach or Brahms' German Requiem are apparent in the first few seconds of each. Once the length of the story is perceived and our internal interpreting scale is calibrated, we are ready to be taken through it, to be moved by it.

To help see this calibration, below is a violation of the expected story length and delivery. Imagine you are a youngster sitting with friends around a campfire in this scene:

> An old, gray-bearded man is telling of the time he was whaling in the North Atlantic when a Nor'easter blew in and the heavy seas were bobbing his ship like a plastic toy. Ten minutes into the story he leans in and lowers his voice. The flickering fire lights his face from below as he squints and hoarsely whispers:

> "Then, in the howling wind, I got my leg TANGLED in the HARPOON ROPE! I reached down to untangle it, the wind died down, and we all went to sleep."

Poof, the expectation bubble is burst and all the little listeners are disappointed.

In order to keep our interest and attention, successful large-scale works take us through contrasting expressive phases. We stay on the ride if these phases are connected psycho-logically. Passions are given time to dissipate before the calm. If the build-up is too short, the arrival will be weak. If humor follows too closely behind the heartfelt plea it robs the plea of its authenticity. If the stillness before an interruption is too short then the shift is less noticeable, if it is too long it becomes boring. There is something like inertia in the rising and falling of emotions; it takes a couple of minutes for some feelings to subside.

The musical onset of an emotion and the rate at which it dissipates in human music is most effective when it relates to the human rate of response. A fine composer is sensitive to the time taken for the onset and dissipation of different emotions and is able to regulate the flow of the music accordingly. Love and euphoria are felt gradually – rising more like a glow than a reflex; musicians who are tugging the audience toward expressions of love do so incrementally. The euphoric ending of Stravinsky's *The Firebird* ballet, for example, builds very gradually. Other emotions such as fear and anger can be immediate. The infernal dance from the same ballet owes much of its excitement to its shatteringly explosive opening.

One performer who had a deep understanding of natural emotional inertia was the cellist and pedagogue William Pleeth. When I heard him make the following comment to a student who had played a transitional melody in the Schumann concerto, it was all I needed to make me go to London to study with him for two years: "Don't get so soft so soon! How quickly can you un-spin your passions?" In the music of great composers, the pacing of the emotional tides coincides with human nature, and performers must understand and convey this emotional flow.

Any of the composers who have had their likenesses carved into marble busts knew this: the more psycho-logical the sequences, the deeper and clearer the expressions, and the more varied those expressions, the greater the work.

The Power of the Unexpected

Unless, that is, the psychological change is intentionally illogical. Consider Oscar Wilde's comment on Dickens' *The Old Curiosity Shop*: "One would have to have a heart of stone to read the death of little Nell without dissolving into tears of laughter." The twist of the last word is especially startling because Wilde has led us down the road to Sympathyville then suddenly turns onto Surprise Party Lane. When music presents an unexpected change it piques interest and attention. Just as Wilde demonstrated, the degree of attention that is generated by the unexpected is related to: 1) the strength of the emotions themselves, 2) the degree of contrast between the contrasting the emotional territories, and 3) the suddenness of the change.

Some of the emotional charge we get from the unexpected in music may be closely linked to Wilde's memorable bait-and-switch criticism of Dickens. Just about any joke we hear ends with an unexpected twist. In general, humor is not an emotion that is well represented in music, but the paradigm shift at the punch line that gets the laugh is very similar to the kind of harmonic shift that signifies a change in the "tonal paradigm" that twitches our emotions.

The expectation that is generated by the composer or storyteller can be fulfilled, delayed, dissipated, or violated. Examples of expectation delayed and fulfilled are countless. Perhaps the grandest of them is the Liebestod at the end of Wagner's opera *Tristan und Isolde*. If you can survive the three hours of unresolved build-up, the climax is a musical orgasm that will leave you luxuriously spent. It is difficult to provide a successful example of dissipated expectation because composers who write music that leaves us hanging don't get to be very famous.

The violation of expectation is found in the music of all great composers and is a hallmark of the works of Beethoven. His control of the dramatic flow is so adept that he is able to make powerful shifts seem somehow inevitable. In his music the party goes on just long enough before the furious patron barges in to break it up, his peaceful landscape is presented with just enough time for us to breathe in its beauty before the storm breaks.

Strong emotions make for strong emotional swings. A patron breaking up a lively party brings more of a sense of foreboding than if he were to break up a game of checkers. Quick transitions also make for surprising violations. In *The Wizard of Oz* the wicked witch of the West first shows up in a ball of flame in the midst of a celebration interrupting the highest note in the celebratory song; and at the end Dorothy melts the witch just at the moment when all seems to be lost. We are left with emotions that are in keeping with those that follow the violation. When we are turned from sympathy to humor the impact is funny, when we are turned from humor to sympathy the impact is sympathetic.

To demonstrate how the direction of the change can leave us with a completely different sense of an idea, follow me into the mind of Mark Twain. He is constructing a statement on the importance of choosing words that express ideas clearly and in combinations that are unusual enough to keep the reader's attention fresh. He decides to make a comparison wherein the difference of a single word completely alters the meaning. Staying true to the nature of humor, he puts the twist at the end of the sentence:

"The difference between the right word and the almost right word is the difference between the lightning and the lightning bug."

Our premier humorist and satirist chose to present his depth and insight in the garb of wit. His audience is enlightened, charmed and amused.

Now let us imagine that old Sam awoke one morning on the serious side of the bed and decided to get the same point across with more weight than wit by reversing the order:

"The difference between the almost right word and the right word is the difference between the lightning bug and the lightning."

This reversal leaves an image of a turbulent night sky containing mysterious, powerful, and explosive forces and the echo of thunder resonating in the air. Each of these statements describes the same concept using exactly the same words. One tickles the funny bone with a bug while the other touches the awe inspired by lightning.

In Carole King's "You've Got a Friend" the introduction begins in the major key then immediately turns to the relative minor just before the vocal line enters. This unusual and unexpected modulation introduces the melancholic expression of the opening verse: "When you're down and lonely and need a helping hand..." Then the expressive heart of the song, *the point of the story*, is sung in the major key of the chorus: "You just call out my name, and you know wherever I am, I'll come runnin'..." The introduction begins with the essentially positive message of the song before a harmonic and psychological modulation enhances the somber nature of the first line. The veering itself makes the new emotion more apparent. A change of heart and direction can create contrasts that enhance the listener's appreciation of a newly introduced mood.

In one study of people's response to music, subjects were instructed to move a joystick when they felt any emotional response at all. They tended to move the stick when the music contained something unexpected. An example of the unexpected turn in music is the deceptive cadence, a harmonic shift to the relative minor chord when we expect to hear the tonic major chord. We are touched by the deceptive cadence, and composers have been drawing from its well for six hundred years. It is often used to extend the final cadence as in *Bridge Over Troubled Water*: "Like a bridge over troubled water I will lay me down [at 1:16 in the original studio version we hear a deceptive cadence to the minor "sixth" chord] Like a bridge over troubled water I will lay me down [this second time, at 1:27, the melody is the same as the first but the harmony cadences to the major "one" chord]."

Familiar/novel is an emotional win-win that is fundamental to our enjoyment of music. We tend to enjoy the familiar; it defines our surroundings, our world, ourselves. On the other hand we tend to pay attention to the new; changes in direction, weather, and personal intrigues seldom fail to center our focus. Since we are naturally attentive to a story's direction, if a variation is prepared we feel included and relax in the knowledge that we understand; when the variation is unexpected our awareness is ratcheted up a notch. In the culinary world a fine, well-balanced dinner would never comprise a parade of similar courses. ("Tonight the soupe de boeuf et pommes de terre, will be followed by an entree of manzo e insalata di patate, followed by the main course of beef with potatoes, and finished with a delicious desert: carne de la patata crema.") No, the warm liquid soup contrasts with the cold, crisp salad, and the sorbet clears the way for the savory course followed by sweets. Each transition highlights the tastes and textures of the new dish.

The enjoyment of food, perfume, and music are facilitated by our perception that favors new information. One reason a multi-course dinner is more likely to be more enjoyable than a single course is because the strength of a given taste diminishes over time. Similarly, an ever-present odor diminishes after a few minutes of exposure in order to enable us to recognize other smells. Listening to music without variety and unexpected turns is like driving in Eastern North Dakota.

Unexpected changes stimulate parts of the nervous system automatically, that is to say pre-consciously. The short circuit between incoming sounds and deep brain structures related to motor control and attention allows us to have reflexive responses to sounds. This primary evaluation acts like the triage of sound processing. ("This one has been heard before, send him back to the waiting room. This one is different, send him up to the midbrain using the open elevator marked 'attention'.") The auditory system differentiates between old and new. A redundant sound, such as an echo, is filtered out of our perception, allowing us to more clearly hear the sound signal itself. The opposite happens when we hear a new sound, it triggers our attention and may even startle. When you reflexively turned toward the automatic icemaker after it dropped ice cubes into the bin, the reaction was triggered near the brainstem before the information reached your conscious mind. Musicians have intuitively discovered ways to slip music past the triage of primary auditory processing and into the corridors of the midbrain where emotions reside.

Repeated patterns in music sound more "alive" and natural when performers imbue them with subtle differences. A stiff, less talented school girl singing a popular song will sing exactly as the music is printed on the page. Even if she is in tune, the audience hears it as a straight and inexpressive performance. A fine singer imbues the song with variations in timing, melismas, and tone colors that serve to change the patterns enough to provide aspects of newness.

Subtle variations allow each verse in a song to be heard from a new perspective. In the song "Whither must I wander?" by Ralph Vaughn Williams, for example, there is a phrase that ends a sequence of musical patterns set to the words "I go where I must." Normally the musical interpretation of the phrase would arch in the middle "I go WHERE I must." following the arching line of the melody. But in the marvelous interpretation of Bryn Terfel, he sings "I go where I MUST!" This accent makes sense when spoken, but is surprising when sung on the last note of this musical phrase; it provides a sincerity and newness to the projection of the spirit of the song. To hear me singing this phrasing go to www.davidteie.com and click on V. Williams or listen to track 14 on the CD.

Instrumental performers also use contrasting sound colors and dynamics to bring variety to interpretation. The great cellist Gregor Piatigorsky asked a friend of mine in a lesson "If you play forte (loudly) all the time, how will we know when you play forte?" And the insulting moniker that Dmitri Shostakovich reserved for the weak performer who would play everything at the same middling volume was "Mezzofortist".

A variation of a pattern that is unexpected and distinctive can powerfully enhance the expression. Aaron Copland spoke of writing "the note that costs". It is the musical counterpart to the uniquely turned phrase exemplified by Mark Twain's comparison. In keeping with an aesthetic principle observed by Francis Bacon: "There is no excellent beauty that hath not some strangeness in the proportion." music veering in an unexpected direction will often prod our awareness and our emotions. The poem that ends with a word that "costs", the melody that is made from a single, but varied theme, the soft light that falls from the left in a painting by Vermeer, the short, bold, brilliantly colored brush strokes of a late painting by Vincent Van Gogh, these "variations on a theme" are so important that it could be said to distinguish art from craft. A merely crafted work could very well contain no variations in the repeated patterns, but most deeply communicative art contains variations that allow us to see or hear each design anew.

The unexpected turn may also be structural. Beethoven often teased the listener with false recapitulations as if to say: "You think you're home, eh? Not yet." Brahms went out of his way at times to *hide* the return. In the first movement of his fourth symphony the great symphonic return/arrival of the sonata-allegro form, the recapitulation, is blended into the texture slowly at first and we only realize that the music has returned when the tempo is restored in the middle of the theme. In this movement, a climactic moment of arrival would have been incongruous with the plaintive quality of the opening melody. The blended return enhances the intimacy of the melody rather than calling attention to it; the slow, soft return expresses an introspective shyness. Just as it was in the story of the delicious ice cream, Brahms uses a quality of voice (quiet violins) at the point of emphasis that is in keeping with the emotion that caused the telling of the story.

The novelty bump can be achieved when words and music are paired that are dissimilar or even conflicting. In David Bowie's "Let's Dance" the moment of arrival in the song is well prepared by a continuous crescendo in the driving pulse, a repeating stasis preparation in the solo vocal line, and the extremely directional harmony of stacking a dominant seventh chord (i.e. in Twist and Shout the" aah, aah, aah, aah" before "c'mon, c'mon, c'mon baby, now") then delivers a hard-hit arrival with a high, complex scream-like vocal sound on the word "flower". The pairing of the violence in the quality of his voice with the delicate image of a flower forces the listener into a paradigm jump-shift that brings newness to the appreciation of each.

Stories that provide variations, expected results and unexpected twists, generate anticipation. Anyone who has been hooked on a soap opera or serial reality show or the regularly published chapters of Dickens' novels knows how tantalizing expectation can be. Anticipation is inherent in changeable stories and is possible to evoke it in music. One of the keys to fulfillment is to prepare a climax with a carefully paved period of expectancy.

The Presence of Absence

Fishermen know that the gradual process of reeling in a large catch is often interrupted to "let the line out". Composers and performers of effective large-scale works are well acquainted with the fishing technique. Rostropovich used to say: "The audience is like a dog on a leash, sometimes you have to let them go, but I do know when to pull them in again." These are the times when music is intentionally inexpressive. The music may conjure images of a ship becalmed in the sun or a still forest where large snowflakes drift to the ground on a gray afternoon. The stillness and non-expressive playing are capable of providing the bias-relief that highlights by contrast the dimensions and colors of passionate playing.

While music of Eastern cultures often reflects the inner peace that may be found in the absence of desire, Western cultures tend to put more emphasis on desire. Accordingly, music of the West is thick with passages of longing and expectation. Success in competition and sexual fulfillment are felt more passionately if the satisfaction is delayed, and so it is with the euphoria of musical arrival. Musicians intentionally delay the orgasm. When performing a long, gradual crescendo lesser performers get too loud too soon and let the tempo move forward. In such a passage the great performers hold the reigns on the tempo and delay the crescendo. But when the time comes for fulfillment all restraint is lifted. In a memorable rehearsal of the swinging, rocking theme in Gershwin's *American in Paris*, Lorin Maazel called out to our brass section (they are usually held in check since they are capable of blowing everyone else off the stage) "Let it go!" The performance was like sonic fireworks.

If a piece of music contains a crucial stasis area it usually immediately precedes The Arrival. The stasis anticipation is the "ahh – ahh – ahh" before the "CHOO!", the calm before the storm, the slow, creaking ascent of the dark staircase by the knife-wielding woman before the screaming appearance of the psycho, the lowered hoarse whisper of the old gray-bearded man at the fire before telling his wide-eyed audience:

"Then the dislodged harpoon washed overboard and my LEG was pulled under-NEATH me as easy as you'd break a TOOTH-pick and I grabbed the jib line and cried out 'CURSE YOU DAVEY JONES, YOU WON'T GET ME TONIGHT!'"

Happy Endings

If the story structure ends with the emotional emphasis like that, how do we explain the descending tail at the end of musical structures? The musical story structure prepares the characters and situation before delivering the emotional point, but rarely stops there – the musical storyline continues past the point. If the first two lines set up the story and the third delivers the high point, then the fourth ends the verse. It is the "And they all lived happily ever after" of the musical world.

One function of the fourth verse/musical tail is to give a musical representation of the reception and sympathy that the storyteller was seeking. Stories are followed by responses. Imagine that the stories that were previously used as examples received no reactions: the husband listens to the tale of little Harry grabbing the vase and immediately after hearing "WOULD NOT LET GO!" he silently turns and walks away, or after the Frankie Valli sighting is reported the listening girl stands mute and expressionless. The very social nature storytelling dictates that the entire shape of the communicated story contains a time for response and settling.

The exceptions to this are tales that end with triumph. The last musical picture in *Pictures at an Exhibition* by Mussorgsky and the final victory celebration in Stravinsky's *Firebird* are examples of triumphal endings. The sound resembling cheering voices singing of victory is the shining silver thread that is common to all celebratory music. Hear the sound made by a fan of the victorious team in a big game against an arch-rival after the final buzzer: "AAAYYY!!" Now picture the same person in the same scene, but the sound is a low, soft "oh". You could attend every game in your area for a hundred years and never hear that combination. Music of triumph could not be formed from the contrabasses and violas slowly weaving tunes in the low register. Triumphal endings finish abruptly because we don't need the sympathetic spin-out time; we are all celebrating together.

Breathing Life into Characters

We normally communicate emotionally charged stories to people who are close to us – to those who are most likely to respond sympathetically. In music and drama, sympathy for the characters must be established before the audience's emotions will be touched. Characters that possess qualities that we admire, are in need of help, or that we *relate* to in some way will tend to receive our sympathies. The ability to establish characters that will engender sympathy and empathy is as important in music as it is in drama.

Contained in the dynamic forces of dramatic structure are: the histories of the characters (position and power), their desires (attraction) and fears (repellence) and their relationships to the others in the story (relative movement). These relationships, forces, and movements give life and meaning to storylines.

In one performance of the second movement of Shostakovich's first cello concerto I was thinking of a Soviet winter landscape as I played the haunting opening melody. When the melody returned later in the movement I thought, instead, of a young girl I had seen on the sidewalk in East Berlin in 1980. That year I was a member of the Baltimore Symphony Orchestra as it became the first Western orchestra to play on the other side of the iron curtain. East Germany was a prison. The East Germans could see the wealth and color on the other side of the razor wire, land-mined, concrete barrier but lived in the faded, colorless cold of grey buildings and dim lighting. One day as we passed in a bus I saw a girl, not yet 10 years old, in a dress holding her arms out to her side and slowly turning in circles while looking down. There was no one else around. The spacious boulevard was completely empty at midday except for her. The price of alienation and socialist severity was somehow personified by this lovely girl dancing in solitude. The repeated melody that I played with this personal image in mind was much more affecting than the first had been. Later, when I listened to a recording of the performance my impression was confirmed. The differences were very subtle; the dynamics and bowings and contours were identical. I didn't change the interpretation consciously, and yet the second version was unquestionably more meaningful.

The musician's understanding of character changes the way we intone the musical line in the same way that the meaning of anything we say changes the way we say it. The words: "I am leaving now." spoken by a child after a happy playtime will have a very different meaning when spoken by a villain who threatened to commit a murder that evening. A happily married Stanley Kowalsky crying out "Stella!" to ask her where she keeps the crackers will not qualify as one of the great moments in theater. The portrayal of character is the soul of drama.

Like the forces of stored kinetic energy in a motionless but leaning tree that can be violently released if the snapping point is reached, a drama will have potential energy resulting from the characters' desires and relationships with others. In the theater, an understanding of the movement that results from the stored dramatic energy colors and informs the actor's communication. In music as well, performers enhance the listener's understanding of the meaning behind the music when they enhance the portrayal of character and inter-personal dynamics.

The following is an example of how a performer's understanding of context and character movement can deepen the listener's appreciation of the expression. The melody and harmonies of a beautiful berceuse by Manuel de Falla contain an aspect of poignancy in that is not indicated in the lyrics: "Sleep, my child, under the stars." A performer who imagines movement and direction in the characters and their relationships can broaden the expressive possibilities. Let's take those lyrics and try to see inside them – imagine a history and envision a fate of the woman singing the lullaby.

A maid in the service of a Spanish Duque bears his son. The Duquesa learns of the son and insists that the maid leave the domain. The Duquesa, herself unable to conceive, gives the maid two choices: she could take the son with her or she could leave the son behind to be raised by the royal couple. The maid decides to allow her son to be raised by his father and the Duquesa in a rich and privileged environment rather than subject him to the hardships and poverty of a life as an outcast. The night before the maid gives up her baby and leaves the castle she sings this berceuse to him.

Just as that story would be told with more inflection by the maid's brother than by a news reporter, the melody of Manuel de Falla's lullaby is conveyed intimately when it is played with those people and that situation in mind. You can hear a cello and piano version of this berceuse at www.davidteie.com and click on de Falla or listen to track 14 on the CD.

Subtle and intuitive performers play with nuances that are based on expressive qualities of speech. As such, the listeners intuitively recognize them. The tempo slows, the tone quality is pure but a bit unstable, the nuances between the notes and inside of the notes are intimate, and the last notes are drawn out as if the mother doesn't want the song to end. Through these inflections the most expressive performers project complete characters. The workaday player reads the notes, plays the slurs and the dynamics, and calls it a concert. The artists that we revere recognize the personalities, relationships, and dramatic structure behind the notes. In their hands the music becomes a story.

Musical lines without lyrics can also be understood and interpreted by performers in the context of a dramatic structure. As I studied and practiced Benjamin Britten's first suite for unaccompanied cello (written for Mstislav Rostropovich) a storyline seemed to emerge from the music. There are hints of the story in the titles of the movements: Serenade, Lullaby, Song, March, but there is no description of characters or a story in the sheet music. In one of my lessons with Rostropovich, as I played the opening of the Serenata movement I was thinking: "Here he wakes up." This awakening was not only something that I had conjured up in my study of the suite, it was in the front of my attention as I played. Rostropovich interrupted me exclaiming: "More! This is where he wakes up!" I thought: "ARRRGHH! What more can I do?" I would eventually come to understand that the role of the performer is not only to possess ideas but also, and more importantly, to project them. Clearly Rostropovich understood there to be a character and a storyline in the suite, and we may assume that the character existed in the composer's imagination as well, but the imagined storyline that a performer may attribute to a piece of music does not necessarily originate in the composer.

I heard an unforgettable story in music the first time I heard Rostropovich play live with the Minnesota Orchestra in Northrup Auditorium in 1972. The reader should understand that (non-Minnesotans please forgive the ice hockey comparison) Rostropovich was the Wayne Gretzky of the cello. He was the best there had ever been by quite a margin, billed at the time as simply "the world's greatest cellist". He had more great compositions written for him than any other performer on any instrument in the history of music. That evening in Minneapolis he played two concertos, one by Lutoslowski and the other by Haydn, even though concerto soloists usually play only one concerto on an orchestral program. One of the bargains that he often made in order to convince presenters to program the music that had been written for him was to agree to play a second, more standard concerto if he was allowed to play the contemporary work. I had not heard the Lutoslowski before this. From the moment he began playing it was not so much music coming from a cello that I heard as much as it was a story being told, a story about a prison. In the last dinner I was ever to have with Rostropovich, I mentioned this to him. Nadia, his long-time friend and translator, said that it gave her goose bumps to hear how the music had affected me because, unknown to me at the time, the concerto is, indeed, a musical story of a prisoner. Rostropovich remained unmoved and unimpressed that his playing could have communicated something so clearly to a naïve boy. He knew and assumed that such experiences were common in his audiences.

To help his students to understand how this can happen he told us of the time when Stalin was purging enemies, intellectuals, and artists in the Soviet Union and Rostropovich had not slept for days. It was the only time in his life that he considered suicide. At the urging of his friends he agreed to be seen by a hypnotist. The first thing the hypnotist did when he arrived at the apartment was to ask for his 10-ruble fee. Rostropovich reluctantly paid him although he was wary of giving payment to someone who had yet to earn it. The man said: "So, you haven't been sleeping." "No, I have not been able to sleep at all for days." Then the man looked at some vases on the shelf and asked: "These are lovely. Where did you get them?" "Those are from Venice. I bought them from a glassmaker when I was playing there." "Hmm. And these porcelain dishes, where did they come from?" "They were bought in Amsterdam." "They are beautiful." Then the hypnotist said goodbye and left the apartment. Rostropovich's first thought was that it had been a complete waste of 10 rubles. Soon, however, he slept. He slept from that afternoon until early in the evening of the following day and slept normally after that.

Later, when he met the hypnotist at a gathering, he asked him how he had accomplished something so remarkable. The man said that the words he used were different than the intent behind the words. While using the words that describe porcelain dishes he was thinking of and infusing the words with the meaning: "You are tired and you will sleep tonight." Rostropovich wanted us to understand that the intent and meaning must be in our minds and hearts in order to convey them through the notes.

Involved Storytellers

Most of the aspects of music described in this chapter are created and appreciated naturally, without the assistance of conscious direction. When we recognize a pattern it is not accomplished by paying attention to the repeated curves or motives, the recognition is triggered automatically and may not even make it up into our consciousness. The same is true of pattern creation, the character-situation-event sequence of our stories, the anticipation of an arrival, as well as the violation of those expectations. All of these owe most of their creation and appreciation to the intuitive, parallel-processing subconscious mind.

Conscious thought is overrated. These thoughts have to wait in lines worse than the DMV. Conscious thinking is like constructing a building by using only one small group working in one place at a time. Intuitive divergent thought, on the other hand, gives over routine tasks to many groups at the same time through second nature and consults with a broad array of architects simultaneously. Emotionally grounded divergent thought can erect elegant structures in its sleep.

Here we come to the issue of sincerity, exemplified by the words of Pablo Casals who said: "Either you believe in what you are doing or you do not. Music cannot be turned on and off like tap water." He also said "In music, the primary role is played by intuition." When a musician allows the divining rod of emotion to lead to the well of divergent thought and intuition, the results are heartfelt and sincere. This simple approach to music allows performers to tell their stories in the first person.

Whereas a painting may represent a scene, a book may communicate a story, and an actor portrays a character, music *is* sound. An actor can portray Richard III but he cannot *be* Richard III. Music, however, does not need to represent something other than itself. The booklet-sized score of a symphony that may be held in your hand is not music; it is only a sketch of the intentions of the composer; it is no more music than the blueprint of the Parthenon is the Parthenon. Our art is incomplete until it sounds. The musical performer does not *re*create anything but is a part of the creative process. When a performer understands and internalizes the directions and intent in the score and gives voice to the music it can bring the mind and emotions of the composer to the minds and emotions of the listeners through his or her own fully involved self. Whether directly from a singer/songwriter or from a genius from another age expressed by a sincere performer, in music the sound is the art.

5

STRUCTURE AND PATTERNS

We recognize patterns so naturally that most of us are unaware of the enormous cognitive complexities involved in recognizing patterns in sounds. If you were to hear an orchestra play "Happy Birthday" in D major with the melody passed from the violins to the violas, then hear a different version in B major with different harmonies where the melody is passed between the oboe and the flute, you would have no trouble recognizing that it is the same tune. In other words, your auditory and cognitive processing easily recognizes the pattern of the melody of "Happy Birthday". While this type of pattern recognition is automatic for most people, it is still far beyond the capabilities of today's biggest, fastest computers. A child could do it incidentally while paying attention to building blocks, but Big Blue, Tianhe-1A, and Watson are all stumped.

Nearly all music is built from repeated patterns. The ability to recognize patterns and design has played an important role in the development and survival of our species. This ability was important enough for us to have evolved emotional responses to pattern recognition. When designs are recognized the reward centers of our brains are activated. Just as conscious calculations are not involved in a "sense of direction", the enjoyment of patterns does not require conscious analysis. Our naturally pattern-sensitive minds recognize logic in the design and then the reward centers of the brain deliver the smile of approval.

Computer scientist Jürgen Schmidhuber has suggested that our enjoyment of patterns is related to our ability to compress information, an important feature of memory storage. Nicholas Hudson has shown that the music of Beethoven is more compressible than techno music; the complexities of Beethoven are created from reducible motives. For example: 12 12 12 12 12 12 12 12 12 12 can be compressed to 10x12. When we compress information we categorize, allowing us to better understand our world. Our subconscious processor sees that 26 26 26 26 26 26 26 26 26 26 can be compressed to 10x26 and recognizes that both of these have "10x" in common and belong in the same category. The enjoyment comes into play because important human functions are likely to be supported by our internal reward system. It would seem that we are rewarded with a pleasurable feeling when we perceive simplicity in apparently complex information.

Subconscious pattern recognition is associated with our sense of beauty. A number of recent studies have shown that symmetry is directly related to perception of beauty in the human face; the more symmetrical the features, the more beautiful the face. Cate Blanchett and George Clooney each have one side of the face fairly well mirrored on the other. Duplication = symmetry = repetition = pattern = aesthetically pleasing result.

Although the appreciation of patterns is highly developed in humans, we are not the only members of the animal kingdom with a preference for symmetry and design. According to a study of Capuchin and squirrel monkeys, they prefer symmetrical pictures and designs with elements repeated at common intervals to pictures of random patterns. The subconscious enjoyment of design is also indicated by studies that have shown that infants prefer gazing at symmetrical pictures. Since conscious recognition, as we understand it, is not available to monkeys or infants, it cannot be involved in the preference for symmetrical patterns. I imagine a baby with dangling legs front-packed on her mother at an art museum removing her own pacifier to say: "Notice how the eye is drawn through the curvature of the flowing gown up to her sensuous, curved lips."

Three aspects of repetition are musically significant:

1. Repetition is symmetry. Shapes are made from repeated components. A spiral has an outer beginning and an inner ending and the self-contained repetition that defines its design. A circle has an inherent repetition in the continuing curve that meets itself, and a square is made from four repeated lines and four repeated angles. Since melodies are simply collections of notes, a pattern would not be apparent unless it was repeated; the patterns that make up melodic motives and structural sections are patterns *because* they are repeated. In music and geometry, the repetition defines the pattern.

2. The repetitions in music are directly associated with vocalizations that are generated in the emotional centers of the limbic system such as the "ha ha ha" of laughter. Emotional calls throughout the animal world tend to transmit these repeated patterns. The eminent zoologist E. O. Wilson noted that animal communication is "repetitious to the point of inanity." The communications that humans use when giving voice to emotions that originate in the primitive mammalian midbrain such as sobbing, laughing, and moaning are all comprised of varied repetitions of a single vocalized sound.

3. Repetition allows recognized patterns to be stored in compressed files in the brain and, therefore, categorized and understood on a deeper level, leading to a pleasure-triggering "aha" moment in the brain. Music that sounds complex but is reducible to simple patterns will benefit most from the string of pleasurable "aha" responses that are felt as the music plays. The famous "dit-dit-dit-daah" motive from the first movement of Beethoven's fifth symphony arrives to the listener's ears as often as players hitting the ball in a quick game of ping-pong, and every hit scores a pattern reward point.

The fractal branched pattern seen in rivers and trees is an elemental and natural design. The water carves crooked rivulets in the soil that drain into larger crooked creeks that drain into larger crooked streams that drain into larger crooked rivers. Similarly the veins in a leaf, sprigs of a branch, and branches of a tree all have similar and proportionate designs.

A human construct based on this architectural organization is found in the Pantheon in Rome. The exterior is comprised of a dome, a rectangle, a triangle, and columns; the interior contains all of these produced in a smaller scale, with columns separating rectangular recesses capped alternately with domes and triangles.

And Frank Lloyd Wright regularly used shapes and designs in the details of his buildings that were smaller expressions of the overall design of the buildings themselves such as the nesting arches of the Marin Civic Center:

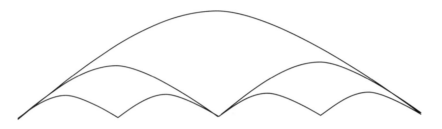

These artistically rendered organic extensions are a part of our natural lives and world and indicate harmony that we enjoy; the single destination of each small step is a miniature of the destination of the walk/journey just as the veins in the leaf resemble the branches that resemble the tree.

Unlike the static grandeur of great architecture, music is alive; its architecture progresses through time. When performing music of pure and exquisite design it is possible to sense the awe in the audience as if they were looking up into the arched, vaulted ceiling of a great cathedral. Of all of the works that I have performed, none stills a room more quickly that the Prelude in G major for unaccompanied cello by J.S. Bach. This is as true of the kindergarten class as it is of an evening crowd in a concert hall. In the first *two* seconds it presents an arch that is replicated in the larger phrase. The following are three visual representations of the opening seventeen seconds:

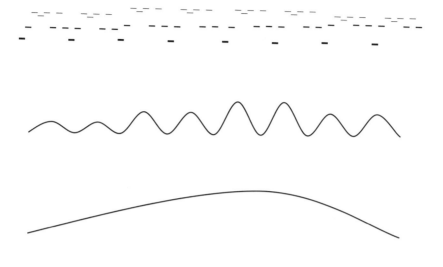

Below are those first seventeen seconds, the first four measures, of this Prelude in musical notation. The upper staff shows the music as it was written, the lower three staves show the same music separated between lower, middle, and upper lines. Eight repeated Gs are the pillars at the foundation of the music providing the bass and the pulse. Above this foundation the inner line peaks on the note of greatest tension, the highly dissonant leading tone, at the height of the phrase before advancing to the note of resolution at the end of the phrase. The shape of the upper line expresses home, movement away, and return.

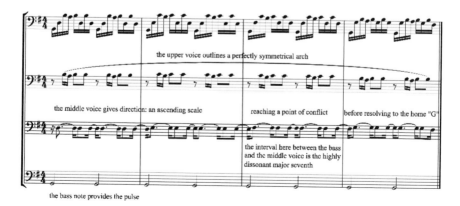

Bach has created a rainbow that establishes the home key and predicts in the shape of the phrase the shape of the movement as a whole: in it the repeating arches move to the relative minor key toward the middle section where the celestial arches of the opening yield to an earthly turbulence, giving way to an extended, rising, tension-filled anticipation that prepares our return to G major home.

While the performance of some kinds of music demand that the performer be personally and passionately involved in the action of the drama, this music is better served when the performer is a clear window. Some composers strive to create works that go beyond self-expression. Beethoven strived to illuminate his music with noble human aspiration and Bach often points toward a spiritual, unifying deity. Performers affix their attentions on these ideals as well. Instead of taking the role as the personally impassioned voice of the composer, the performer joins the composer in a presentation of something more universal. The result can be as if the performers and listeners are all looking in the same direction at a single vision.

The anticipation that can be felt by listeners when hearing this Bach prelude is felt even more dynamically by the performer who must predict the gradual crescendo before creating it. One of the greatest pianists of the 20th century, Sviatoslav Richter remarked: "If I feel a storm, the audience will feel a breeze." Just as a welling emotion rises before an exclamation, the generation of a heartfelt and communicative crescendo begins in the belly and grows until it reaches the arms, and only then is it made sound and heard by the audience.

Playing this prelude is like dancing. The cello requires a real physical involvement to produce a full, ringing tone: the bow arm swings in pendulous curves as if conducting the instrument and this movement speeds circulation just enough to awaken and enliven the senses. The cello rests against the chest so the cellist directly absorbs the resonance from the instrument. The low notes transmit the most palpable sensation, so the steadily repeated low G in the opening rumbles into the cellists body. Cellists must be careful to present the trance-inducing pulse without becoming entranced themselves. Many a performance has been marred by players who have not kept their concentration out in front of the ongoing music, having been seduced, as it were, by their own sounds.

Human Music

Repetition and Hypnosis

The hypnosis of repetition distracts conscious thought; by doing so it may open the door to a more imaginative, sensory experience. When repetition keeps our attention turning in place the attention itself tends to become a bit paralyzed, focused on the lulling pattern. The meditation mantra and concentration on breathing have this same effect of stilling conscious activity. When music presents cyclic repetition it can slip past the dozing conscious mind and fall into more subjective, emotionally connected, and intuitive perception.

At times an insistent repetition can be profoundly moving. In the middle of the last movement of the cello concerto by Edward Elgar is a theme based on only four notes. Beginning around 8 minutes (into Jacqueline DuPre's gold-standard performance of the movement) it evolves, is repeated over and over, passed between the solo cello and the violins without any other motives to break up the repetition, and finally (around 10:20) dissolves into the theme from the previous slow movement. The varied apparitions of this single four-note statement take up more than two full minutes. The concerto was written in England during the last period of Elgar's life after the enthusiasm and romance that characterized his earlier works had been crushed by the devastation of the First World War. The British casualties in The Great War far exceeded the total of all the previous wars in their long history. The repetition of loss, the grotesque length of the grim parade, the sheer *numbers* were what made the war so difficult to bear. In this passage of the cello concerto I imagine that Elgar refuses to reduce any human loss to a statistic; each of the fallen deserves his full recognition regardless of the time that such attention requires. It is as if each repeated motive acknowledges another individual. When I think of this passage I also can't help but remember the man on the cell phone talking to his wife as he knew he was speeding toward his own annihilation onboard one of the aircraft involved in the September 11 tragedies. His last words were the constantly repeated: "I love you, I love you, I love you..."

Human Music

Poetic Patterns

Some impassioned poets also find themselves unable to fully communicate powerful emotions unless they employ the repetition of litany in sequenced phrases such as in Elizabeth Barrett Browning's:

How do I love thee? Let me count the ways.
I love thee to the depth and breadth and height
My soul can reach, when feeling out of sight
For the ends of Being and ideal Grace.
I love thee to the level of everyday's
Most quiet need, by sun and candle-light.
I love thee freely, as men strive for Right;
I love thee purely, as they turn from Praise.
I love thee with a passion put to use
In my old griefs, and with my childhood's faith.
I love thee with a love I seemed to lose
With my lost saints, --- I love thee with the breath,
Smiles, tears, of all my life! --- and, if God choose,
I shall but love thee better after death.

The most obvious similarities between the rhythmic patterns of speech and the rhythmic patterns of music are found in rhymed verse. Here again, our enjoyment takes place under the radar of conscious awareness.

The following sonnet by Lord Byron is predominantly iambic tetrameter but we do not need to know that for us to recognize it as a pattern:

She walks in beauty, like the night
Of cloudless climes and starry skies;
And all that's best of dark and bright
Meet in her aspect and her eyes:
Thus mellow'd to that tender light
Which heaven to gaudy day denies.

We also do not need to know that "Humpty Dumpty sat on a wall" is a fast 6/8 meter for us to recognize the character of its rhythm. We internally comprehend the pattern, and sense the humanity in the design.

Pattern and Purpose

A pattern usually begins to sound banal if it is repeated often enough without variation, but the degree of complexity of the patterns in music and the amount of change that is represented in the variations of the pattern depends on the purpose of the music. Music that is intended for attentive listening evokes interest, attention, and emotion through variation. Music that is not paired with lyrics or dance or cinema is designed to provide a complete artistic experience, and tends to be highly complex, appealing to the pattern-sensitive mind.

On the other hand, dance music and hypnotic music that is intended to induce relaxation usually contain few small, slowly evolving variations. Too many variations may be distracting to the dancers and the hypnotized. If we accept that some dancing is as George Bernard Shaw described: "The vertical expression of a horizontal desire legalized by music." then uninhibited dancing is easier if we turn our attention to the rhythm and turn off our conscious thinking; simplicity is best if the purpose of the music is to pave the path of procreation.

The fellow soberly listening to techno dance music (instead of drunkenly dancing to it) may complain that it is too repetitive. It is tempting to label the music as bad and simple-minded since it tends to sound that way from an armchair, but the music may be well suited to its purpose as a rhythmic prod designed to move Joe Hormone toward the dance floor. Joe does not have music on his mind and complex, nuance-laced melodies will just not do.

Pattern recognition and Repetition

A repeated pattern can be as simple as equally spaced drumbeats or as complex as the repetition of the opening seven minutes of a symphony by Brahms, but in each case, the pleasure we receive from innate pattern recognition is immediate, intuitive, and subconscious. It is tempting to think that we only appreciate patterns consciously since we are able to look at each motive and repetition, turn it over in our minds, talk about it, point out specific features, give it a name (iambic pentameter), and recall it at will, but the two pleasures are distinct. For most listeners the more common and more important recognition is subliminal. Perhaps the following example will provide convincing evidence that pattern recognition is natural, not conscious, and essential to our perception of beauty in music.

Paul McCartney dreamt the melody of the song "Yesterday". He worried that it was a melody that he had heard on the radio and subconsciously remembered. In his biography, *Paul McCartney: Many Years from Now*, he recalled: "So first of all I checked this melody out, and people said to me, 'No, it's lovely, and I'm sure it's all yours.' It took me a little while to allow myself to claim it, but then like a prospector I finally staked my claim; stuck a little sign on it and said, 'Okay, it's mine!' It had no words. I used to call it 'Scrambled Eggs'."

John Corigliano showed me the elegant structure of this song in one of my first composition lessons with him. The motives used in the melody of *Yesterday* are repeated, turned upside-down, and slowed to half speed exactly the same way subjects are treated in fugues. Let's look at the subconsciously created patterns in the song.

The first three notes of the song form a descending motive in a long-short-long rhythm are set to the first word:

    Yes -

        ter day

Then there is an ascending scale sounding with the words:

                            so

                      seemed

                  bles

              trou

          my

      all

At this point in the song, we have heard *all* of the motivic elements of the entire verse. The opening three notes form the predominant motive, the foundation of the song itself, containing the title and the rhyme. The scale connects the repetitions of these motives to each other.

Following the first scale is a restatement of the original three-note motive, but twice as slow in:

far

a -   way

Then a descending scale (the original scale turned upside-down):

now it

looks

as

though

they're

followed by another statement of the first motive, but twice as slow again:

here

to   stay

Then a brief, new motive breaks the repetition: "oh, I believe in"

followed by an upside-down *and* twice as slow version of the first theme:

ter   day

yes

The first verse is now complete; the second verse is a repetition of the first with different lyrics. That is to say, the entire verse is a large, repeated pattern. This song is the product of a pattern-sensitive mind writing intuitively for listeners who listen intuitively with pattern-sensitive minds.

These patterns are not coincidental. Leonard Bernstein wrote an explanation for why we will not be running out of original melodies any time soon. He observed in his brilliant book *The Infinite Variety of Music:* "...the maximum possible number of vertical and horizontal combinations of 12 notes or less comes to a figure which is expressed in 106 digits." And that figure does not account for rhythmic differences. In brief, these patterns do not occur randomly, they have been designed.

The Fugue

Varied repetitions of singular motives are the hallmark of a musical form that has a reputation for being highly cerebral and mathematical: the fugue. It is a musical form that represents the pinnacle of compositional skill commonly used by German-speaking composers of the 17th, 18th, and 19th centuries.

The principle melody of a fugue is called the subject. The most often-used manifestations of the subject are: twice as slow, twice as fast, upside-down, backwards, and any of the various possible combinations of these. After the subject has been played alone it is paired with an accompanying melody, the countersubject, which can also be turned upside-down and backwards and all the rest. Most fugues have been constructed entirely from the elements of these two melodies. Below are examples from fugue #2 in the *Well-Tempered Clavier, Book 2* by the acknowledged master of the fugue: J.S. Bach (1685-1750).

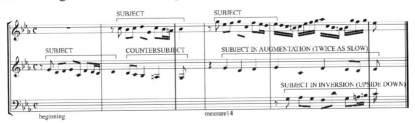

It is a highly structured form with many rules, not unlike the rules of accent and rhyme that must be followed when writing a sonnet. Richard Strauss chose a fugue to provide a musical depiction of intellect in *Also Sprach Zarathustra*.

When I first set my hand to writing a fugue I summoned all of my limited mathematical skills and novice knowledge of counterpoint, and failed miserably. Creating counterpoint, the art of composing two or more lines that sound simultaneously, is the key to writing a proper fugue. Without belaboring the details, the primary difficulty of writing counterpoint is that each voice must follow a set of rules that are determined by the interval or distance between the voices. The relationship between voices is calculated in intervals that must be kept in strict accordance to those rules that prohibit parallel 5ths, require resolution of dissonant intervals, prefer contrary motion, etc. As I tried to construct my first fugue I would change a note in the middle line so that it would fit with the lower line, but then it didn't fit with the upper line. If I decided instead to choose the only note that follows the rules the line itself sounded unnatural, so I changed a note in the upper line. But now the upper and lower lines didn't fit together, and so it went. Eventually my fugue sounded like a Frankenstein's monster of patched-together intervals with band-aids on all of the stitches. My composing ground to a stop mired in math.

So I pitched the scratched-up paper with erasure holes into the trash and tried a different approach. I took my fugue subject and played it a few times on the piano. After a while I began to imagine and sing an accompanying tune to go along with the subject. Once I was satisfied with my Baroque-sounding countermelody I wrote it down underneath the subject. Then I played those two lines together until I could hear and sing a third voice along with them. I continued this way until the fugue was finished, writing out the subject upside-down, singing an accompaniment to it and writing that down, etc. I found that I had very little fixing to do as I went through the finished fugue to edit the places where I had broken the rules; my ear and imagination had followed the rules. I had spent years singing traditionally written counterpoint in chorales and played countless contrapuntal lines in orchestras. The texture and sound of good counterpoint had soaked into my intuition.

Despite its intellectual reputation, fugue writing can be just as intuitive as songwriting. Bach and Mozart could each sit down at an organ and improvise a fugue. I should add here, and will elaborate on this further in the chapter devoted to inspiration, that the kind of intuition that allows someone to improvise a fugue can be thought of as intellect in hyper-drive – a parallel-processing information storm that accesses and employs many different areas of the brain at the same time. In the minds of these genius musicians, the facilities for playing a keyboard instrument and composition were so engrained and well-practiced that they became second nature; they could improvise music as easily as a well-spoken individual is able to compose complete, grammatically correct sentences while simultaneously employing a host of finely-tuned musculatures in the vocal tract to convey them.

I submit that a listener's appreciation of a fugue can also be more intuitive than intellectual. While listening to a fugue, the educated listener will have many opportunities to receive pips of "a-hah", little doses of pleasure from his or her recognition of elements of the design: "The subject is long; this will be a great fugue! There's the counter-subject in the bass voice. Isn't that the subject in retrograde inversion (upside-down and backwards)? A-hah!" But, the point of all of this is that the emotional power of a great fugue may be felt by a listener who doesn't know a double fugue from a double espresso. I frankly doubt that an explanation of where the subject is inverted adds very much to the listener's enjoyment of a fugue. The pleasures of conscious recognition are genuine but *secondary* to the emotional response resulting from our natural sense of design and the strong emotional tug that can be felt when we sense the movement and variation in melodic lines, that is to say: when we appreciate the patterns subconsciously. Perhaps our appreciation for the depth and beauty of a Bach fugue would be more enhanced if, rather than appealing to the intellect to understand it, we simply close our eyes and breathe deeply.

I once composed a fugue that appeared at first in my mind disguised as a funky rock bass riff. I was in Lincoln, Nebraska in the late 1980s where fellow cellist Steve Honigberg and I were playing the concerto for two cellos by David Ott with the Nebraska Chamber Orchestra. The concerto has a brilliant, high-octane cadenza near the end of the piece (www.davidteie.com click on Ott or track 15 on the CD) and I wanted to write something for cello and piano that could set a concert on fire like that.

One morning in a practice room at the University of Nebraska I was trying to imagine just such a piece. I was like an excited dog sniffing around to find a scent trail. I was pacing and hearing/murmuring a strongly grooved beat and pulse with tom tom-like booms. Gradually the booms became organized into a pattern: boom – (silence) – (silence) – (silence) – boom – boom – boom –(silence) – (silence) – (silence) – boom – boom – boom– (silence) – boom– (silence) – boom... Then I began to hear pitches in the booms. I sketched out what I was hearing and worked it out on the cello. I liked the sound and feel of this theme, wrote out the first 15 seconds or so and set it aside. Sometime later, while I was looking out the window of a train, I was letting the theme play in my head, hearing it grow and evolve as I pondered the best way to structure the piece. Ahah! It's a fugue. In the already completed opening there it was: the statement of the subject immediately followed by the subject in the dominant with a countersubject, a brief transitional episode, and a restatement of the subject in the original key. Now that it was clear to me how the music wanted to be structured, I studied some of the fugues of Bach. Since I already had an eight-second subject, I paid particular attention to the relationship between the length of the subject and the length of the whole fugue in the works of the old master. In Bach's fugues the relationship between the length of the subject and the length of the fugue itself is similar to the balanced relationship between the size of the arch and the size of the building in classical architecture - the larger arch supporting a larger building. You can hear my completed fugue at: www.davidteie.com and click on Fugue or listen to track 16 on the CD.

In fugues as well as in songs such as *Yesterday* repeated motives are the building blocks of music. It has been noted that when a short, spoken phrase is repeated it sounds like music. Try it yourself sometime, rewind and play a phrase over and over and you will probably find that the pitches and rhythms begin to sound musical. What you will hear is the seed of music. Repeated phrases do not simply resemble music, they are its bedrock foundation, its origin. If a repeated phrase spins in the mind of an intuitive composer it can expand and evolve into a complex and decorated work of art.

Rule of Three

Repeated patterns in nature tend to be recognizably different from one another. When we repeat a sequence, it is expressive of the living nature of the pattern to subtly change the colors and balances of the pattern to "give it life". Variation occurs naturally in sequential poetry where the stresses change as the words change. There is variety in the repetition of every tree, every flower, every day's passing brings new versions of the repeated patterns of our lives. In music, it would seem that the third repetition in a sequence is the one that is often given a varietal twist, the one that turns toward a new direction.

If Goldilocks had listened to the bears' music she might have decided: two repetitions is too few, four is too many, but three is just right. The sensibilities of most Franco-German composers led them to elaborate on the third repetition in a sequence, I think of it as the Rule of Three. The following is a linguistic version of the third repetition leading to new melodic material:

Go to sleep
Go to sleep
Go to sleep as fast as you can.

My daughter came up with that little lullaby when she was three. The notes of the descending melody are:

1:	C-B-G
2:	C-B-G
3+:	C-B-G-F-E-D-D-C

Once the third repetition has been extended you can get right back to the first again, as in the following more famous example:

1:	Happy birthday to you
2:	Happy birthday to you
3+:	Happy birthday dear Insert Name… (and then we can get back to the original)
1:	Happy birthday to you

This "Happy birthday" version of the Rule of Three is similar to the standard limerick pattern:

1:	There was on Old Man of the Isles,
2:	Whose face was pervaded with smiles;
3+:	He sung high dum diddle, and played on the fiddle,
1:	That amiable Man of the Isles.

(Edward Lear)

Another brief example of the Rule of Three is found in the rhythms of Peter's melody from Prokofiev's *Peter and the Wolf*:

Hybrid Structures

The Rule of Three is combined with leaf/branch/tree design and the setup-and-deliver of story structure in one of the most famous rock songs of all time: Led Zeppelin's organic masterpiece "Stairway to Heaven" by Jimmy Page and Robert Plant.

The first three notes Robert Plant sings form the head of the melody and predict the structure of the entire song. The song begins with two words "There's a" that prepare an arrival on the word "LA-(dy)". These first three notes of the melody and the first three words of the lyrics create a miniature story structure that may be seen graphically as:

1 – 2 – 3 +

1	*Setup:*	(the lowest pitch)	"There's…"
2	*Setup:*	(higher pitch)	"…a…"
3 +	*Deliver:*	(highest pitch)	"…lady…"

Two lead-ins culminating in a stronger three are found in each progressively larger incarnation of the motive: the structures of the verse, the motives of the instrumental bridge, and the song as a whole. The tradition of extending the third repetition of a motive into new material are used for each of the small, medium, and large patterns in the song's design.

The second level of this pattern is heard in the first sentence, the verse:

1   *Setup:* (six syllables in the lowest pitches) "There's a lady who's sure…"

2 *Setup:* (six syllables in higher pitches) "...all that glitters is gold..."

3 + *Deliver:* (ten syllables in the highest pitches) "...and she's buying the stairway to heaven."

The third level of the pattern is heard in the architecture of the song as a whole:

1 *Setup:* (verses, lowest pitch center) 0:53 minutes into the original studio version

2 *Setup:* (instrumental break, higher pitch center) 5:34

3 + *Deliver:* (third section, highest pitch center) 6:43 "And as we wind on down the road..."

The emotional impact of this third section is enhanced by the instrumental break that leads into it. Page plays a lead guitar solo that drives an exponential crescendo where the music gets increasingly faster and higher, hanging onto its highest note just before the arrival of the climactic third section – the emotionally emphatic point of the song.

Additional manifestations of the pattern are found in the three strumming figures played by the guitars at the beginning of the instrumental break (5:34):

Larger scale:	1	2	3+	
Smaller scale:	1 2 3+	1 2 3+	1 2 3+	
	G ----	G ---	G ---	G ---
	F# -	F# -	F# -	F#
	E -	E -	E -	

And the pattern is also found four times slower and inverted in the guitar accompaniment that begins the third section (6:43).

The result of all this fluid, interconnected organization is that this song fulfills the expectation and arrival of a story within an elegant design of nesting patterns. The listener is taken on a Rule of Three ride through the gear-shifting, increasingly revving pace augmented by Plant's singing that climbs from a crooning beginning to a visceral scream near the end. The cohesive design sustains this song for more than 8 minutes.

The Rule-of-Three is an example of a musical tradition that has been handed down by pattern-creating musicians through the generations. If you were to ask Mozart or Plant or Page about the Rule-of-Three each of them would say he had never heard of it. However, it seems likely that if you were to ask their compositional advice on a melody where you play a repeated sequence that goes on past four or five repeated statements of a motive, you might hear them advise you to cut out a repetition or two.

Not so if you were to ask the same advice from Tchaikovsky. Russian and early Italian composers were more likely to extend the sequences beyond three, particularly if each successive phrase is transposed higher or lower:

He is going

    He is going

        He is going

            He is going to school today.

Have a listen to a passage in Tchaikovsky's 1812 overture: www.davidteie.com and click on 1812 or listen to track 17 on the CD.

In this transition (infamous among orchestral musicians) Tchaikovsky presents no fewer than 41 consecutive statements of a four-note descending scale motive in a single melodic line without accompaniment. You couldn't possibly count up all the musicians who view this passage as a thin, uninteresting line that has been disastrously overblown into tedious nonsense. Yet, not one of those musicians will ever be as highly regarded as Tchaikovsky, and the 1812 overture remains one of the most popular pieces of classical music. The long, repetitive transition represents the retreating French army and immediately precedes the victory bells and the anthem *God Preserve Thy People*. Tchaikovsky often presented music of extreme simplicity and repetition to prepare important passages. Just as a loud blast is more effective if preceded by soft playing and the victory celebration is more effusive if it was hard-won, a musical change of scene is more recognizable if some time is spent with the curtain lowered. Tchikovsky's extended repetitions were designed to enhance expectation.

Extended sequences are also often found often in the music of the Italian baroque masters Vivaldi and Domenico Scarlatti. Perhaps my favorite Scarlatti sonata is K. 27 (L. 449) in B minor (www.davidteie.com and click on Scarlatti or listen to track 18 on the CD) that contains a sequence that is repeated six times without variation, like a broken record. When I was growing up we had one of those old vinyl records of Emil Gilels playing 5 Scarlatti sonatas and I would put it on and lie on the floor to listen. I have heard other performances of this sonata that are played quickly, but in Gilels' hands the music flows in tender trickles. It had the effect of clearing my mind. The purity of this music, without the distraction of words or stories, almost defined me. In much the same way that some of Schumann's music touches a place inside of me that I wouldn't know was there were it not for that music, the Scarlatti seemed to reveal an aspect of me to myself. Not the personality-wearing self who might be more callous with the guys and more polite with mom, but the quiet self who sits alone in the room that no one else will ever see, where all armor and pretentions are left in the hallway. Somehow this Scarlatti sonata found a way into that room and put up a mirror there. Perhaps the hypnosis of the repeated sequences was the key to the door? When I listen to it now I remember how it felt to be 12 years old lying on my back absorbing this music and feeling: "I love this music. I am this music." I listened without conscious awareness of any patterns or sequences; it is not necessary for the hypnotized to know the secrets of the hypnotist.

There are occasions when a composer uses an extremely simple continuously repeated motive and colors and varies the repetitions so skillfully, blending it into the texture so seamlessly, that the motive itself becomes almost imperceptible. The opening four minutes of the second symphony of Rachmaninov is built entirely from the irreducible element of the scale-wise movement of one note to another. Every line in every voice, nearly every note in the entire introduction to the first movement is derived from the opening two-note motive.

Two notes! Every instrument plays a melodic chain made from the links of this one motive. The first statement of the motive is heard in the first two notes of the first movement, in the cellos and basses: B to C up one scale step. If you listen to the opening of this symphony you will hear an instrument or section of instruments enter on a note and the second note is always a single step away from the first and all successive manifestations of the motive are made from the scale-wise steps outlined above. He used almost no rhythmic variation. Whatever note you hear from a given instrument the next note will be the same duration and one step down or up. Rachmaninov fit these two-note motives together to make scales and lines of melodies resulting in such a variety of rich harmonies and linear movements that the listener becomes involved in the complexity and beauty and will most likely be unaware of the simplicity of the motivic element. In fact, I have little doubt that there have been many performances of this symphony where not one person in the hall was consciously aware that every note heard for those first four minutes was built from the first two notes of the piece. The point is: it doesn't matter. It is understood subconsciously; the sinewy texture, the smooth ribbons of interwoven melodies are perceived as naturally as the colors in a beautiful tapestry. Examining the tiny thread that was used to weave this grand tapestry may increase our respect for Rachmaninov's compositional mastery but will not enhance our appreciation of the expression or beauty of the music itself.

The Power of Design

As noted earlier, pattern is repetition. It is heard in the high realms of poetry and oratory as well as in the primal realms of animal calls. Repetition is the essence of design and the beauty of nature around and within us. Nesting repetitions of fractal patterns are seen in the trees' trunk - arms - branches - leaf veins as well as in the rivers' rivulet - brook - stream - river - delta.

The time continuum of music is perfectly suited to the presentation of repeated patterns as well as the setup-deliver sequence of stories covered in the previous chapter. When these two are merged they become mutually supportive and expressively super-charged. By inducing different emotions for different reasons at the same time, through pattern recognition on the one hand, and through social connectivity on the other, music is capable of creating hybrid emotions. The origins of these magical, blended emotions have remained elusive until now, but when we tease out the variety of emotionally resonating elements that are synchronized in music, we begin to understand the power of the concoction.

Structural design is normally understood as a product of linear thought, the result of consciously applied rules of order. In music, however, design can be intuitive - the product of highly creative divergent thinking. Designs spring from the minds of composers who process music so naturally that they do it in their sleep. These intuitively generated designs are often subtle, elegant hybrids of story structure and nesting patterns. Our appreciation of these structures is every bit as intuitive as the creation. Conscious thought was not necessarily used by creators to construct these designs and conscious thought is not necessary for listeners to appreciate them. The automatic pattern recognition in your subconscious does the analysis so you can sit back, relax, and enjoy the musical ride.

6

MOVEMENT

Movement is life. To animate (from the Latin *animare* to breathe) is to move. Movement is contained and implied in e*motion*, and we refer to being *moved* by music. The ability to interpret and understand movement is one of the most impressive characteristics of the human brain and is central to dance, drama, painting, sculpture, and music. It is life-evidence, enabling the flow of communication and the expression of artistic spirit.

Imagine taking a pen and placing its point on the left side of a blank sheet of paper. Now look to the other side of the page and move the pen across the paper until you reach it. There you have one of the essential actions of artistic expression. The pen-track that is left on the paper expresses relationship, connection, line, destination, desire, fulfillment, shape, and movement. If your progress was slow and even it was the movement of the lion stalking its prey. If you began slowly but accelerated to the arrival you moved like a falling stone. If you traced an even, shallow arch then you proscribed the path of the winter sun. Evidence of the nature of a movement is contained in the shape of the line that remains.

The 18th Century English painter William Hogarth proposed that the S shaped line expresses life and movement. If Hogarth had drawn the line described above it might have looked something like this:

Hogarth's "line of beauty" implies direction and movement. The movement suggests purpose, journey, and an arching climax. This line is also something of a visual representation of the story structure that prepares, develops, and then delivers the crucial point before finishing, as we saw in the previous chapter.

The first great cellist of the twentieth century, Pablo Casals said: "All music is a succession of rainbows." Melodies are often shaped in successive arches. Notice the rise and fall of the melody of the *Londonderry Air*:

And look how similar the arching melody of *White Christmas* is to Hogarth's line of beauty:

And there are plenty of other examples to choose from: Ave Maria (Schubert), Frere Jacque, and the national anthems of The United States, Great Britain, France, and Germany, to name but a few. The arch formation is a common and typical way to deliver a well-rounded tune.

The Crescendo Moving Towards You

Ever had that feeling that music is rushing towards you? Many composers create or accentuate movement in music by variations in loudness, simulating a sound source that gets louder as it approaches or getting softer as it recedes. When a sound approaches the listener at an even pace the perceived loudness increases exponentially; that means the sound level of an approaching noise doubles every time the distance is cut in half. If a virtuoso singing an aria from 40 feet away started walking towards you, the sound of his voice would double in the first 4 seconds, and then double again in the next 2 seconds and so forth until he was bellowing right next to you.

The composer proscribes the path in the map of the musical score but it is up to the performer to evoke a perception of movement that feels natural – by simulating approaching movement with a crescendo that increases at exactly the right rate. If I am preparing a repeated motor rhythm crescendo, for example, I might imagine standing next to a train track watching an engine approaching from the distance at an unstoppable speed. In the last moments before reaching me the ever-increasing sound and power of the train culminate in a blast of wind and rattling as the engine passes. Then I close my eyes and play the passage with that train approach in mind and practice it until I feel that the passage conveys the image. In the best performances, the image is realized; the music *becomes* the train and the audience feels the expectancy of the exponentially increasing crescendo before the rattling blast.

Gravity causes another variety of movement that can be implied with the same crescendo technique. We all possess an internal sense of gravity; we have learned to sense when we will touch the ground after jumping from a platform, or when we throw a stone to skim the water. I remember that we were told in the preparation for a parachute landing that we should not look down to anticipate the landing because the steady pace of the parachute descent throws off our natural ability to predict the touchdown. (I looked anyway and thought I was still at treetop height when I hit the ground.) All of these graduated types of movement are a part of our experience and perception. Music that emulates our world sounds natural to us and evokes a sense of the natural dynamics of our environment. In musical jargon we even refer to the gradations of loudness as dynamics.

When I teach the exponentially increased crescendo to cello students I refer to it as the Balanchine crescendo. A master of body movement and expression, the choreographer George Balanchine sometimes had his dancers express energy with accelerated movements. Try it yourself: with your right arm point to your left across your body, then move it to an extended position pointing away to your right. First make the gesture with a steady pace, then do it again and accelerate your movement as you move to the right, as if a magnet were drawing your hand and increasing its speed as it moved until the sudden stop at full extension. The Balanchine crescendo expresses vigor and life.

This would be an example of a gentle crescendo and diminuendo (getting softer) in a pastoral phrase:

Row, row, row your boat gently down the streeeam merrily, merrrily, merrily, merrily, life is but a dream.

This would be an example of an exponential Balanchine crescendo and diminuendo:

Row, row, row, your boat gently down the streeeam merrily, merrrily, merrily, merrily, life is but a dream.

The Comforting Swing of the Pendulum

The pendulum's swing contains a curve, acceleration, deceleration, and a bit of the bounce sensation that we felt in the womb when our mothers were walking. The swing is as regular as the pulse we heard in the womb, perfectly symmetrical, and contains aspects of drive, impetus, arrival, and release that can serve to direct a musical flow. The pendulum is seen and felt in the tick-tock of the metronome as well as in the arced swing of the conductor's baton. Nearly all music is built around these movements; they are the visual and sensory expressions of footfalls and pendulums, the timekeepers of ordered movement.

Take yourself back to your childhood and sit your young self down in your favorite swing set. Kick-start and pull and push hard. Continue reading only when you are in full swing. Ready? Now, from the weightless rear apex where you are looking down at the ground you fall and accelerate into the nadir at the bottom where you feel the added g-force weight of your body in the seat, and the propulsion of the torque carries you up until you slow to weightlessness again and experience a moment's pause in the sky, before returning to the backwards fall. The repetition, power, and consistency of swinging motion in music has three expressive purposes: 1) it is reminiscent of the cycle of alternating weighted/weightless sensation that we experienced in the womb while our mothers were walking, 2) it establishes a portal of trust: the listener is attentive to the ordered movement, and 3) it is hypnotic: the listener can be placed in a mild trance and, through it, enters another, deeper portal, into the subconscious circus of desires and fears and dreams.

One example where a pendulum motion is brought to music is in the introduction to the Beatles' song *Come Together.* It begins with:

shhhhu – rising bass – cymbal – du-dle-a-du-dle-a-du-dle-a-dum
shhhhu – rising bass – cymbal – du-dle-a-du-dle-a-du-dle-a-dum

A swing that would create the tempo for that song would have ropes about 20 feet long. Picture the "shhhhu" at the low point of the swing, then the bass tune rises you up then Ringo's first tom-tom note of the "du-dle-a-du-dle-a-du-dle-a-dum" comes precisely at the moment that the swing has reached the top before the pendulum begins it's return. The gentle hypnosis of repeated accompanimental figures such as these are mainstays of song introductions. Musicians play these to become the hypnotists with the swinging pocket watch: "You're getting sleepy. Relax and enter the dream world of the subconscious."

The Fulfillment of Arrival

Music often conveys direction and the fulfillment of arrival. These are all passionately expressed in the climactic ascending scale in the first movement of Elgar's cello concerto. When I play this passage I think of the lighting of the Olympic flame in Barcelona where an archer stood with a flaming arrow aimed at the cauldron high above the stadium. He released the arrow and it flew, slowing and arching near the destination and finally ignited the huge basin. Listen to the scale crescendo (www.davidteie.com and click on Elgar or track 19 on the CD) while closing your eyes and imagining the flight of that flaming arrow and you will get an idea of what it feels like to play this brilliant passage.

Composer and Performer Moving Together

In Classical music the composer may provide indications in the score that imply movement, but it is up to the performer to interpret the intent and project the expression. The rope of music can be unraveled to examine the many overlapping and mutually supportive threads. Classical performers are generally responsible for different threads than composers. In jazz and rock music the performers are responsible for all aspects of the creativity; these musicians originate the music as well as perform it. Back when Mozart and Beethoven were performing their own compositions they were more like jazz and rock musicians in this regard, they were creators and performers in one package. The separation of duties in classical music today, however, is fairly rigid; the composers wrote the music and the performers play it. Composers are the demigods of music who sketched out instructions for the performers and then died, leaving only ink on paper behind for performers to interpret. The principal domain of the composer is the determination of the pitches, tempos and harmonies. The composer also chooses the basic timbre by assigning the instruments that are to be played. It is the performer's responsibility to follow the indications printed in the score and turn the sketches into sound. The performers are expected to make the sketch sound the way the composer intended. This separation of powers gives us an opportunity to see how the realm of composers differs from that of performers and by examining these differences we can see how music is a coordinated soundshow made up of many different elements.

One example of the complex and often overlapping responsibilities of composers and performers is the regulation of loudness. Until the middle of the 18th century composers left most of these decisions to the performer; very few indications were placed in the score to indicate how loud a given passage or instrument should be. By the middle of the 18th century composers began placing some general dynamics into the score. That said, it is common in the music of Mozart to find only a single notation of *piano* (soft) that applies to an entire minute or more of music. It was assumed that the players would contour the line within that general dynamic. Casals used to say that: within a *piano* passage, some notes may be as loud as *forte*. As the years progressed composers indicated ever more clearly how the contours should be performed and how the timbre of the instrument should be adjusted.

By the time Tchaikovsky was composing in the 19th century the dynamic indications were often explicit and demanding. It seems that Tchaikovsky had a difficult time getting musicians to play loudly or softly enough to satisfy him. In musical notation f indicates "forte" meaning strong or loud and ff indicates fortissimo: very loud. I imagine that Tchaikovsky heard players playing ff and thought: "No, that's not enough." so he wrote fff fortissISSimo. Sometimes even this wasn't enough so he added another $ffff$, fortissISSISSimo! When I see Tchaikovsky's indication $fffff$ I imagine him saying to us from beyond the grave: "More, more, I want to hear your hearts tearing!"

I took part in this kind of ramping up when I was in the Baltimore Symphony. Michael Tilson Thomas was conducting the second movement of Tchaikovsky's symphony #5. In this masterpiece of romanticism there is an indication for the strings to play fff *con desiderio* "with desire". I don't know of any passage in any other piece that contains this instruction. It occurs in the ascending scale passage in the strings about three and a half minutes into the movement. This is a sustained passage where the strings slowly increase the volume and pitch; the tension in the resisted movement of the melodic line is like the restrained stretching of an elastic band or the last few clawing meters of an exhausted climber nearing the summit. In the rehearsal Michael stopped and said that our volume of sound was not enough and that the quality needed to be more gripping. We played it again and he stopped again and said: "No, I'm sorry. That's simply not enough." At this point most conductors would have moved on and left well enough alone, but Michael refused to give in. We played it again and he stopped yet again and insisted on more. He had the sound that he wanted in his imagination and what he heard from us did not equal his imagination. Finally, we broke through and played this passage with a huge, ripping, wrenching quality of sound that was thrilling and powerful. "Yes, that is the sound." he said. In my three years with the highly refined Baltimore Symphony of the early 1970s, that was the only occasion that the string section created exactly that kind of passionate sound. The ascending crescendo took on a quality that made the *desiderio* palpable.

Direction itself implies desire. To begin in one place and end up in another evinces a purpose behind the movement. Most of us don't have visionary dreams of staying in the same place; we dream of something more, something better, something fuller, richer: a movement to a place *other*. Desire is the heat in the balloon, the fire in the piston, and the magnetism between lovers. The hot-blooded hedonism of Western culture was distilled into a simple and elegant equation by Tennessee Williams: desire is the opposite of death.

Desire is expressed by giving the musical line direction. Performers who understand the profound relationship between desire, movement and expression use all of the dimensions of music: time, pitch, harmony, volume, and timbre, to enhance and project the sense of direction in musical lines. In order to clarify which aspects of music are the responsibilities of the performer, let me take you on a backstage tour of the performer's mind. As I mentioned previously, a musician must always be thinking ahead. When desire and direction are the called for, I turn my attention to the arrival in the distance. Only by keeping in mind the impending culmination are we able to meaningfully calibrate the crescendo and the tempos. Peaking too soon is never fulfilling, is it? There are times when the music may accelerate toward a fulfillment, but most often the basic pulse must be kept at a consistent tempo. In these cases a cellular motive or phrase within the larger framework can be played a little early, or stretched at the beginning and rushed at the end giving a sense of urgency and impatience. When the performer keeps the arrival in mind the music that leads to it tends to be imbued with direction.

As a performance becomes more openly expressive the dynamics become more exaggerated. One of the top priorities of the performer is to make the movement in the score come alive. The performer expresses this by contouring lines in volume and/or timbre, but may also bend the pitch in the direction of the desired movement, use faster or slower tempos, or bring out certain voices that enhance the quality of a harmony that contains a desire for movement to another pitch or chord.

A well-practiced performer expresses emotion through these techniques as if by second nature. The cellist who plays louder and more accented when expressing forceful determination is not necessarily consciously manipulating the dynamics any more than you would consciously make your voice louder and pronounce your consonants more clearly when you express forceful determination. You feel the feeling and your voice manifests that feeling in sound. So it is with performers who absorb and reflect the feelings of the composers. Once the soul of a musician has marinated in years of practice and exposure to great interpreters, these subtleties become less conscious decisions than they are spontaneously generated expressions. Just as your voice is connected to your emotions, so it is that some of us feel that we can express freely and naturally through our instruments.

When I am waiting in the wings before a performance I take time to recall the essential spirit of the music I am about to play. Most often the offstage time for recollection of the spirit of the music helps to create a higher fidelity performance - as if I were painting on a larger canvas with more vivid colors. I remember preparing for one performance of the Shostakovich Piano Trio, a work that was written as homage to those slain in the Holocaust. In one of the rehearsals violinist Zino Bogachek and pianist Anna Balakerskala talked about how the victims had suffered and died for nothing. I said that these people still have voices in Shostakovich's music. The warnings and stories of these victims can still be heard today when we play this music; the victims speak through us. When the time came for the performance, the extremes of lamentation and horror were so vivid that I was repeatedly overcome with emotion and in danger of losing control of the cello.

The very best performers are those who can open themselves up to freely express and convey the spirit of the music. I heard the legendary cellist Piatigorsky remark to a student who was playing in a reserved, refined manner: "In life conceit is stupid. In music modesty is criminal." Rostropovich said: "I open my heart and play for *all* the people." Performers who are the most vibrantly alive, furious when angry, animated when happy, soothingly tender in lullabies and immoveable blocks of stone when proudly principled, these are the musicians who command the stage and communicate to audiences. The auditory difference between the mediocre performer and the communicator is most evident in the expressive range. The forte passages are powerful and the softest passages are barely audible.

Most classical performers believe that expression should be conveyed entirely in sound. We tend to move little when we perform. Richter used to play with only one lamp onstage illuminating the music stand; he didn't want the movements of his body or the image of his face to distract from the music. The iconic master of the classical guitar, Andres Segovia, sat motionless when he played and insisted that his students do the same. Arthur Rubinstein could be seen gesticulating in his youth, but in his mature years as the consummate master of the piano and of music he moved no more than was necessary to play the instrument.

Most often, we classical musicians don't even move our heads with the beat. Visually, this may seem to indicate a lack of involvement. Rock and pop musicians bob with the beat because the beat is consistent. Classical rhythm, however, is flexible and reactive; you go with the lead melody or the line with the fastest notes. If I keep the beat in my body it is like creating a bubble with only myself inside; I will be less able to react to rhythmic subtleties of my colleagues. Truth be told: when a soloist playing with an orchestra nods conspicuously to the beat you can bet that the hairs on the back of the necks of the orchestral musicians are rising. That kind of bobbing translates to us as: "I will not listen to you, you have to listen to me." People have occasionally remarked to Ken Harbison, a percussionist in the NSO, that he must have a great sense of rhythm. He tells them: "I haven't put three beats together in the same tempo since I got into the orchestra. We are constantly adjusting to what we hear."

Body Movement

When I was in high school I went to a concert by the band Three Dog Night. This was decades before huge screens and light shows were a part of live rock acts and we were seated far from the stage so there wasn't a lot of visual interest. As they performed the song that brought them their first gold record, *One* by Harry Nilsson, I leaned forward expectantly waiting for my favorite place in the song: just after the second time Chuck Negron sings "It's just no good anymore since you went away" the moment when the other two singers enter on a dissonant interval in the high register singing: "num-ber" (1:53 into the song). Countless times when hearing this entrance on the radio I had taken a break from the world around me, squinted my eyes closed, made a fist, tightened my stomach, and felt these notes burn through me. In the concert the two singers simply leaned slightly toward their microphones, sang the notes, and leaned back again. I was a bit crestfallen. That's it? No singing on their knees while leaning back and holding their mics in the air? No gyrations?

We equate music and physicality so naturally that we often expect one to partner the other. The ancient associations between dance, synchrony, and music have received a good deal of attention from researchers recently. A thumbnail sketch of the body of this research shows that there are deep connections in the brain between the emotional and the motor control centers, as well as profound social connections between individuals who interact with coordinated, repeated movements.

Repetitive movements require less cognitive processing than changing movements. People walking or tapping fingers, fish and birds flapping are examples of short cycle repetitive movements that can be repeated with little attentive involvement. Motor repetition allows your attention to be affixed to more interesting objects, like your dance partner. Since repetitive music foments repetitive movements, music is the ultimate dance partner.

Why Dance?

As usual, it is good to get a fresh perspective – let's look at it from space. An orbiting alien taking notes on the behavior of *Homo sapiens* would have a clearer picture of us than we have ourselves. Ask a human: "Why do you dance?" and you may get something of the anthropomorphic view that we usually have: "Because I like it." "Why do you dance at that tempo?" "Because it feels good."

Let's look at the notepad of the alien: firstly, dance tempos are determined by the size of the human body and the strength of gravity on earth. We have seen how slowly the astronauts walked on the moon; the moon samba would have to be considerably slower than the earth samba: about as slow as the hippo samba. The primary rhythmic pulse of the dance is rooted it the duality and tempo of walking. We may think of walking as a smooth, easy pattern of movement, but next time you are walking pay attention to how active the body is, and how all of its movements are synchronized to the same (dance) tempo.

Care for some more reader participation? (If you were embarrassed by vocalizing out loud with a lowered larynx, you will love this one.) Start by walking in place. Now say out loud some rhyming verse, any one will do, Humpty-dumpty will be fine, and keep the rhythms of your speech in phase with the pulse of your walking. Now move your arms to match the syllables of your speech. Now look in the mirror and see what you're doing. The rhythms of speech with bipedal movement synchronize with the body movements of rhythm; any speech aligned with the pulse of walking or bouncing will create the foundation of dance music.

So dancing and music are proportional to the human scale, but why do we enjoy it? The bounce of walking was one of those early experiences that informed the developing brain in the womb. The tactile sense is normally the first sense to develop in the fetus. You felt the bounce of your mother's walk even before you heard her voice. Research has shown that infants respond more to being gently bounced than they do to being gently swung. I learned a technique for calming infants from Michael Weinreb that we called "the dad walk" that is remarkably effective. The success rate for calming a crying baby with the dad walk in my 4-children experience is well over 90%. You hold the baby upright on your shoulder in the burping position, gently but firmly hold the baby against your chest, then bounce twice per second as you walk, alternating deeper and shallower bounces: LUB – dub – LUB – dub, etc. The firm, surrounding hold and the feel of the bounce in the tempo of the maternal heartbeat make for a sensory familiarity from the womb that soothes any but the most riotous infant.

When we dance we are often lighting up the earliest of all memories stored deeply and permanently in our brains. The cerebellum, often referred to as the reptilian brain, is responsible for guiding movements and keeping the timing of the repetitive oscillations of walking and running. The cerebellum is strongly connected to the amygdala, one of the brain structures responsible for emotion. In the regions of our minds that are out of range of the searchlights of our attention, emotion and movement are in constant communication. Deep within these well-connected emotional and motor sensory areas of our brains are remnants of the very first things we learned about our environment. That first environment that calibrated our minds is one of the primary underpinnings to our enjoyment of dancing.

In dance as in music, there is no single, silver-bullet reason that fully explains why we do it or why we enjoy it. Dancing appeals to us in a number of different ways: prenatal experience, coordinated social bonding, alpha demonstration, sex appeal, storytelling, as well as art forms that combine these and more in stylized forms.

One of the favorite coupling of arts and certainly the one that boasts the most enduring relationship is the marriage of music and dance. There are many films without music and poetry readings are common, but we rarely see a dancer without music. Music invites the dance. A dance that begins with the dancers dancing, then the music joining in plays in the mind like a mistake. The flowering of so many variants of dance and music gives us a spectacular array of expressions in bodily movement, but since the purpose of this book is to examine the foundations of emotion in music, the primary interest is in the foundations of dance. In keeping with that goal we should consider how dance affects music, how music affects dancing, and how they are combined to create hybrid emotional experiences that transcend each experienced alone.

One example of how the physicality of dance influences music is found in the arcane detail in the proper performance of the waltz mentioned in Chapter 1. The rhythm of the waltz gives us a clue to the connections between the human body, gravity, and the music that was designed for them. When Viennese musicians play a waltz so that the second beat arrives a bit early after the first then pause a bit before the third beat to allow the dancers time to float up on their toes, it is a musical manifestation of a physical characteristic of movement. Musicians have learned to shadow the earth-natural movement of an object thrown in the air and hanging at the apex for a moment before falling again.

Communication between dancers and musicians concerning tempos is usually dominated by the dancers, and rightly so. We are able to play in a wide range of speeds, but gravity insists on a much more limited range for the dancers. This became clear to me when I played *The Swan* by Camille Saint-Saens in a performance with one of the principals of American Ballet Theater. I remember looking into the program and seeing that it was listed as *The Dying Swan.* I hadn't thought of my swan as sickly, but I was willing to give it a go. After a few seconds of my playing in the rehearsal the dancer stopped me and asked for a slower tempo. I smiled and agreed and began again, this time more slowly. Soon she stopped again and said that it was still too fast for her to dance to. I assented again and began playing the piece much more slowly than I have ever heard it performed. Half way through she stopped again, apologized for all the trouble she was causing, and asked that it be slower still. I suppose my eyes widened a bit with my smile this time as I was thinking that if the tempo gets any slower it would come to a stop and go into reverse. She danced beautifully and, sure enough, she fluttered and expired at the end. It left me relieved and wondering what bizarre recording she must have been listening to in her practice.

When many dancers are aligned with the unifying beats of music the emotional effect can be profound. Synchronized group dances enhance the sense of unity in the participants. In a group dance people of high station and those of low station are evened out, everyone simply belongs. A unifying beat seems to be The Great Equalizer for the living. There are often reports from those who experience the synchronous movements of marching that they have a feeling of awe inspired by a sense that they are attuned to a higher purpose, a calling beyond individual needs. Daniel Levitin writes in *The World in Six Songs*: "Humans around the world report not just strong emotional bonding from synchronized, coordinated movement together, but feelings of a spiritual nature – a sense of there being a collective consciousness, the presence of a superior being, or an unseen world that is larger than what we immediately experience."

This feeling of awe related to a collective consciousness has been placed by evolution into our emotional systems because it encourages societal behaviors. Ants are programmed to display behaviors that benefit the society over the individual, and so are we. We may attribute good feelings associated with social synchrony to a purpose beyond the self. That purpose is to support the structure of the group itself. Rhythmic synchrony in groups enables war dances to unify and to inflate the resolve and commitment of warriors and also enables hymn singing in churches to illuminate a commonly felt sense of deity.

Music, Dance, and Sex

Rhythmic movement is rewarding to many of us as a simple, internal enjoyment, but dance can also be highly communicative. We enjoy watching. In music as well as in dance, we appreciate both the skill and the expression of the performers. Dancers *express*. Ferris Bueller's air guitar display notwithstanding, most people don't dance alone unless they are practicing. Good dancers expect people to watch them. John Travolta's character in *Saturday Night Fever* may be all we need to point to in support of the idea that human dancing can serve precisely the same purpose as bird dancing: "Watch me, I am the male for you."

One of the foundations of the partnership of music and dance is, of course, sex appeal. Dancing can be an invitation and prelude to another exiting and often rhythmic pairing. Young people of an age when their sexual arousal is easily piqued and consumed with the desire to find a partner will be the people most likely to be seen limbering their pelvises at the dance clubs.

The rhythms in those clubs are about the same as the rhythms of copulation. The headboard hitting the wall of the adjacent hotel room and the accompanying vocalizations constitute the ultimate dance music. Since emotions serve the selfish gene there is no better place to introduce a pleasing response than pre-procreation, and Mother Nature did not pass up this opportunity. I will not spend much print space on this topic since this theory of human music is intended to map the mysteries of emotion in music – the reason that some dance music makes pleasurable emotions light up like Vegas is no mystery.

The music of immediate physical attraction and the music of long-term committed relationships draw from different emotional wells. We don't often hear pulsing, gyrating music played as Our Song at a wedding. If you were to hear such a wedding song it might be reasonable to calculate:

length of time until physical attraction wanes
+ a few months
= duration of marriage

Human Music

Slow Dance

Most love songs are ballads. The fetal associations of the heart-rate pulse and treble voice combined with poetry make slow songs an ideal language of love. Most of the songs that get airtime are love songs. In related news: guys get into the music business for the chicks (classical musicians generally excepted). Love songs, poetry and prayers contain the kinds of appeals that are set to music - pamphlets on how to assemble outdoor grills are not. If one were to read such a pamphlet aloud, the speech would not be touchingly musical. If one were to ask a prospective lover to stay the night, *that* speech would be musical!

Said the troubadour
to the troubadee:
"How my song means more
when I sing for thee!"

The ballad that the newlyweds slow-dance to at the wedding reception evokes a womb memory that was established before the recognition of self as a separate entity. A common understanding of human psychology holds that the old brain/subconscious will "see" a strongly imprinted person from our past in someone who resembles them in the present and fire off emotional responses accordingly. A child who lacked approval from her father, for example, may try to win approval from a father figure as an adult. The conscious brain knows the difference but the behavior-controlling emotional brain only sees the ghost. Music of love targets the subconscious that harbors our earliest memories and is capable of switching on mysterious emotions. The source of ballad music is the heartbeat tempo, consonant, tonal treble melody, and storyline phrasing heard in the womb. Music of the womb is a part of the emotional foundation and history of each, bride and groom alike. The slow-dance ballad projects the emotionally remembered image of that which they each desire: to become one with the other.

Although this section is only intended to outline some of the underlying connections between body movement, emotion, and music, it seems appropriate to tip a hat to the art forms of dance that have evolved from these primal origins. Perhaps art is something that can only be defined for one's self. My definition is that art is expression. Not all expression is art, but all art is expressive. A review of the connections between music and dance must include mention of the art form of dance that is purely expressive, one that may not be related to wars or mating or love or community, but that includes every facet of human expression. The art of dance is expression through movement. The viewer perceives the movement and understands the intent.

Our visual processing is finely tuned to perceive the meanings of human movement and also designed to call our attention to certain kinds of movements. Just as we are predisposed to process resonance-enhanced periodic sounds made by vocalizing animals, we are predisposed to pay attention to directed movement, the kind of movement that animals make. Music follows this predisposition to our enhanced attentions when it is processed visually. The following section describes movements that are perceived to be within the music itself.

Visually Perceived Movement

The mind interprets music in a spatial context, using the same apparatus in the brain that processes the movement that we see around us. This is why we "see" music as a series of movements in our mind's eye. And why music taps into emotions that are related to our reactions to movement. When music enters this part of the brain it trips wires that are set up for visual cues. A melody that "moves" from one note to another isn't actually going anywhere, but the nature of its perceived movement will cause the mind to trigger emotions that would have been triggered by actual movement.

There are three basic categories of movement that we detect that are relevant to music:

1. Perfect Movement: the arcing movement of celestial bodies

All celestial movements that are visible to the naked eye are smooth and perfectly ordered. This perfection in the movements in our sky has led civilizations to perceive it as the realm of gods and heaven. This kind of movement is proscribed in the opening of the Bach Prelude in G described later in this chapter.

2. Turbulent Movement: the random movement of terrestrial forces

Turbulent terrestrial movements are chaotic. The unpredictability of the movements of eddies, whirlpools, and gusts of wind led the ancient peoples to believe that the spirits of these forces were impulsive. Our brains tend to ignore turbulent movements such as tall grass waving in the wind since these kinds of movements distract from the recognition of other movements that may benefit our survival. Our recognition of turbulent chaos and our natural ability to ignore it is the first cognitive filter in the process of comprehension. Our visual processing tunes out the unimportant movement of grass in the wind so that we can focus on the critically important movement of an animal in that grass.

3. Directed Movement: the purposeful movement of humans and animals

Perhaps the most important perceived movement is human or animal movement, recognizable because it has been logically directed – someone, or something, is moving into our line of vision and we need to work out whether it presents an opportunity or a threat.

It is the directed movement that enables us to create an audio performance on our mind's stage. Some aspects of music are processed in the same part of the brain as vision, and make us react to musical scenarios in much the same way as a visual scene. The celestial can make us feel spiritual, the turbulent uneasy, but for a real adrenaline boost you need the threats and rewards inherent in our perception of directed movement.

Directed Movement and the Power of the Periphery

Visualize a landscape horizon where you see a deer walking in the distance (melody) and out of the corner of your eye you see something slowly and steadily coming toward you (descending bass line). The peripherally perceived movement will stimulate a dose of fear; your emotional director will insist that you turn your attention toward it to see if something is stalking you. Like the deer, the melody receives our object-tracking attention. Since peripheral vision is so sensitive to movement, the movements outside this area of attention can hold even more emotional impact for us than the deer's attended movement. This phenomenon is one of the reasons that harmonic movement may touch us deeply when the melody without its contrapuntal counterpart leaves our senses quiet.

Purposeful, logical movement is generated by living beings. The necessity to avoid being eaten has made the perception of directed movement a priority for nearly all animals and insects. Predators have evolved hunting movements that are designed to hide or mask the direction. Cats stalk directly toward their targets because movement that follows the prey's line of sight is very difficult to see. Chameleons waver when they stalk their prey so that their movements will be seen as random, like a leaf in the wind.

The lion feels an attentive response to directed movement. The deer feels a startle response when unexpected movement is directed toward it. Accordingly, the emotional response in various species will differ depending on the needs of the species and the nature of the perceived movement. As both predator and prey, humans have evolved both of these emotional responses to visual perception of certain basic movements. One is relevant to pursuit, the other relevant to being pursued.

The hypothesis of emotional response to visual movement offers two types of movement that heighten attention in humans:

1. Change in direction of linear, overtly attended movement, such as a hunter (predator) reacting to the movement of a running animal (prey)

This relates to our abilities as predators. Our awareness is heightened when we perceive the directed movement of an animal we are hunting. This movement is kept in the clearly focused line-of-sight, the fovea of the retina. Any variation in the movement of the prey necessitates a reaction from the hunter, like a defender in the secondary covering a receiver in American football. The movement of prey under attack is most often crooked and evasive while the movement of an attacking predator is reactive. This reaction is reflexive and emotionally stimulated.

We humans, who are pack-hunters by nature, also have a highly developed ability to keep track of the other hunters in our group while keeping an eye on the movement of the prey. The emotional thrill we feel when we successfully employ this instinctive ability is found in pack-hunting based sports where every participant keeps a relationship to a single object, usually a ball, and coordinates his own movements relative to the pack (team). Think about how closely the bounding movement of an air-filled ball resembles the movement of escaping prey species.

When viewing a team sport in a stadium the spectator is able to share in the enjoyment of tracking concurrent movements. This emotional response is subtly tapped when we track perceived concerted movements in music.

2. Peripherally perceived, steady movement, such as the hunter (now the prey) perceiving a crouching lion (predator) in the undergrowth to his right

The peripheral vision – movement at the sides of our sight – demands the most vigilant awareness. Threats tend to come from stage left or right, and we automatically keep track of what's lurking in the corner. This is one secret to music's ability to light up awareness, attention, and emotions: our naturally heightened emotional reaction to movement that is seen in our peripheral vision. Even though peripheral vision is blurred, it is highly sensitive to movement. In particular, logically consistent movement causes the peripheral attentions to stir and it is this type of movement that we are most concerned with here.

When the lurking, stalking, shadowy figure approaches the shower in the film Psycho we want her to "LOOK OUT!" Our peripheral vision is permanently attuned to pick up lurking, stalking figures and the connections between these perceived movements and emotional attention/startle responses are set on a hair trigger. The eye naturally turns toward peripherally perceived directed movement: that movement picked up out of the corner of your eye that could be worthy of attention. Ever noticed how you keep looking over to that muted but visually active television screen in the dentist's waiting room? Every time the picture changes our ever-vigilant vision directs the momentary glance: "what's that?" This emotional response is similar to the "ahah" that we feel when we subconsciously recognize a pattern. The next time you are driving and stopped at a traffic light, notice how often your eye glances toward peripherally perceived movements. We do not consciously take note of all the turning signals, pedestrians, and blinking signs because they are usually irrelevant, but our eyes still tend to be drawn by the changes and movements. In visual perception, change defines movement. The observed object was there and now it is over there – we witness and anticipate change when we observe movement.

To get a sense of the difference between attended and peripherally perceived movements, try this demonstration: stand and look straight ahead and imagine that you are surveying a savanna landscape. You see that the horizon is splitting the viewing area in upper and lower halves. Imagine seeing the turbulent chaotic movements of the windblown grasses in the lower half. Those movements are naturally filtered out of your notice but the determined movement of a mammoth moving laterally near the horizon draws your attention. Your alertness is enhanced; heart and respiratory rates rise preparing for the hunt. Now imagine, in the same field of view, something moving steadily toward you in the bottom-right-hand corner of your sight. The emotional state that is aroused by this movement is powerful and immediate. Your peripheral vision has informed you correctly as you turn and see a saber-tooth tiger stalking you a hundred feet away, and your adrenaline pumps hard as you freeze and prepare to fight or flee.

In our two-dimensional field of view seen from eye level 4 to 6 feet above the ground, any movement toward the position where you are standing will be seen as a downward movement. The trajectory is straight down if it approaches from the front, and progressively shallower as the perceived movement comes from the sides. From the perspective of standing humans, downward movement below the horizon is movement toward the observer and would be the type of movement that would most likely be a danger to the observer. This theory holds that peripherally perceived downward movement in the lower half of the field of view will trigger a stronger attentive/fear response than other types of movement.

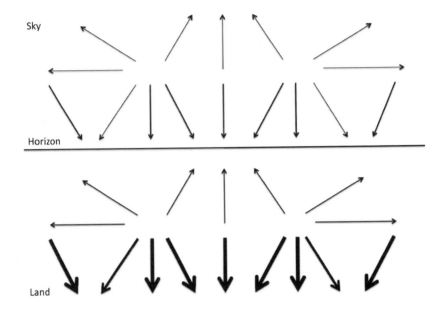

Since we process music visually – a scale goes *up*, a scale goes *down* – **any inherent emotional response to a given type of movement may be triggered by a musical representation of that movement**. A descending musical scale is understood in our subconsciously deducing mind to have the determined straight-line movement of animals as well as the downward movement that indicates that the thing is coming nearer. Since it is perceived in the "peripheral vision" of the music, away from the melody of our attention, it presents you with the cousin of the fear response you would feel if you saw a stalking creature approaching out of the corner of your eye.

The musical version of steady, downward movement perceived away from the center of attention is the descending bass line. It is an example of an element of music that deserves a herald introduction.

Counterpoint

A single musical line is a melody, adding a second or more lines to it represents counterpoint. It is the keystone of Western music. Harmony and chord progressions are children of counterpoint. The ability of counterpoint to present lines underneath the melody allows it to draw from the well of our emotional responses to peripherally perceived movement.

Since the movement of a contrapuntal line is more difficult to follow than the movement of the attended melody, these peripheral voices are heard more clearly when their movement is slow and stepwise.

This is the one point in the book when hearing an example will illuminate more than a hundred pages of explanation. With access to the internet the reader could become the listener. Go to www.davidteie.com and click on Bass line demo or listen to track 20 on the CD. This demonstration involves only five notes, but shows how a descending scale may create the sense of peripherally perceived movement. The upper sustained note played on the cello represents the melody, the object in the center of view. The lower notes in the piano form a descending bass line representing the directed movement seen in the periphery.

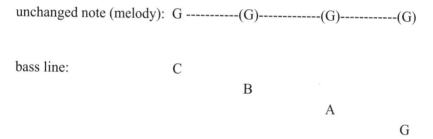

The more you enjoy music and listen attentively, the more you are likely to feel the vibrancy of counterpoint. Practice sharpens our perception. An experienced animal tracker is able to point out footprints and minor disturbances in a pathway, often able to judge how fresh the track is. The hours of attention and practice have boosted the brainpower of the relevant senses and perceptions in the tracker while experience has shown what to look for. In the same way, those who listen attentively or who play instruments or sing in choirs are enhancing their abilities to follow musical lines other than the melody. This means that the enjoyment of this aspect of the music will tend to be culturally specific. Music is, indeed, the universal language in many respects, but appreciation of counterpoint is less universal than, say, the understanding that high, soft, pure tones sound lovely while low, loud, harsh tones sound aggressive.

A single musical element may have more than one way to affect our emotions. One example is the change in direction of a line or harmony. It could light up our humor-related violation of the expected like the twist at the end of a joke and at the same time piquing the attention pursuant to a tracked object changing direction. These two reactions are mutually supportive and contribute to the overall feeling that we get when listening. Later you will find a more thorough description of combination sensitivity and why the accumulation of small emotional reactions adds up to more than the sum of the parts. For now, I think it is worth noting again that there is no single secret to music's ability to evoke emotions. The fragrances of music come from many different flowers. When they are presented in a bouquet, the accumulation of aromas leads us to inhale and smile.

The descending bass line demonstration introduced above produces of a number of expressive features that are related to storylines and vocal sound quality – adding more flowers to the bouquet. Each of the notes in the bass line combines with the upper note to create a different interval (the distance between two notes played at the same time). Each interval has its own type of emotional charge and the sequence of intervals implies a progression. Listen again. This time pay attention to the character of each interval and to how the progress of the "story" implies a home, a journey, and a return home.

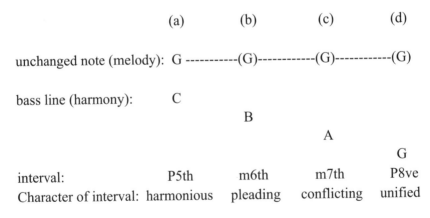

	(a)	(b)	(c)	(d)
unchanged note (melody):	G ----------(G)------------(G)------------(G)			
bass line (harmony):	C	B	A	G
interval:	P5th	m6th	m7th	P8ve
Character of interval:	harmonious	pleading	conflicting	unified

(a) The upper note G played with the lower note C creates the interval of a perfect fifth, a consonant interval. The term Perfect denotes the consonant-perfect harmony. The sound of this harmony is settled, the sound waves are synchronized and in-phase.

(b) Then the lower note moves to a B below the G, there is a perceived downward movement in the bass line and the harmony is changed. The interval now is a minor sixth. In the expressive intonation of the spoken non-tonal languages this is an emotionally charged interval, often expressing pity and mourning.

(c) When the bass line moves to an A it is perceived as continuing its downward movement creating a minor seventh, an interval found farther along the harmonic series and is, therefore, more dissonant. The sound of this interval is unsettled and out of phase. The conflict presented by the relative dissonance of this interval drives the movement of the harmony. The movement of the bass line combined with the conflict of dissonance creates a sense of direction and a yearning for resolution. The consonance-to-conflict-to-resolution structure of dramatic movement is contained in the combination of the scale in the bass line perceived as downward movement and the increasing conflict found in the intervals.

(d) The bass line continues to a G: the conflict of the dissonance is resolved and the resulting octave is the most perfect consonance.

The movement of the bass line has colored the melody of my sustained G. The resulting intervallic relationships between the bass note and that melody create varied, increasingly dissonant, and emotionally charged intervals that eventually arrive home at a perfect octave. In this example the melody is a single, inexpressive note. The emotional implications and the home/conflict/resolution storyline are expressed in the movement and *relationships* between the upper note and the lower line; the expression is in the counterpoint.

This system of musical progression is designed to create direction and fulfillment. Dissonant harmonies that require resolution are the primary levers that drive harmonic movement. When one note sounds as if it leans toward another, such as the third note A in the above example leaning toward the last note G, we interpret the movement as conflict-resolved. This action of dissonance toward consonance moves melodies, harmonies, and tonal centers.

There is another subtle shot in the emotional cocktail of the descending bass line. The polarity of Morton's rules come into play: remember that low pitches sound ominous to us because humans (and other mammals) are aggressive in the low register and submissive in the high register and that we are instinctively attuned to this difference. The bass line, as its name suggests, sounds in the range of the low male voice. A man who speaks in a low, full voice when introduced to a baby will most likely be greeted with pouts and cries. Our auditory systems are predisposed to pay attention to tones in these low frequencies.

Visuospatial Music

"We don't see the world as it is, we see the world as we are."
- Anaïs Nin

Prepare yourself for a paradigm-shifting reality check. I am writing about lines, but what we are actually hearing are more like dots. The brain connects these dots to make lines that imply movement, but movement in music is all in our minds. Just as the screen in the movie theater presents rapidly changing still images that are perceived as movement, so do the successive tones in music create an impression of movement where there is none.

The perceived "lines" in music are supplied entirely by the interpretation of the sounds in the brain of the listener. The movement I refer to here is the perception that a melodic line goes up or down. The ability to perceive this kind of movement has been *adopted* by music.

The dominant perceptive ability of primates is vision and the most important extension of that visual foundation in the human mind is spatial reckoning. Perception of movement is a highly developed capability for recognition that is permanently up-and-running in the brain. The mind is predisposed to organize information spatially and music has benefited from this capability. When we hear a succession of notes, our interpretation connects them and perceives movement just as it connects dots to perceive shapes. In this part of the mind, music is a guest.

Although the ear is responsible for picking up sounds and detecting where they come from, the movement in music referred to here happens entirely in the mind. A fellow who is sitting close to an orchestra will be able to tell what instruments are on the right and what instruments are on the left, but we have to look deeply into his brain to find his perception of high and low pitches.

Why do we say that a flute is high and a bass is low? Why is there an up and down to our perception of frequencies, the faster frequencies labeled as higher and the slower frequencies as lower? We don't refer to the faster frequencies of light as up (blue) and the slower as down (violet), but when we hear successive tones of ever faster frequencies played on an instrument we say that we hear the scale ascending.

The answer lies in our visual representation of pitch. If we hear a given instrument play 262 Hz (middle c) followed by the same instrument playing 247 Hz (b natural) we say that it has moved down. The successive sounding of pitches from the same source is interpreted and stored in the brain as a kind of spatial, visual memory.

Can you name this tune? Each of these pitches lasts 1/4 second (each number represent a frequency in Hz): 206, 310, 468, 440, 468, 310, 468, 310, 206, 310, 468, 440, 468, 310, 468, 310. Perhaps it is fairer to ask if you can name the tune represented like this:

Give up? It is the opening measure of the Prelude in G major for unaccompanied cello by J.S. Bach, heard often in commercials and film scores, the one we met earlier in the book. The pattern that actually strikes the ear is 206, 310, 468, 440, 468, 310, 468, 310, 206, 310, 468, 440, 468, 310, 468, 310, but we hear it more like this, as it is represented in musical notation:

In the same way that our eye connects these dots to create a line, our brain processes successive tones as a shape. This all takes place in the visuospatial right hemisphere where our brains process incoming images from the eyes. Recent research into visual processing has given us insights into how the brain connects dots to perceive shapes and movement. When we see a yellow ball rolling across a table, the color is processed in one part of the brain, the shape in another, and the movement in another, and then combined into a single recognition of the moving object. This same visuospatial part of the brain also supplies the missing information between the notes, translating it into the music that we can enjoy. When we hear successive pitches sounding with the same timbre, the brain fills in the gaps and recognizes the sequence visually as movement.

Seeing the Shapes of Sounds

Musical designs often derive tension and movement from the diametric opposition of the low, dark, turbulence of earth to the clear perfection of the high heavens. When music passes through our visual perception it is judged according to the principles of the world we see:

high	sky	bright	light	sublime
low	earth	dark	heavy	profound

In our world gravity pulls away from the light. The heaven of perfect movement and perfectly organized space is the ultimate destination for the devout as well as the adventurous. To rise above nature (notice the use of the word above) means to rise above the terrestrial chaos and the bestiality of life consuming life. Dark, chaotic music will seldom be heard in worship services; music of celestial perfection and harmony serves to point in the direction of our hopes and aspirations.

Our musical representations of these concepts are consistent with the interpretations of the dualities of light/dark up/down that seem to be natural to us. Slow frequencies also tend to have a visual association with darkness. Perhaps this association is due to the lack of clarity inherent in the bass register. Higher frequencies are easier to locate and distinguish. Low frequency wavelengths are so long that determining the location of origin is difficult, and the sonority is "muddy". I heard a concert by Metallica in Washington, D.C. where the sound of the bass and the sound of the pedal drums were virtually the same. That kind of extreme lack of clarity is easily classified in the mind as muddy.

I hope you are beginning to get a picture of music as a cascade of charged sonic elements that induce emotions, lighting many different sparks inside of us. Even five notes in two lines are capable of illuminating a number of different emotional lights. Counterpoint is not linear movement *or* consonance *or* dissonance *or* harmony, but all of these. Bottom line: when we uncover the secrets of music we find that there is no "or", we find only "and, and, and...".

Harmony Moves

"Music resembles chess. The Queen (melody) has the greatest power, but the King (harmony) decides the game."

- Robert Schumann

Schumann also wrote: "We have learned to express the more delicate nuances of feeling by penetrating more deeply into the mysteries of harmony." but a protégé of Schumann, Johannes Brahms believed that the key to writing music is the mastery of counterpoint. Harmony and counterpoint are best understood as two facets of the same jewel.

This connection is demonstrated in the round:

```
                                        stream
                                the
                    boat   gent-    down
                    your            ly
Row,    row,    row
```

The note sung on "Row" is the key note or "tonic" of the round. If you sing an F on "Row" then the song is in F major. "Row", "gent", and "stream" which are sung at the beginning, middle, and end of the first part of the round make up the notes of the F major chord: FAC.

When two voices are combined they constitute two contrapuntal lines:

```
                                              stream
                                        the
                  boat gent-      down                  boat
             your              ly                  your
Row,   row,  row              Row,   row,       row
                               ^      ^          ^
       At these moments:      here   here   &   here
```

The two lines combine to form the intervals of a major third, another major third, and a perfect fifth, again forming an F major chord. The second entrance in a round creates counterpoint; the relationship between the two voices creates harmony.

Schumann and Brahms were referring to the one and the same secret to composing effective and expressive music, the ability to write each line in such a way that it will have a melodic contour of its own and at the same time creates nuanced harmonies resulting from its relationships to the other voices.

In Brahms' music, the contrapuntal melodies are often as beautiful as the principal melody. The genius in his contrapuntal technique was his ability to write interior lines that express the same spirit as the melody itself. In the second movement of Brahms' fourth symphony there is a passage for strings where each of four different lines is a richly expressive melody in its own right (you will hear an all-cello version of this passage if you visit www.davidteie.com and click on Brahms 4 or listen to track 21 on the CD). We played this symphony on tour with the National Symphony and I remember thinking in a performance in New Jersey while playing this passage: "I feel so fortunate to be playing this line. And the violas next to me – their line is just as beautiful as ours – and neither of us is playing the melody!"

The varied harmonies that are formed by interior lines augment and enhance expression. Harmony is often thought of like a vertical CT scan of the music, the chord beneath the melody, but the secret to the ability of harmony to touch our emotions lies in its movement. Another simple demonstration of the expressive power of counterpoint can be heard at: www.davidteie.com and click on Counterpoint or on track 22 of the CD.

In this recording I begin by presenting the separate elements. You will hear six different intervals, one three-note melody, and a three-note bass line. I think you will agree that very little expression is conveyed when these are presented as independent slices. When these elements are combined as two related lines at the end of the demonstration the expression in the music is revealed. Each of the three bass notes creates a unique background for the melody, coloring it and providing variations to the pattern. I hope these few notes presented in different ways will help to illuminate the nature of the blended roles of harmony and counterpoint and allow you to hear how the colors of harmony can change the meaning of a melody.

All of the movements in the melody and the bass line in that demonstration are stepwise. The slowly stepping scale is the musical movement that is the most apparent to our perception. The connection between clearly perceived movement and emotional response to music is demonstrated by the near universality of the reaction that audiences have to certain pieces. If you think of a deeply moving piece of music, the chances are that it contains slow, stepwise movement in the bass, and will very likely have slow, stepwise movement in the interior lines and the melody as well. The heartbreaking longing and resignation in the opening of the slow movement of Mahler's 4th symphony is a tender, slowly ascending scale in the cellos. The Adagio for Strings by Samuel Barber is similarly woven from slow, stepwise melodies and countermelodies.

The movement that harmonic changes provide can imply a sense of direction and arrival. Music often conveys a sense of longing – to be *there* – whether *there* is the savannah of our prosperity and safety, the celestial perfection of heaven, or just to know the end of the story. The ongoing nature of music and the movements implied in tonality can combine with the shape of the story structure to provide music with a sense of arrival that may be stronger than in any other art form.

Movement is the last piece in the puzzle of music. Now we can step away from the board and see how the pieces mingle and weave. Since the major players in the array of musical features that are capable of inducing emotions have all been introduced, this will be my last warning against giving undue credibility to any idea that names a single feature of music as *the reason* for its emotional appeal. From this point forward I will present the same concept from another perspective: all of the elements of music combine to create varied tapestries of emotions. The elements themselves are much less important than the mixtures; each element supports the others. Even polar opposites, such as dissonance and consonance, can be mutually supportive when presented in succession: the dissonance trips a momentary awareness and fear-based unease that awakens our perceptions making the affectionate consonance that ensues more relieving and satisfying than it would have been standing alone.

7

INTUITION AND
INSPIRATION

The musical sensation high point of my life happened in Williamsburg, Virginia. It was in a performance of the Brahms C major trio on a tour that I played with the Amadeus Trio. In the rehearsals I had held most of my own interpretive suggestions in reserve, hoping that my opinion would count for more if it were offered rarely. I used my ace-in-the-hole request in the second section of the third movement. Violinist Tim Baker and pianist Marian Hahn were accustomed to playing it faster than I wanted to play it. I asked for a slower tempo and included in the plea that so much of Brahms' music is turbulent and longing, but that this section is a singular musical depiction of the sweet ecstasy of the fulfillment of his passion. Brahms' purest (but probably unrequited) love was for Clara Schumann, the composer, pianist and wife of Robert Schumann. There is evidence in his notes and letters that when he wrote in C he was writing for Clara. The striking horn theme near the beginning of the last movement of his first symphony, for example, when the music sounds as if it is suddenly bathed in sunlight, is an Alpenhorn melody that he sketched on a birthday postcard to Clara with the inscription: "Hoch auf'm Berg, tief im Thal, gruss ich dich Viel tausendmal!" "High on the mountain, deep in the valley I greet you many thousand times!" I asked that we soak ourselves in the beauty and glory of the fulfillment of this deeply felt yearning that he had endured for many years. Tim and Marian agreed and we played this section broadly and with a sense of languishing freedom. Goosebumps usually waft over the body like a gentle breeze on a summer day, but the thrill that I felt in this performance lasted from the first note until the last of the entire second section of the third movement; I experienced more than two full minutes of euphoria in waves of bliss.

Presently, no one can fully describe everything that is involved in such a phenomenon. It is becoming clear, however, that many different features of music come into play. In my experience in the Brahms trio, even though there are many different facets of this music, it was the tempo alone that accounted for the difference between simple enjoyment and ecstatic euphoria. David Huron, a researcher who has been looking into the mechanisms by which music affects the emotions, has identified six activating systems of listening that all receive and interpret sound information concurrently. Huron has also defined two characteristics of music that he believes to be necessary for goosebumps: it must be loud and it must present some kind of unexpected change, but neither of these is contained in the two minutes of chill bliss that I experienced in the Brahms trio. This is just one indication of how difficult it is to ascribe specific causes for the waves of thrill in music.

Emotions that are induced by music are composite cocktails made from adding together responses from many different cues. Huron has compared the enjoyment of music to the enjoyment of a fine dinner party where scintillating conversation and wine-induced release of inhibitions combine with the ever-changing aromas and flavors of a multi-course meal to create a unique sensory experience. I would add to this that the emotions involved in the dinner party of a piece of music need not be all pleasant. When mild fear-related cues such as dissonance are resolved into the consonance of affection it is like taking the table at the dinner party on a little roller coaster ride and then bringing it to a stop with a smile. The attentiveness it provides enhances the experience of all the accompanying emotional cues.

Emotional responses tend to be activated easily. The emotion of fear, for example, shoots the adrenaline first and asks questions later – whether the body is primed to fight, flee, or freeze. Our attentive and startle reactions were calibrated by the needs of our hunting and foraging ancestors. If a fearful response should turn out to be a false alarm, well, no harm done. If, however, a dose is needed but is not delivered, the resulting lazy reaction might spell doom for the inattentive. The vanguards of attentiveness in the mind tend to be over-protective.

The emotional center of the brain directs our behavior with rewards that are often subtle, like the miniature doses of emotional pings you feel when you solve a problem, recognize a rebuttable flaw in a statement made by an opponent during an argument, or observe an object changing its course. The pleasure we feel from the recognition of a pattern could hardly be described as euphoria, but it is, nevertheless, pleasing. And so it is with emotional reactions to sounds that are recognized from the earliest times, the origin of our formation. Sounds that remind the subconscious of heartbeats and mother's treble melodies in the womb include most of the popular songs that you know from the hymn *Amazing Grace,* to Elvis' *Heartbreak Hotel,* to Motown's *Ain't No Mountain,* to Michael Jackson's *Billie Jean* but that does not mean that we will assume a fetal position whenever we hear a song based on the sounds of the womb. A subtle recognition is there, however, and leaves in its wake a trace feeling of self-identity.

The emotional recipes of music often include the activation of potentially powerful responses delivered in very small doses; the more the response benefited the species the more powerful it will tend to be. If the fear of being stalked is only half-awakened by a line that descends the emotional valve will open ever so slightly, dripping where it was designed to gush. Similarly, the internal alarm that is designed to go off when we hear a human voice in a threatening tone subtly murmurs when we hear a dissonance. Bear in mind that even ultra-harmonious Mozart often sprinkled dissonances into his music. The 6th and 8th measures of the famous opening of *Eine Kleine Nachtmusik* contain a chord where the dissonant intervals of a major 9th, a major 2nd, and a major 7th all sound simultaneously. If you were to sustain this chord in isolation (www.davidteie.com and click on Mozart dissonance or track 23 on the CD) it would be disturbingly dissonant, but Mozart resolves the dissonances in measures 7 and 9 and the result is delightful. The attention of his dissonances is immediately replaced by the dopamine of affection when he resolves the music to a consonance.

Human Music

Music Presents a Bouquet of Hidden Influences

Oftentimes the things that set off our emotions are not consciously identifiable. When we consider the host of complexities and nuances involved in our emotional responses to different events and thoughts we can understand how difficult it is to tease out each thread that influences our feelings. If each of us were able to consciously identify the fundamental causes of all of our emotions psychiatrists would have a lot of free time on their hands.

The complexity of the experience of listening to music and the inability of conscious attention to understand subconscious processes clouds our recognition of cause and effect in our emotional responses to music. The blend of feelings touched by pattern recognition, womb memory, and fear stir us in ways that are hidden to the listener.

Our inability to distinguish the exact cause of many of our emotional responses is the primary reason that the connection between emotion and music has been so impervious to examination. We tend to attribute the cause of the feelings induced by music to things that we *are* able to pay attention to. In 1962 Stanley Schachter and Jerome Singer conducted a study that demonstrated the variability of our interpretations of emotional response and the psychological phenomenon of false attribution whereby, for example, a fellow who has been depressed for three months will point to the recently leaking faucet as the reason he's depressed. In this study, some subjects were injected with epinephrine, an arousing drug, and the control group was injected with a placebo. They were then taken into a room where an actor, posing as another injected subject, behaved as if he were either euphoric or angry. The results indicated that the subjects who had received the epinephrine usually associated their own feelings with those of the companion in the room and began to behave likewise. The subjects in the control group who had not received the arousing drug did not respond sympathetically to the actors. We all do this: we feel a feeling and then we look around to find the cause. Naturally, we can only choose from those causes that are available to our conscious attention.

Emotional Build-up

When we consider the accumulated effects of the many subconscious cues contained in music, however, the roadmap to our emotions becomes clearer. The mild sensation resulting from a faint stimulus to an instinctively powerful reaction has a more pleasing effect than a genuinely triggered full-flow response. Consider the feeling in your belly that comes from driving quickly over the crest of a hill; my children used to call a road that had a few of these hills in succession the "whee way". The fear of falling, when controlled and mild, can be enjoyable for a child, or for the child in all of us. This same hard-wired emotional response is turned up to the thrill level by the roller coaster, and to wide-open fear in skydiving. A faint and enigmatic fear response is capable of deepening and broadening the impact of entertainment, drama, and beauty.

What we describe as a feeling results from what is often a complex array of neural responses and chemical cocktails produced by our emotional centers. The limitless variety of musical and extra-musical elements that combine with a particular recipe of emotional responses stimulated by music produces a unique reaction to every piece.

The electro-chemical responses that result from the emotional triggers take time to dissipate in the body's system. A strong emotion will remain in the system for quite a while; it may take some time to get over the anger at the guy who cut you off in traffic. Milder emotions such as the pleasant feeling that a major chord induces won't last too long. An accumulation of consonant/pleasant – dissonant/attentive chemicals can result when an extended passage triggers many small responses that build up in the system from the chords, movements, and harmonies. Listening to music is not so much like a single bright light turning on in our emotional centers as it is like a field of fireflies in June, a host of tiny twinkles. Each little illumination lets out a bit of a dopamine-related pleasing feeling, occasionally spiced-up with the adrenaline of attention. Just as having one drink per hour will keep you tipsy but one drink every half hour will get you drunk, the accumulation of chemicals in music can be like sipping from a different cocktail every few seconds. If the passage is built so that the chemicals accumulate more quickly than they dissipate, then you have the recipe for an emotional rush. Most of us have a few favorite musical rush moments. Mine include the last two minutes of Wagner's *Liebestod,* the climax of Puccini's *Nessun dorma* from Turandot, and the final dirge in the last minute of Tchaikovsky's *Overture to Romeo and Juliet.* In each case the rush is strongest when the climax is well prepared, when the emotional pumps are primed and flowing.

Similar responses will tend to support each other to create a stronger cumulative reaction. If I were to write and play an introduction to a lullaby love song, for example, the composer part of me would probably include a slow, regular pulse, a treble-register melody, and sweet, consonant harmonies while the performer part of me would play softly with a smooth tone. Each of these components expresses calm and affection.

Mind you, I would have done these things long before I had consciously learned or discovered any of the origins or emotional cues that are outlined in this book. It's no secret that most artists work intuitively. If the lyrics express a deep, lasting love then a musician setting the words to music will simply feel the atmosphere created by the words and write and play the music that emerges from that feeling.

Decades ago when I began to commit more time to composing I found myself getting up early to write songs. One of the first was a song about a man who was outwardly content but "what he really wanted was to be twenty years old and falling in love in Boston." I congratulated myself on my ability to empathize with this imaginary character. You may have guessed that I was writing about myself, but it would be years before I would figure that out for myself. The internal, subconscious demand for honest expression is often an engine for artistic expression.

As outlined in the chapter on the voice, music is partly constructed from the elements of speech that communicate emotion. Accordingly, musical performers intuitively parallel the expressions of emotional speakers. The intuition of an expressive performer is the very same intuition that we use to communicate with each other every day.

When you meet someone for the first time, in addition to the words you hear your senses are simultaneously absorbing and interpreting facial contours, postures, and tones-of-voice. It is wonderful to think of how much we can tell about someone in five seconds of conversation. Hidden senses are absorbing impressions as well: if your subconscious mind sees the likeness of someone you already know and love in the face of a woman or man you just met it is probable that she or he will be immediately attractive to you.

We take in the essence of music in much the same way. All of the patterns, timbres, harmonies, dissonances, consonances, interior movement, familiar structure and more are absorbed and understood in the interior mind of intermediate level awareness, meanwhile the womb remembrances are understood by our emotional center as belonging to the most essential and original aspects of ourselves. The inner source of such a musical embrace originates in the mind and heart of the composer, is transmitted through the mind and heart of the performer, and communicates directly to the comprehending mind and resonating heart of the listener.

This kind of communication happens all at once and is understood in a moment. We all communicate varied and complex expressions of the languages of body, face and tone quality and can understand this human discourse in all its ramifications immediately and intuitively. We don't take out the flashlight of our conscious thought and shine it on every aspect of the communication, one at a time, before adding them together and coming to an interpretive conclusion. The parallel-processing, emotionally connected, pattern-recognizing, exquisitely subtle communicating and interpreting abilities are the ones that are tapped by intuition and inspired thought. A real understanding of musical inspiration has been elusive precisely because this kind of processing is hidden from conscious attention.

The abilities that we have evolved to express subtleties in language have endowed us with the sophisticated and intuitive interpreting abilities that helped to make the development of music possible. The following is a scene containing some of the highly evolved varieties of perception that have been infiltrated by music:

> Imagine that you are having a conversation with a woman who is a dear friend. You are seated outside across from her on a sunny, breezy afternoon. You hear a train whistle (it has a faint echo, allowing you to recognize that it is in the distance) and you hear the intermittent noise of the wind rustling leaves in nearby

branches. Your friend is telling you about the recent death of someone who was very close to her. Tears well up in her eyes as she says: "I don't know. I'm sorry, it's late. I have to go." Her voice has a high, hollow quality. As she says the words "I have to go" her voice cracks and you feel tears come to your own eyes, a slight tightening of your throat, and your belly squeezes out a puff of breath.

In that scene your conscious attention may be on her words, but it is the sound of her voice, the quality and the cracking of it that moves you, the words themselves mean little. The poignancy and beauty of the entire experience, including the shushing sound of the leaves in the breeze and the sunlight flickering on the face of the grieving woman, are absorbed simultaneously. While your attention is focused on: "I'm sorry, it's late. I have to go." there is an accompanying sensory symphony that is touching emotions of sympathy and beauty.

In the very same way musical expression is carried through many different layers of sound received in a parallel flow and interpreted in hidden places of our minds; much of this interpretation occurs in the complex, sophisticated emotional centers of the brain. We understand speech by paying attention to the words spoken, but the simultaneous projection of the grammar, syntax, tone-of-voice, facial movements and body language of the speaker are all taken in through an intermediate-level awareness. We listen to music similarly. As we pay attention to the melody or lyrics, we also have a peripheral, intuitive awareness of the pulse, the harmonic movement, the directions of the contrapuntal lines, and any of the other two dozen facets of music that have been outlined in previous chapters. Our ability to listen to music is not unlike our ability to appreciate many varied aspects of a painting in a single gaze or to make judgments of perfect strangers in a moment.

Here is a blow-by-blow account of some of the features of *Over the Rainbow* (see the score below) that touch our emotional soft spots: (1) The pitches from the accompaniment produce the periodic waves of vocal sounds that receive priority treatment in our sound processing, allowing the music to pass through the background noise filter. It contains strings playing softly and with light, fast bows over the fingerboard to create a pure, warm tone that blend with the pure tones of the harp; these pure tones are characteristic of affectionate speech that awakens our sympathetic emotions. (2) Judy Garland sings with the full, warm voice of a lowered larynx that hints of emotionally charged speech. (3) The combination of melody and harmony create the aligned overtones of a consonant sonority that communicate affection. The harmonies in this song are predominantly consonant. Rather than covering the page with indications pointing out the many consonances, I will call attention to the occasional passing dissonances. (4) These two adjacent notes are a major second apart creating a mild attention-piquing dissonance that is resolved into another consonant chord after the first barline. (5) The melody begins with an octave leap, the most consonant interval. (6 and 7) More passing dissonances are like adding lemon to the sweet cheesecake. (8) The first pattern is repeated giving us the pleasing sensation we feel when we recognize symmetry and order. (9, 10, 11, and 12) Three lines, including the bass line, move downward in stepwise motion giving us the sense that we are perceiving directed movement that may be worthy of our attention. Some of the notes in these descending lines create the arousing zest of passing dissonances. The second staff (the lines that begin with: "there's a...") includes all of the 12 features of the music that are found in the first 4 measures and includes (13) another pattern that is repeated twice.

Over the Rainbow

These are only the musical features, and not all of them are listed above. I have not listed any of the subtle differences of tone quality, contoured pitches, stressed and unstressed notes within the phrase – that is to say: the list does not include any of the many vocal qualities that make Judy Garland's singing so much more expressive than that of an average singer. Each of these features is also triggering emotions in us because we are naturally and exquisitely capable of interpreting tones of voice. When all of this is added to the mysterious and evocative lyrics we can hear that this single musical sentence is not so much a flower as it is a bouquet. Or, to use a culinary analogy: in the recipe of music a beautiful phrase contains many delicious ingredients. Instead of appealing to the taste buds the ingredients in music appeal to the emotions. All of this is accomplished intuitively, simultaneously, and subconsciously.

The upshot of all this should be put in neon lights: The essence of aesthetic awareness of music is not achieved through conscious thought.

The parallel-processing intuition that allows listeners to appreciate music is used by composers and performers to create music. The intuitive flow is reversed just as it does if you listen to someone speak to you then your emotions swell within you and you have something to say. Creative musicians appeal to the intuitive emotional centers to supply the substance of the music the way a lover writes a love letter or speaks imploringly to the loved one.

Performers defer to the second nature of intuition because the simultaneous, real-time necessities of reading music, adjusting for balance, intonation, rhythmic variations, and all the rest are best accomplished when conscious attention is focused on the spirit of the music being played. Attention to each of the details of technique is required during the hours and years of practice mastering the instrument, but while performing it is important to be able to allow the hands to do what they have been trained to do, unencumbered by conscious tinkering. Rostropovich used to say: "If you ask the centipede what his 54th leg is doing when his 23rd leg is moving forward, he will lose the ability to move."

So what do we do with our conscious attention while our hands are making the music? A bored session player on the fourth take might be thinking about what to have for lunch. I have often conversed with players about what they were thinking about when playing a familiar piece in a rehearsal. Some make mental lists of errands they need to do while others are planning conversations with stubborn children. It is not uncommon for musicians to play through an entire movement before awakening to realize that it is finished.

Distracted, automatic playing is a trap that results from the repetition that is necessary in order to master the techniques. Once a passage has been perfected, the player must play it over again and again and again. Each repetition can lead the attention ever further into distracted thoughts. Oftentimes this perfected playing and distracted thinking is taken into a performance and then the musician may receive a dangerous and subversive gift: the compliment. Well-intentioned praise is the lovely devil who camouflages the opening to the trap of programmed, automaton playing. I spent many years mired in this trap and was only evicted when a bomb went off in my musical world that destroyed the foundations of my confidence.

When I was 13 years old I received a very nice review from the judge at the State music contest in Wisconsin following a performance of a relatively simple, student sonata by Romberg. During the performance

I had been looking off in the distance and thinking about: the sunshine outside, wondering why so many people were in the room, and how I hoped that my endpin would not slip in the tiled floor. The success of the little performance convinced me that it was okay, possibly even good, to be distracted when playing in public.

I was studying at the time with Johan Lingeman. I hasten to credit him with the well-established technique that allowed my mind to wander, but I take full responsibility for the pitifully mundane objects of that wandering. He was an old school gentleman who regarded music as something that is sacred. He had been born in 1888 in Holland and, among other career highlights, had played in the Concertgebouw conducted by Gustav Mahler. I enjoy thinking of Mr. Lingeman as a direct connection to the epicenter of the world of classical music. The year he was born Brahms was 55, Tchaikovsky was 48, Puccini was 30, and Richard Strauss was 24. He told me that technique was important but "you don't want to become like Heifetz." I was dumbfounded because Heifetz was the god of the violin and I did not possess a hundredth part of the talent or ability of such a supreme master. He explained that he had heard Heifetz and Kreisler each play the Beethoven concerto within a few weeks of one another. After Heifetz's performance Mr Lingeman got up from his seat thinking that it was not possible that the violin could be played better than that. After Kreisler's performance he was so moved that he could not get out of his seat. Mr. Lingeman was quick to remind me that, good reviews aside, the ongoing quest of the musician is more than just technique: it is to communicate the spirit of the music.

I applied that advice to my preparation of the music, but I made the mistake of not applying it to the ongoing attention during performances. I used to prepare music like a sculptor: lengthen this note, shorten that one, vibrate these and not those, crescendo here, etc. I then took these practiced interpretations to the performances and received the confirmation of applause, modest success, and smiling praise.

Then, in my early career in 1980 my smug confidence was destroyed. I was 25 years old and playing in the Baltimore Symphony at the time, having enjoyed enough success to make me believe that I was on the right track. I had reason to believe that if I kept working away down the path that I was on that I would eventually reach the level of artistry that I hoped to achieve. That year I went to my first international competition in Budapest and, despite playing my sculpted best, did not get past the first round. As I was sitting in the hall listening to the second round I could see a woman in the row in front of me flipping through the pages of the program for the competition wherein her companion had written comments on each of the players in the first round. She was getting to the T's and I eagerly waited to read what was written there about me. On my page was scrawled a single word: semmi! I wondered what this Hungarian word meant. Perhaps it meant great, or wonderful. I later asked the woman who looked after the dorms about it and she said that the word meant: nothing. I asked: "Do you mean that it's a nonsense word like Yippee, or is it the Hungarian word for nothing?" She said: "It's the Hungarian word for nothing."

There it was, the worst possible review. I was alone in an extremely foreign place and the entire structure of my approach to performing burned to the ground. In this state I went back to the competition to hear Alexander Baillie play the Brahms E minor sonata. He was a giant of a performer. Hugely expressive and spontaneous, he was completely involved in the ongoing drama of the music. At one point in the first movement he fell back into his chair while playing as if he had just been told that a dear friend had died. I tried to imagine myself in his chair doing what he was doing and realized that I had never played the way he was playing. Later that night I took my cello to the basement of the dorm, closed my eyes and tried playing with the freedom and spontaneous emotional outpouring that Baillie had exemplified. I was musically reborn in that basement and set myself on a new path that would eventually lead me to study for two years with one of Baillie's most influential teachers, William Pleeth.

This kind of emotionally committed approach is exemplified by another of my heroes: Geraldine Walther who was the principal violist in the San Francisco symphony the year I was there. She is a fully committed, passionate player who personifies Piatigorsky's dictate that whenever you have the instrument in your hands you must be 100% involved. She plays every note in every concert and every rehearsal with an absolutely relentless focus on the emotional intent of the music. I remember rehearsing the Brahms G minor piano quartet with her, violinist Jorja Fleezanis, the concertmaster of the Minnesota Orchestra, and pianist extraordinaire Garrick Ohlsson. I was filling in for their usual cellist, the principal of the San Francisco Symphony, Michael Grebanier. One moment Geraldine would be sipping tea in smiling conversation and the next she would have the viola in her hands like a lightning rod that veritably crackled with rhythm and purposeful expression.

Playing such as hers comes from an emotionally connected parallel-processing mind. The composers' access to inspiration and the performers' access to heartfelt playing are opened with the same key, it allows the intuitive interpreters of sound in the mind to create rather than receive. This is the reverse of the multi-faceted experiences such as the conversation described earlier where your friend is sitting in the flickering sunlight with the train whistle in the background describing the loss that she feels. Just as the reception of an entire scene is taken in as a whole, the inspired creative mind accesses emotionally directed, parallel processing thought that is far superior to the linear/serial process of conscious attentive thought.

One way that musical performers can work to achieve access to intuitive thought is through a process of directed imagination that works like this: 1) The musician plays an empty, ghostly version of a passage. This playing is deliberately void of interpretive expression – its only purpose is to get the passage into the memory. 2) In a quiet room, he or she imagines the Absolute Master of the instrument playing the passage. In the imagination of a skilled player who has spent years attending to music, this imagined performance can often be perceived in great detail. There is an expressive unity to the phrasing, sound, dynamics, and movement that is possible in one's imagination since it does not need to simultaneously cope with the technical demands of the instrument. 3) After hearing the imagined performance, the musician attempts to play exactly as the imagined performer did. This is attempted as a whole, just as a dancer would see a choreographer demonstrate a series of maneuvers and then imitate the series without having to think through each of the details of the separate movements. 4) This is followed by an often painstaking interval of practice and polishing to achieve in real sound the imagined performances. As this practice technique is used over the years the process speeds up and becomes more fluid. Sometimes, when all cylinders are firing and the performer gets into a zone, the imagined Absolute Master and the real player become a pair in tandem flight - the imagination is streaming just in front of the performer, who at once absorbs and performs the imagination-directed music. I have the sense that the noted cellist Yo-Yo Ma spends a lot of time in that zone.

Yo-Yo demonstrated that he had earned his legendary stature in a rehearsal of the great Dvorak cello concerto with the NSO at Wolf Trap a few years ago. Rehearse wouldn't be the right word to describe the time spent on the piece; he simply played through each movement a couple of times with us to give us ideas about how he may interpret the concerto in the performance. Every phrase was slightly different each time he played it. If he stressed the middle of the phrase in the first reading, as if he had said: "He was a GENEROUS king." he might stress and lengthen the beginning of the same phrase in the second reading: "HE... was a generous king." No matter where the phrases peaked or how the tempos moved, the music always flowed naturally. Clearly he didn't know exactly how he would play the passages before he began, but the playing was consistently expressive, balanced, and *human*. He has so completely mastered the art of using the voice of the cello to communicate emotionally expressive nuances that his imagination and his playing fly as pilot and co-pilot.

I began developing the practice technique outlined above after a lesson with Rostropovich where he taught me to hear the quality of sound first, and then create that sound on the cello. Normally a cellist will work in the reverse order: playing with his or her own sound first before trying to modify it. One day, while working on the Schumann concerto, I decided to stretch the imagined sound beyond a single note and try to hear an entire passage. The passage that I chose was one that I had played many times and heard others play often (visit www.davidteie.com and click on Schumann transition or listen to track 24 on the CD). I think of the fourteen notes in this transitional passage as a musical portrayal of a character whose furious mood turns tender, as if, in his anger, he looks up to see the innocent face of his daughter who has been frightened by his temper. When I opened my eyes after hearing my imaginary cellist I was thunderstruck. I could hardly breathe. As if she had been waiting there all the time, the imagined cellist who played for me looked and played very much like Jacqueline Du Pre' even though I had never actually heard Miss Du Pre' play the Schumann concerto. It was as if my supercellist had appeared to me in a dream - seated on the stage of the Liszt Academy in Budapest (perhaps because it was there that I had heard Alexander Baillie). The performance that played in my mind that day was unlike any I had ever heard by anyone; it was so compelling, so heartfelt, so passionate, and so *human* that I thought "Of course! That is the only way to play it!" The differences between the imagined interpretation and the one that I had previously been playing were so many and important that I had to change most of my fingerings and bowings to accommodate the newly imagined interpretation.

The simultaneity of intuition that created the complex, nuanced, multi-colored, organic playing of the supercellist informs our interpersonal communication every day. Perhaps actors use a dramatic version of the process: An actor considers his line: "If I go now, I will be lost." He imagines the scene, the face of the one he will be speaking to, the context of the line, the emotional state of his character - then sees and hears the character saying the line in his mind. He takes in his movements, his face, hears his tone of voice and the cadence of his speech - all in one, complete vision. In this way an actor could open up the access to our naturally intuitive understanding of human behavior.

Just as the mind of the actor fills in countless details of the character, rich with movement and expression and tone, naturally conveying the sense of the scene and the lines, the mind of the musician hears complete and blended details of nuance, timbre, and movement that manifest the spirit of the music in sound. When music is created in the intuitive, unattended mind it can often have an organic consistency, a blend, which is difficult to achieve with conscious calculation.

The projection of this blend in interpersonal communication is the image of personality. Imagine: In a conversation with a friend, I learn that she will be moving away. A sadness colors my tone when I say "Oh, no. When are you leaving?" I say it with a high, soft, hollow sound in descending pitches with an ascending minor third interval between "you" and "leav-" and descending minor tenth between "leav-" and "-ing" while reaching my hands out with open palms as my face creases the area between my brows and my head tilts slightly to the right. All of these elements of communication come to me naturally, I haven't thought about any of the many aspects of vocal, facial, and body language to express my feeling of impending loss after receiving the news that the friend would be moving away, but they are expressed clearly. In much the same way, once music has become a part of the second nature of a musical performer, the feeling and thought come to mind, and then intuition blends the quality and quantity of sound, the character of the connections between the notes, the speed of the movement, and the distribution of emphasis in the phrase. This second nature is available because the elements of musical expression have been taken from our vocal expression; the ability to communicate emotions through pitch and quality of sound has been built into us all.

I think of the second movement of the Schumann cello concerto as a statement of Robert to his wife Clara that he will miss her when he's gone. He knew that his sanity and health were in decline when he wrote this, his last important piece. When I play this movement I put myself in his position. More to the point, I transplant his predicament into my life and sing through my cello as if to my own dearly beloved wife. (You can see and hear me play this movement with the Eclipse Chamber Orchestra conducted by Leonard Slatkin at www.davidteie.com and click on Schumann concerto, or listen to it on track 25 of the CD.)

Casals said "In music, the primary role is played by intuition." Not all of the elite artists who are able to tap into the fluid stream of heartfelt intuition are household names. The soprano Geraldine Tucker was a homemaker turned voice teacher for the 1974-75 academic year at the University of Wisconsin-Oshkosh. Her voice was like clear, sweet liquid, her phrasing was pure and naturally contoured, and she could spin impossibly long, arching lines on a single breath. Perhaps most remarkable was the quality that she lacked: there was absolutely nothing affected or grindingly "*sopraanooooo*" about her singing. I once heard Garrison Keillor remark that the only music that he does not enjoy is music made by operatic sopranos. Even many of us who do enjoy the genre understand what he's talking about. There are plenty of hyper-contrived and overblown divas out there. I'm quite sure, however, that Mr. Keillor never heard Geri Tucker. She gave a recital at UW-O with Dr. Bruce Wise at the piano that included the Four Last Songs of Richard Strauss. By the end of the performance my face was wet with tears as were the faces of nearly every person around me. Her singing so seared my memory that despite spending the next 35 years in concert halls including hundreds of concerts that I attended in a two-year stint in London, the classical musical capitol where all of the highest-fee artists appear regularly, Ms. Tucker's Strauss remains the single greatest performance that I have witnessed.

Classical musicians have not cornered the market on parallel-processed intuition; it is essential for jazz improvisation and is in evidence in a great deal of popular and rock music. It may be surprising to my classical musician colleagues that I used Led Zeppelin's music to demonstrate superb, organic structure rather than, say, Beethoven's. When I was researching the literature on musical aesthetics and musical philosophy I couldn't help but notice that the writers generally seem to feel that any music worth appreciating had already been written by the end of the 19th century. This may be a good place to remind or inform the more highbrow readers that the talent pool for popular music is enormous, the emotional resonance is genuine, and that sincerity, dedication, and integrity are found in musicians working in all styles.

There are plenty of examples of classically trained musicians crossing into the pop music world. Some groups such as Radiohead and Muse even include the classical styles of their nurturing in their albums. When Metallica was still an upstart band, bassist Cliff Burton used to bring recordings of Bach to the rehearsals. These exceptions notwithstanding, the strictly aural and physical nature of rock and jazz performing produce the most fully formed creative artists when they are not chained to the anchor of classical music: the printed page. In other words, it is good that they don't read music.

The reflexive rap against many pop and nearly all rock musicians is that they can't read music, presuming this to be a handicap. I can testify that a far greater problem is that so many classical musicians won't *stop* reading music. It often prevents a host of subtleties and flights of imagination from entering many classical musical performances. All too many of us think that we are finished interpreting if we have faithfully executed everything we see in front of us. Wagner noted that most of the musical nuances necessary for expressive performance could not be written down, *including all of the important ones*. I would also like to point out that learning to read music is a hundred times easier than learning to read, say, classical Greek. Reading music could be learned by almost anyone in a week and a half. Since the rock musicians that I know are also among the hardest working musicians I know, I believe that if they thought that their music would improve by learning to read it, they would do so.

Perhaps if I relate an experience I had while recording the first Echobrain album, it might enhance the reader's appreciation of elite rock musicians. Bass player Jason Newsted, while still a member of Metallica, formed Echobrain, a group that played in a broad range of popular musical styles. I wrote the string arrangements and played the cello solos on their first album. One of my improvisatory solos in the song *Sweet Summer* was like a miniature parade of musical personalities: a hint of John McLaughlin gave way to Stephan Grappelli, it even included a ditty from the Shostakovich cello sonata (this can be heard if you visit www.davidteie.com and click on Echobrain solo or on track 26 of the CD). It was something of a musical version of the scene from Dorothy's bedroom after she had been struck by the flying window in The Wizard of Oz: there goes a woman knitting, then there's a couple of guys in a rowboat, etc. The last two notes of my solo were the third and tonic of the home key played as artificial harmonics. These notes were a tiny quote from the end of "She's Leaving Home" where John Lennon sings "Bye-bye". I placed them there because the last word that Echobrain's singer Dylan had sung in the song was "bye". I assumed that it would remain a little inside-joke-tip-of-the-hat that no one would notice. The moment I finished playing these last notes in the recording session Jason stood up in the control booth, turned on the mic and asked:

"What's that from, man?"

"The Beatles"

"Oh yeah, 'She's Leaving Home.'"

He had identified two notes from the background vocals of a thirty year-old song that was not a hit.

Inspiration

Here is a kind of balance point between the realms of musicians, psychologists, and philosophers. The presence of inspiration virtually defines art and yet has received relatively little examination. The musician who has access to it is reluctant to discuss it, reluctant to question the source lest it disappear. Mozart consistently refused to describe his process of composition to a doctor who was persistent in his request to know how he composed. Surely Mozart and others feared the loss of the mysterious source of their inspiration, or that the magical imagination would cease if it were to be defined "...like a face perceived in a dark room, once recognized as a configuration in a pile of clothes, impossible to re-imagine as a face." (Tolstoy) Most composers believed that the spontaneously appearing strains of music were delivered by God. Beethoven, in response to a violinist complaining of the difficulty of a certain passage reportedly said: "I have been inspired by God. Do you think I am concerned with your puny violin?" And Puccini made the statement that *Tosca* had been written by God, and that he had merely held the pen.

Among those who might be expected to examine the nature of inspired thought are musicians who would hope to acquire it but have been foiled by the difficulty of examining something that they have not personally experienced. Inspired musicians are often not able to explain their own flights of inspiration in any but the most general and associative terms. Meanwhile those who long for inspiration can see the iconic masters through the glass ceiling but are unable to ascend through it. You can't buy it. You can't learn it. Or can you?

Psychologists have done some valuable work examining the neural pathways of transformative thinking, but they still tend to be surprisingly willing to declare the non-existence of inspiration. In any case, it would be exceedingly difficult to study such a rare and fleeting mental event. Given that scientists have had such success using serial, linear intelligence to build a wealth of detailed information brick by double-blind-tested brick, it is understandable why they would consider an intuitive leap hidden from attention to be suspect. But stories of intuitive leaps are often found in the stone-tablet history of the sciences; there are countless examples of rockets of intuitive inspiration that are later proven to be valid.

Spontaneous Composition

There are times when, doing something unrelated to music, I will hear a strain of music in my imagination. This spontaneously generated music can be as simple as a brief melodic element or as complex as a passage that is complete with orchestration, repeated and varied patterns, and accompanying harmonic movement. As much as a full 10-second passage will fly into my mind unbidden and fully formed. This is music that I have not heard before, although, when it comes to me it is as if I am hearing a familiar melody popping into my head.

I use these passages as the building blocks in compositions that I construct. Compositions that are made out of the material that comes from this spring of inspiration are constructed consciously. The attentive mind plays the role of editor and organizer. The intuitively presented material is adjusted, tweaked, doubled, halved, transposed, cut up and reconstructed, combined with appropriately modified other material and then written out. We know from their letters that this was the process of composition of Mozart and Beethoven and was surely the process of countless other composers.

Personal views of creative inspiration are hard to come by because deeply felt music often has its source in buried memories and emotions that the composer would rather not dig up. The emotional disinterment required to create works from these sources is difficult enough to accomplish without extending the disturbance by spending time discussing the process. In the interest of clarity, however, I will do so here: In the course of writing my cello concerto I became stuck at one point in the third movement, the Elegy. It contains a turning point in the emotional flow after a sustained and increasingly tense first half of the movement leads to a cathartic blast-release where the roar of the orchestra swamps a screaming solo cello line. I had planned to follow the blast with music of reconciliation and peace. I tried many times to write the end of this movement. Some attempts were completely finished and orchestrated before being discarded. A single, simple melodic theme insinuated itself into every version, sometimes it would come through in an oboe line, sometimes in the solo line, once as an answering motive in the flute. It had a melancholic expression, though, and I deleted it from every version on the grounds that it was not in keeping with what I had *decided* was to be the peaceful nature of the second half of the movement.

One morning as I was looking at the score, it seemed to speak to me. It said: "I am about forgiveness." I realized that the motive that kept reappearing and that I kept trying to eliminate was expressive of the true spirit of the movement, my true reason for writing the Elegy, something I had previously only dimly understood. As I was thinking about forgiveness, music began sounding in my head like an underscore to a scene of a deeply contrite composer sitting in the morning sun. I thought of the larger kind of forgiveness, not to be forgiven for what I have done, but to be forgiven for who I am - the kind of forgiveness that is more difficult to ask for and more difficult to grant. I wrote down the music that I had been hearing and when I had finished I sat on my bed and cried. The music that I heard in my head and wrote out that morning received little subsequent revision.

It may be surprising to hear that not all intuitively generated music is worth writing down. I have had melodies come to mind that could only lead me to believe that inspiration has a sense of humor. In such a case my conscious mind addresses my muse: "You must be joking. You expect me to make something out of that? You go right back to the hilltop and don't come back until you have something I can use."

It would be a good bet that no similar conversation ever took place in the mind of J.S. Bach. I believe it did, however, in the mind of Brahms. He literally burned much of what he wrote. By his own admission, if his heart was not in it, his music was dismally unappealing. If he had been talked into writing a work for a pharmacist's convention celebrating an anniversary of the invention of aspirin we would no longer be hearing it in our concert halls. Nearly all of Brahms' music is still heard in our concert halls because anything that he wrote that did not have its genesis in deep emotions didn't get past his fireplace.

It is possible to incorporate a flaky, ditty of a tune in a piece, leaving it to consciously directed compositional skill to turn it into something charming. That is what happened in the following mind-boggling pairing: here we have lyrics that are so simplistic that they barely qualify as lyrics at all, married to an equally simplistic melody of a single note in two different octaves. In Roger's and Hammerstein's *Carousel* the chorus sings in celebration: "Juuune, Juuune, June, June, June". Only brilliant guile or clueless idiocy would allow creators to have the courage to include that passage as a part of their work. Yet, these non-lyrics and the one-octave drop non-melody form a stasis section (miniature dominant pedal) that prepares an ebullient finish that projects a delightfully innocent spirit in a wildly popular musical. Brilliant guile wins.

Most musical material is not found complete and edible like manna from above. The modeling of musical themes and structuring is often intuitive as well, but the bulk of the contrapuntal details, transitional requirements, as well as practicalities such as the limits of the ranges of different instruments are the domain of attentive craft. We see one example of this in Beethoven's sketches that contain three different versions of the opening of the second movement of his 5th symphony. One version had an even rhythm coupled with a predominantly leaping melody and the other version coupled a lilting rhythm with a predominantly stepwise melody. In the final version he paired the leaping melody from the first with the lilting rhythm of the second.

Often a portion of an inspired motive is tailored to serve a purpose, such as a transition. Perhaps the tail end of an inspired melody will be repeated a few times over, each repetition set in a lower key and played more softly. (Tchaikovsky was fond of using this technique.) As noted in the chapter on structure, spinning the music that forms the road from one "scene" to another in the time appropriate for the latter expression to dissipate and prepare for the former is a part of the compositional craft of structuring large-scale works.

Composers of large-scale works must weave together musical material into a tapestry that provides a dramatic flow that sustains interest. The masters of epic construction create contrasting sections and transitions between them that are attuned to the natural paces of the ebb and flow of human emotions. The length of time that an anticipatory crescendo can be sustained or a stasis tone maintains suspense must be carefully regulated. Since it may take days or weeks to complete the composition of these passages, composers keep a large-scale frame of reference in mind like a painter who first draws a pencil sketch on a large canvas.

I'm sure there are superior methods of plotting music over time, but what I do is lay out a row of sheets of music paper that I have subdivided into evenly spaced segments, each representing about two seconds. Then, while keeping the beat in real time, I sketch dashes and notes on the pages as if I were playing the paper. This gives me a somewhat secure sense of the timing of sections and the gradations needed for building up and dissipating energy. I will have prepared for this sketching "performance" for some time accumulating themes and rhythms in my mind and notebook. I did this when I wrote the *Nightmare* movement from one of my first fully produced compositions: a three-movement theater piece for mime and string quartet entitled *The Shadow Dance*. You can hear the movement by visiting www.davidteie.com and clicking on Nightmare or listen to track 27 on the CD. This piece had its genesis in a dream. I awoke one morning having dreamt of a performance for mime and string quartet on the stage of the National Academy of Sciences auditorium. I immediately sketched out the story and the ideas as completely as possible, then spent the next few months actually composing the piece.

Songwriters have less of a need to work from broadly calibrated sketches because a song only needs to sustain our interest for only a few minutes at a time. Free from the conscious tasks of stringing together calibrated transitions, the songwriter often composes from pure inspiration.

Imagine

A song can be a kind of emotional hairball - if you lick your wounds long enough you will eventually cough up something that can be sprayed and trimmed and put under a glass. One song = one feeling. The songwriter puts him or herself in a state of mind, thinking about the subject of the song-to-be, and on a good day a song will come to mind. Some tinkering may be needed: rhymes discovered – accompaniments filled in, bridge sections built – but the ability to construct sections that flow from one scene to a very different scene in a way that carries the listener through the long ride of a symphony is not needed by a songwriter.

Which of the following do you think best describes the process that John Lennon followed when he wrote "Imagine"?

(a) He determined, firstly, to write a five-note motive with a grace-note leading to the fifth. Then he decided to repeat it three times to establish the key and provide the "hypnosis". Then he transposed the motive up a perfect fourth before singing the leading tone of the key three times in an accented fashion to provide the middle of phrase with the key-related tension that gives it shape and structural dissonance requiring a resolution. He followed that with a construction of a wistful resolution in "you-oooo-oo-oo"... etc.

(b) He had a thought, felt a spirit of hope and imagination, picked up his guitar and some time later, after discarding and replacing a few rhymes, had a song.

The structural elements described in this fantasized play-by-play of how the song could have been constructed are both perfectly valid. The important question is: where did the building of it take place? The answer is: it was built in the same place that listens to it: the laughing, weeping, directing emotional center and all of its cousins - the interconnected creators and receivers that provide the capacities for appraisal in our minds. Remember that two of the previously dissected Beatles tunes are historically confirmed self-starters: Paul McCartney was humming the tune of *Yesterday* for two days assuming that it was a song he had heard somewhere that had gotten stuck in his head, and John Lennon lay down in frustration when *Nowhere Man* came to him.

How It's Done

An examination of the nature of musical inspiration must take into account the complexities contained in any given one-second slice of music. The best compositions of the 18th through 20th centuries in Europe combined melodic motives, interconnected rhythms, and varied instrumental timbres. The contrapuntal writing alone required that every inner line have a melodic contour, a relationship between the direction of movement of each of the lines, an intervallic relationship with the other lines that was in keeping with the expression of the passage as a whole, and a large-scale structural design that would result from the combination of lines keeping a relationship to a tonal center. Any one of these elements could be successfully constructed piece by piece in the way a complex algebraic formula could be solved by making one calculation at a time then plugging the results into the formula, but the problem with counterpoint, as anyone who has tried their hand at it will confirm, is that everything changes everything. If, for example, a B flat in the tenor voice doesn't work with the A in the bass, changing it to another note will present a host of possible problems - the result may produce parallel fifths, the chord resulting from the changed note may not be complete, the new note of choice may have been sung often already by the tenor and the melodic contour will be static. To write music like this, one little equation at a time, is like trying to paint a recognizable landscape by painting a single square inch and sticking onto a canvas like a postage stamp, then repeating the process a thousand times.

Fluid, organic counterpoint is best achieved if second nature is involved, the second nature that comes from having mastered the physical performance of multiple lines. J.S. Bach incorporated the mathematical laws governing counterpoint and harmony at a very early age; he absorbed them so completely that they became available to his parallel-processing intuitive mind. The rules of counterpoint had become second nature and he could seat himself at an organ and improvise a complex, four-part fugue.

Do-It-Yourself

To get an idea of how entire sections of music that have been pre-assembled in the intuitive mind can arrive into the consciousness of the composer, picture in your mind a large stadium. When you do this experiment in thought-only creativity, take time at every slash mark to close your eyes and see each change in the stadium before going on to the next one. Let's make the stadium, say 70,000 seats or so/
make them red seats/
set it in a flat landscape in a field of yellow wheat/
on a hot, sunny afternoon/
with a mountain range in the distance/
change that, make them smaller, more distant mountains/
make them darker, a bit purple/
now rim the stadium with colorful flags.

To do that you didn't need to carve out two curves and a few rectangular doors and proportion the bowl to the walls, you simply "see" the stadium. And you didn't need to go in and etch out new little lines and fill them in with purple to make the mountain range smaller. So it is with intuitive musicians who think music: Hear a scale, now add a descending bass line, the first theme appears in the oboe, softly, in order for the oboe to be heard, the bass line should be put into the muted violas, etc. Once the mental listening and designing has been done, the composer sits at a desk and writes out the score.

Collecting the Dots

In Buddhist thought, enlightenment cannot be attained through learning alone, but cannot not be attained without learning; one must climb the mountain in order to be available to receive enlightenment. Climbing the mountain of learning is the first requirement for anyone to be in the position to have the experience of inspired thought. The chemical engineer will not, in a moment of rapture, envision the combination of colors and brush strokes that will capture and express the peculiar quality of light in a particular landscape in the South of France. And Rodin, while pondering the nature of movement in form, will not have an insight into the wave-particle duality of light. Inspiration can be thought of as a novel combination of already existing ideas. The quantity of material that is large enough to be available for new re-combinations can only be acquired through years of study.

A rough guide for the amount of time required in order for something to be installed in our highly adaptive minds and bodies to the point where it can be completely intuitive and accomplished through second nature is 10,000 hours (that's about four hours every day for seven years). Just like the Buddhist seeking enlightenment, studying and performing something for 10K hours will not make you a genius at it, but you will not be a genius if you haven't committed that much time to it. It is well known that while other band members would go relax after a long gig, John Coltrane and Dizzy Gillespie would often head off to practice. Stories of the super-precocious Mozart dazzling audiences with his musical skills as a child are heard more often than the stories of his demanding father who was determined to make Wolfgang into a musical star. Wolfgang's father was a highly skilled musician and composer who created a home for his son that amounted to a high level conservatory with constant oversight over every aspect of his study and practice of music. There can be little doubt that Wolfgang Amadeus had clocked his 10K hours before his 10th birthday. Here's the truth of the matter: Mozart was born with an exceptional capacity for learning, but he *earned* his genius.

Another requirement for inspiration is the presentation of a problem. The problem or question posed could include an artistic creation yet to be conceived or a new path to a given destination. The answer to a problem often lies in a new and logical arrangement of existing ideas. A maxim of cognitive researchers is "neurons that fire together wire together". The neural connections that arrange ideas can, if given the opportunity, display patterns in the synchronized firings that form new constructs. As the candidate for inspiration thinks about the subject from different angles and considers varied elements of the problem, the pattern-sensitive mind will discover connections between the elements. When the problem is attended to by linear conscious reasoning these crucial co-incident connections may not be apparent, but when the problem is addressed by the divergent thought that floats above the subject, the mind has a view of the entire field. Importantly, it has the freedom of thought to borrow reasoning from other faculties, allowing the physicist to imagine himself riding on a beam of light as Einstein did or a composer to see the music in geometric shapes turning and connecting in his mind.

Connecting the Dots

An embarrassingly appropriate analogy for inspired thought is the TV game show *Wheel of Fortune*. The goal of the game is to complete a sentence or phrase by the gradual accumulation of single letters and vowels that are added to the board by the lovely and talented Vanna White. Once enough letters have been added for the contestant to be able to mentally fill in the remaining spaces he or she will try to guess the phrase. Convergent analytical thought applied to a complex problem would be like trying to guess the phrase while looking at each letter independently and without the knowledge of the whereabouts of the spaces to be filled in. The aha of inspiration is the moment of alignment and understanding that fills in the blanks, makes sense of the arrangement of letters on the board, and completes the phrase. Divergent daydreaming, musing on the subject in question allows the mind to do its own calculating, free from the leadership of specified attention. While the straight-line reasoning of convergent thinking follows a trail through a windowless hallway, inclusive divergent thinking leaves the windows open so that the mind can wander and, perhaps, see the answer in the distance.

Conscious thought lays the groundwork for inspired thought by flagging the necessary elements by repeatedly paying attention to them; the more often we remember something the more readily accessed it becomes. Generally, a problem solved by inspiration is one that has been the subject of a great deal of recent analysis. After much pondering, the board that Vanna is standing next to has been memorized and the completed phrase pops into the mind. When the requirements of expertise and recent analysis are fulfilled the ground is fertile for inspired thought.

Turbo-driven Brain

The description of inspiration as turbo-boosted intellect is more than just a colloquialism that helps automobile enthusiasts to see into the workings of inspiration. The turbo drive is a device that takes the energy that is generated by the exhaust of an engine and uses it to power a turbine that increases the airflow into the firing chambers, increasing the power of the engine itself. In other words, the engine uses its outgoing energy to enhance its own power. In order for the turbo to add more power that it uses up, a certain threshold of engine output must first be reached.

The turbo-drive of intellect is passion. One who lacks passion for a subject will never experience inspired thought because **passion activates the mental mechanism that is put into service for inspiration: emotion**.

Any incoming information that is accompanied by an emotional response gets priority treatment in the brain's storage/retrieval department. The emotions and increased attention that are stimulated by music tag it for long-term storage and easy retrieval. This memory and recall mechanism is the same one that insures that you will not forget the name of the person that made your heart go pitter-patter. Information that carries stronger emotions receives higher priority. This gives music a built-in mechanism for its own prioritizing. Every emotionally moving phrase enlists the build-it-to-last construction crews in the brain.

If the music is heard again it strengthens the storage and appreciation; it increases its emotional resonance with each storage and retrieval. Music is tagged VIP as it goes in and is imbued with more emotion after being retrieved and worked-on – each cycle adds more rungs onto the ladder, and each time a passage is stored and recalled it becomes more readily available.

Come On Baby, Light My Fire

At last the mechanisms necessary for creating inspired music are in place. The single-piston steam engine of conscious, linear thought has been turned into a synchronized, alcohol-fueled V-12 by the parallel processing of second nature, the turbo-booster of passion is attached, the road has been paved by repeated attention to the elements of the subject and the map of the problem has been memorized. It is time to rev-up the engine and go take a nap.

Improved access to intuition is possible in the state of mind between wakefulness and sleep. It acts like hypnosis, untethering conscious attention, dropping the ballast of distraction, and letting the mind float to a bird's eye view. One famous scientist found this state of mind so valuable that he cultivated a way of maintaining it without allowing himself to follow the natural progression to actual sleep. When he was tired enough to fall asleep, he would stand holding weights in each hand at his side, then he would let his mind drift to the problem that he was trying to solve. If he fell too close to sleepiness, the sensation of the weights beginning to fall out of his hands would awaken him just enough to keep his mind active in the in-between state of awareness.

Schubert used to read a poem before going to sleep and would often awaken with a melody paired with the text of the poem. (How beautiful it would be to awaken to the strains of a new melody by Schubert.) Sometimes he would forget the melody before he had the chance to find his spectacles and write down what he was hearing in his mind. He took to sleeping with his glasses on so that he wouldn't miss the opportunities. Some composers, when tired, will have a cup of coffee and sit down for a little nap and think about the section of music that they have been working on. The resulting push-me-pull-you will often allow consciousness to drift between the dreams, desires, and designs.

And if you should drift into the Land of Nod, well, perhaps you will meet bespectacled Schubert there and reminisce.

8

CONCLUSION

In 1977, under the guidance of astronomer Carl Sagan, a phonograph and a record was placed on the Voyager 2 spacecraft. If the vehicle falls into the grasping mechanisms of some alien life forms they will be able to drop the needle and hear from us. Included on the disk are a greeting from the people on earth and various pieces of music, including Beethoven, Mexican mariachi, and Chuck Berry. Any life form capable of starting up the phonograph will probably already enjoy patterns, but unless they have a respiratory rate of 15 to 20 breaths per minute, a circulatory system containing a pulsing heart that beats 40 to 80 beats per minute, an emotionally directed behavior and emotional communication where complex wave forms are negative and simple wave forms are positive, low sounds that communicate aggression, a tendency to emit high, long, loud sounds when alarmed, a gestation period where the alien fetus was carried long enough to hear the pulses and have the sounds of the womb imprinted on the emotional brain structures, a bipedal form of transportation, a size of 100 to 200 pounds, gravity on their planet roughly equivalent to earth's, a voice, a range of that voice covering the span of 65 to 980 cycles per second, the gender carrying the fetus with a vocal range of 196 to 980cps, a sonic "fingerprint" of their voices that favors the fourth overtone, spacing of vocalized vowels in speech from 2 to 6 per second, and tonal centers and consonant intervals in that speech, then it seems unlikely that they will get much of a kick out of *Johnny B. Goode*. Human music does not sound like the chirps of tamarin monkeys or the screech of eagles or, most likely, the sounds of aliens, because it follows the pathway that is intricately built into our minds that is designed for the sounds of humans.

For a final description of music that follows that pathway, here is an appraisal of the opening seven seconds of the Prelude in G by Bach. (www.davidteie.com and click on Bach prelude or track 28 on the CD) The cello built by Andrea Castagneri in 1738 sounds in the rich register of the human baritone, complete with the sonic "voiceprint" of the formant-enhanced resonance of an emotionally charged voice. The strings are made of sterling silver-wound sheep's gut that has a human vocal timbre. The first note is feathered in – the weight of the bow is applied gradually to the string to give the first sound a soft ahh inception of affectionate speech; this is distinct from the percussive ictus that a standard bow stroke would produce. The tonality that is established in the first three notes is tonality that we recognize from the natural world of harmonics and overtones and is interpreted in the emotional centers as consonant and pleasing. The mild dissonance of the fourth note adds a trace of tension. The pattern of the first eight notes is repeated and the recognition of the symmetry takes hold and gives us a sense of the calibration of the size of the story and the consistently common-time pulse and heartbeat tempo have become apparent. The performer has increased the volume to enhance the arcing shape of the line and to help the listener to "see" the perfect movement. The fourth second of music brings a tension-filled F# that directly conflicts with the ever-present low G and induces a drop of anxiety. That conflict is resolved and the adrenaline of attention that it produced is mixed with a dopamine-related pleasure sensation when it resolves to a perfect consonance. The harmonies form a perfectly ordered circle, returning us to the home of G major and completing the musical sentence. That collection of ten emotional responses results from seven seconds of a single line played by a single instrument.

Human Music

Three Keys to Our Emotions

For those who may have been reluctant to pry open the lid and see how music works and where it came from, fearing that some of the magic might be lost if the gears were exposed, take comfort – your amygdala can't read. Knowing how our emotions are brought to life by music does not diminish its effect. Unlike magic, the enjoyment remains and even increases after we have learned how the illusion works. The conscious brain can deduce and calculate till the cows come home and the emotional center will never know, can never know, or care, how a thing is executed; it will respond as it must.

So there you have it, the map of music in the brain shows that there are three entryways that music takes into our emotions:

1. Imprinting in the brain structures responsible for emotions

- The respiratory pulses and the consonant, rhythmic melodies of mother's spoken phrases are permanently woven into the fabric of our emotional centers.

2. Exapted emotions

- The attention that sudden crashes induce, and the responses to pattern recognition and attention to movement are borrowed from our naturally selected emotional responses and activated by music.

This is similar to the evolutionary process of exaptation, where a part of the body that serves one function evolves to serve a different one. The best example of exaptation, and the most relevant to music is the evolution of the ear. The very ear that music enters evolved from a jawbone. Some primeval bone that was particularly sensitive to vibrations was passed down, improvements were sanctioned by Mother Natural Selection, and the modified jawbone eventually became the inner ear. Similarly, music has exapted capabilities and processes, *plays* on pathways and abilities of the brain that have evolved for other purposes; it is the teenager who has discovered that he can take his dad's delivery truck out for a joy-ride. An example of an exapted response is the attention paid to directed movement in music. The emotional response itself was designed to allow our visual processing to recognize potentially important movement and was adopted by music when we process music visually.

Many of the emotional effects of music derive from exaptations of instinctive responses to sounds, patterns, and movement. Music is capable of creating replicas of the signals that our emotional responses were designed to react to: we are built for hunting in packs but we can get a kick out of playing soccer for fun, we are adrenaline-juiced when we fall and can enjoy the thrill of bungee jumping and roller coasters, and the celestial movement of heaven can be given shape in sound, combined with perfect harmony and order, and can give us a sense of the divine in our personal experience.

3. The connection of sympathetic emotion

Only Connect

"Mature as he was, she might yet be able to help him to the building of the rainbow bridge that should connect the prose in us with the passion. Without it we are meaningless fragments, half monks, half beasts, unconnected arches that have never joined into a man. With it love is born, and alights on the highest curve, glowing against the gray, sober against the fire. .... Only connect! That was the whole of her sermon. Only connect the prose and the passion, and both will be exalted, and human love will be seen at its height. Live in fragments no longer. Only connect, and the beast and the monk, robbed of the isolation that is life to either, will die."

- E. M. Forster

- The most important and profound elements of the language of music are those that sing directly from and to our emotional centers and inspire the sympathetic responses that connect us all. The expressive communication of screams, moans, lowered larynx tone qualities, story structure emphasis, pure waveforms of consonance/complex waveforms of dissonances, cracking voices, the sounds of laughter, cheers, flirtation, dominance, submission, threats, and pity are reduced to their sonic essences and formed into patterns and structures that we innately recognize.

Our primitive emotions are connected in a rainbow bridge to the designs of the highest intellect and form a language of emotion. The aspects of human vocalizations and speech that express our emotions have been distilled and poured into this sonic language. It does not represent anything other than itself, does not bait and switch with simulated fear triggers or remind us of our fetal oneness - it is direct communication through a pure form of our natural emotional language.

The composers who wrote music that is made from the essence of emotional sounds, those for whom music was a means of direct expression through the natural path of emotional contact to the sympathetic emotions of the listener wrote greater, more expressive and connected music as they grew older. Almost without exception, and most of those due to illness, the composers of music written in the language of sympathetic contact wrote their best works near the end of their lives.

Great music originates in the emotional center and speaks to the emotional center. While the direct thrill of the fear of heights and falling is felt by the skydiver, the sympathetic thrill of the same fear is seeing tightrope walkers work without a net. *We feel for them*. The sound of one speaking with a lump in his or her throat is able move another to a heartfelt sympathy; this is how music, like the sympathetically vibrating string, does not communicate, it connects. All of the known and well-understood forces of nature are attractive, connective forces. Love is the ultimate human connecting force, and can be conveyed through the direct sharing of emotion in music.

The contact and resonance of the late works of Beethoven show us how expansive and inclusive musical expression can be. Many would agree that, in form and content, the finale of his ninth symphony is the greatest single movement of music ever created. It is set to the text of Schiller's *To Joy* and includes text inserted by Beethoven in the choral climax: "alle Menschen werden Brüder" (All men become brothers). The famous melody contains only one strong accent and one syncopation, both occurring on the return of the head of the melody on first syllable of the word "alle", thus Beethoven highlights the importance of his statement. In the collection of variations leading up to the climax of the movement, Beethoven included a setting of the melody in a Turkish march. Its inclusion in this movement is a bit surprising. Enough colleagues of Leonard Bernstein found the march campy enough for

Bernstein to feel the need to defend its placement in the work. The Viennese of the time viewed the Turks as the bloodthirsty, invading Ottomans who were feared and despised more than any other potential enemy. What Beethoven was expressing by the inclusion of a Turkish march in a symphony premiered in Vienna was "all mankind" formed a brotherhood, not just our people or people like us or people who agree with us or people of our religion, but *all* people. Those who hear the music feel the directly shared sympathetic joy of this ultimate inclusion. The spirit that connects us all is not merely expressed *through* his music, the music *is* the connection itself.

Our emotions do more than direct behavior that will most likely lead to survival and replication. They represent the foundation of humanity that connects every member to every other member. Emotional expressions in sound communicate directly from heart to heart, unaffected by the differences between us and unavailable to the tinkering of prejudice, allowing our fears, desires, and loves to be felt by those around us as we feel them. Music has extracted and expresses, in a way that is more real and fundamental than we could have imagined, the essence of the emotions that connect us all.

ACKNOWLEDGEMENTS

I would like to thank the love of my life, Pavla for encouraging me to publish this book. It cannot be coincidental that my internal fountain of discoveries began flowing when I met her. I could thank my children, Daniella and Mark, who would certainly have supported my writing if they had been old enough to know what was going on. True, real time thanks are due to my no-longer-children children, Andrew and Sophia who were and remain my most consistent, enthusiastic, and loving supporters. I could always rely on them for lifelines of encouragement when I felt myself sinking in words. I thank my brother, Paul, one of the few people I know who is as passionate about music as I am, for a lifetime of insights and probing conversations on the topic. My dad deserves a hearty share of my thanks for giving me such a shining example of a sterling musician who was among the first to use modern technology to help us to understand the science of music. He also showed me how to recognize and use the rare attribute of common sense. The most important supporter of mine has always been my mother. She did not live to see the publishing of this book, but no other person ever saw me in the light that she did; I would describe it as a bemused affection for her carefree, scatterbrained son who just kept pushing the stone up the hill no matter how many times it rolled back down. Without the confidence instilled by her image of me, I would have easily tired from the many, many failures that are the bricks that must be laid in the road to progress.

This book would not have been readable without the insightful assistance from design to details that I received from my editor, Jennifer

Ryan from West Pier Publishing. There are very few people who are comfortable with one foot in music and the other in science, but Jennifer not only kept her balance but was able to guide me toward keeping the reader balanced as well. Her approach to writing would have work as well if we had been composing a symphony; she showed me how structure, story, emotion, direction, and new information can all be seamlessly woven into the same fabric.

Each of the wonderful teachers that I have worked with deserves special thanks: Karen Barschdorf who instills in her students the passion for string playing that she possesses, Johan Lingeman whose patience, discipline, and the honor of beauty from the Old World connected my head and heart to that source of the greatest music, Ronald McCreery who taught me the extreme value of extreme dedication, Stephen Kates who mentored and befriended me and whose incomparable talent flowed so generously that I feel that I was able to absorb a small part of it, William Pleeth who opened up a world of imagination and color for me, and Mstislav Rostropovich who so often selflessly focused his beam of genius on my playing.

I must thank the founders of the Internet and Tim Berners-Lee who established the World Wide Web. My ability to conduct research in the days of library catalog cards and microfilm was woefully inadequate to any but the most mundane task. The Internet that granted instant access to extant research from my thinking chair allowed me to strive for an informed stream of consciousness with a view of the known world. Internet wings took me effortlessly from stratosphere to molecular design and back, providing a map of territories that were thoroughly explored and, by omission, showing where the unexplored voids could be found.

Although many in the scientific community seem to have trouble seeing beyond their own tests, Jagmeet Kanwal is a delightful exception. He is a man of warmth and vision who has consistently helped and supported my ideas. Finally, I owe the entirety of my second career as an accepted theorist it is to the scientist's scientist Charles Snowdon. Without his support, advice, and collaboration my work would be gathering mold and dust in the basement. I offer my most profound thanks to him for his professional and personal acceptance of my work and me.

REFERENCES

Ball, T., Rahm, B., Eickhoff, S. B., Schulze-Bonhage, A., Speck, O., and Mutschler, I. (2007). Response properties of human amygdala subregions: evidence based on functional MRI combined with probabilistic anatomical maps, *Pubic Library of Science ONE*. 2 doi:10.1371/journal.pone.0000307

Belin, P., Fecteau, S., Charest, I., Nicastro, N., Hauser, M. D. and Armony, J. L. (2008). Human cerebral response to animal affective vocalizations, *Proceedings of the Royal Society, B* 275, 473-81.

Birnholz, J. C. and Benacerraf, B. R. (1983). The development of human fetal hearing, *Science*. 222, 516-8.

Blood, A. J., Zatorre, R. J., Bermudez, P., and Evans, A. C. (1999) Emotional responses to pleasant and unpleasant music correlate with activity in paralimbic brain regions, *Nature Neuroscience*, 2, 4, 382 – 387.

Blood, A. J. and Zatorre, R. J. (2001) Intensely pleasurable responses to music correlate with activity in brain regions implicated in reward and emotion, *Proceedings of the National Academy of Science USA*. 98, 11818-23.

Bowling, D. L., Gill, K. Z., Choi, J. D., Prinz, J., and Purves, D. (2009) Major and minor music compared to excited and subdued speech. J Acoust Soc Am 127(1): 491–503.

Fecteau, S., Belin, P., Joanette, Y., and Armony, J.L., (2007) Amygdala responses to nonlinguistic emotional vocalizations, *NeuroImage*, 36, 2, pp. 480-487.

Fitch, W. T. and Hauser, M. D. (1995) Vocal production in nonhuman primates: acoustics, physiology, and functional constraints on "honest" advertisement, *American Journal of Primatology*, 37, 191 – 219.

Fitch, W.T. and Reby, D. (2001) The descended larynx is not uniquely human. *Proceedings of the Royal Society, Biological Sciences*, 268, 1669-75.

Griffiths, T. D. and Warren, J. D. (2002). The planum temporale as a computational hub, *Trends in Neurosciences*. 25, 348-53.

Gunnar, M. R. and Nelson, C. A. (1992) *Developmental Behavioral Neuroscience*, Lawrence Erlbaum Associates, Inc., Need city of publication and inclusive pages 105.

Herzog, M. and Hopf, S. (1984) Behavioral responses to species-specific warning calls in infant squirrel monkeys reared in social isolation, *American Journal of Primatology* 7, 99-106.

Huang, H. Zhang, J., Wakana, S., Zhang, W. Ren, T., Richards, L. J., Yarowsky, P. Donohue, P., Graham, E., van Zijl, P. C. M. and Mori, S. (2006).White and gray matter development in human fetal, newborn and pediatric brains, *NeuroImage*. 33, 27–38.

Huron, D., & Ollen, J. (2003) Agogic contrast in French and English themes: Further support for Patel and Daniele. *Music Perception*. 21, 267-271.

Kanwal, J. P., Peng, J. S. and Esser, K. (2004). Auditory communication and echolocation in the mustached bat: computing for dual functions within single neurons. In: J. A. Thomas, C. J., Moss and M. Vater *Echolocation in Bats and Dolphins*. Pp. 201-8 (Chicago, University of Chicago Press)

Koelsch, S., Fritz, T., Cramon, D. Y., Müller, K., Friederici, A. D., (2006). Investigating emotion with music: An fMRI study, *Human Brain Mapping*, 27, 3, 239-250.

Mampe, B., Friederici, A. D. Christophe, A. and Wermke, K. (2009) Newborns' cry melody is shaped by their native language, *Current Biology. doi:10.1016/j.cub.2009.09.064*

Mehler, J., Jusczyk, P. and Lambertz, G. (1988). A precursor of language acquisition in young infants, *Cognition*. 29, 143-78.

Morris, J. S., Scott, S. K., and Dolan, R. J. (1999) Saying it with feeling: neural responses to emotional vocalizations, *Neuropsychologia*, 37, 10, 1155-1163.

Morton, E. S. (1977) On the occurrence and significance of motivation-structural rules in some bird and mammal sounds, *The American Naturalist*. 111, 855-69.

O'Connor, D. H., Fukui, M. M., Pinsk, M. A., and Kastner, S. (2002) Attention modulates responses in the human lateral geniculate nucleus, *Nature Neuroscience*, 5, 1203 – 1209.

Parvizi, J., Anderson, S. W., Martin, C. O., Damasio, H., and Damasio, A. R., (2001) Pathological laughter and crying, A link to the cerebellum. *Brain* 124, 1708-1719.

Patel, A. D., & Daniele, J. R. (2003). An empirical comparison of rhythm in language and music, *Cognition*, 87, B35-B45.

Patel, A. D. (2008) *Music, Language and the Brain* (Oxford: Oxford University Press)

Patterson, R.D., Robinson, K., Holdsworth, J., McKeown, D., Zhang, C. and Allerhand M. (1992) . 'Complex sounds and auditory images, ' In: Auditory physiology and perception, Proc. 9th International Symposium on Hearing, Y Cazals, L. Demany, and K. Horner (ed.), Oxford, 429-446.

Porcaro, C., Zappasodi, F., Barbati, G., Salustri, C., Pizzella, V., Rossini, P. M. and Tecchio, F. (2006). Fetal auditory responses to external sounds and mother's heart beat: Detection improved by independent component analysis, *Brain Research.* 1101, 51-8.

Poss, R. M., (1998) Distortion Is Truth, *Leonardo Music Journal*, 8, 45-48 The MIT Press.

Querleu, D., Renard, X., Versyp, F., Paris-Delrue, L., and Crèpin, G., (1988) Fetal hearing. *European Journal of Obstetrics & Gynecology and Reproductive Biology,* 28: 191-212.

Richards, D. S., Frentzen, B., Gerhardt, K. J. McCann, M. E. Abrams, R. M. (1992). Sound levels in the human uterus, *Obstetrics & Gynecology.* 80, 186-190.

Saenz, M., Buracas, G. T., and Boynton, G. M. (2002) Global effects of feature-based attention in human visual cortex, *Nature Neuroscience* 5, 631 – 632.

Schwartz, D. A. and Purves, D. (2004) Pitch is determined by naturally occurring periodic sounds, *Hearing Research.* 194, 31-46.

Wilson, F. A. W. and Rolls, E. T. (1993) The effects of stimulus novelty and familiarity on neuronal activity in the amygdala of monkeys performing recognition memory tasks, *Experimental Brain Research* 93, 367-82.

APPENDIX

Table 1 Mood related features of vocal production

Soothing/Affective:	Lively/Affective:
Raised larynx	Raised larynx
Pure waveform	Vocal waveform
Closed vowel (oo)	Open vowel (ah)
Moderate tempo	Quick, short notes
High vocal range	Mid-high vocal range
Open consonant intervals	Major diatonic intervals
Quiet	Moderate
Sympathetic/expressive:	**Threat:**
Lowered larynx	Normal larynx
Vocal waveform	Complex waveform
Mid-closed vowel (oh)	Open vowels
Slow descending phrases	Accented notes
Mid-low vocal range	Low vocal range
Minor diatonic intervals	Dissonant intervals
Quiet	Moderately loud

Alarm:
Normal larynx
Penetrating waveform
Open vowels
Sustained notes
High vocal range
Dissonant intervals
Loud